CW01669573

Publishing for Twenty-five Years

GLOBALISATION AND GENDER

GLOBALISATION AND GENDER

Changing Patterns of Women's Employment in Bangladesh

Edited by
Rehman Sobhan
Nasreen Khundker

Centre for Policy Dialogue
The University Press Limited

The University Press Limited
Red Crescent Building
114 Motijheel C/A
P.O. Box 2611
Dhaka 1000
Bangladesh
Fax: (88 02) 9565443
E-mail: upl@bttb.net.bd

First published 2001

Cover design by Ashraful Hassan Arif

ISBN 984 05 1581 0

Published by Mohiuddin Ahmed, The University Press Limited, Dhaka. This book has been set in Times New Roman by MNS Computer Printers, Dhaka. Designer: Babul Chandra Dhar and produced by Abarton, 99 Malibagh, Dhaka. Printed at Akota Offset Press, 119 Fokirapool, Dhaka.

To the Women Workers of Bangladesh
and
their Brave search for new horizons

Contents

List of Tables

List of Figure

List of Annex Tables

Abbreviations

AAFLI	Asian-American Free Labour Institute
AIDS	Acute Immune Deficiency Syndrome
ASA	Association for Social Advancement
ATC	Agreement on Textiles and Clothing
BBS	Bangladesh Bureau of Statistics
BGMEA	Bangladesh Garments Manufacturers and Exporters Association
BIDS	Bangladesh Institute of Development Studies
BIGWU	Bangladesh Independent Garments Workers Union
BRAC	Bangladesh Rural Advancement Committee
BRDB	Bangladesh Rural Development Board
BSIC	Bangladesh Standard Industrial Code
CAD	Computer-Aided Design
CMI	Census of Manufacturing Industries
DTA	Domestic Tariff Area
EC	European Community
EPB	Export Promotion Bureau
EPZ	Export Processing Zone
FDI	Foreign Director Investment
FGD	Focus Group Discussions
GATT	General Agreement on Tariffs and Trade
GATT	General Agreement on Tariffs and Trade
GO	Government
GOB	Government of Bangladesh

GSP	General System of Preferences
ILO	International Labour Organisation
ISS	Industrial Surveys and Studies
L/C	Letter of Credit
LDC	Least Developed Country
LFPR	Labour Force Participation Rate
LFS	Labour Force Survey
MFA	Multi Fibre Arrangement
MFA	Multi Fibre Arrangement
NGO	Non-Governmental Organisation
NICS	Newly Industrialised Countries
NUK	Nari Udyog Kendro
QR	Quantitative Restriction
RDRS	Rangpur Dinajpur Rural Services
RMG	Ready-made Garments
RNF	Rural Non-Farm Sector
ROO	Rules of Origin
SAARC	South Asian Association of Regional Co-operation
SAPTA	South Asian Preferential Trading Arrangement
SSC	Secondary School Certificate
STD	Sexually Transmitted Diseases
UTPS	Unity Through Population Services
WASA	Dhaka Water and Sewerage Authority
WTO	World Trade Organisation

Contributors

Rita Afsar is currently working as Research Fellow at the Bangladesh Institute of Development Studies. She was previously a Lecturer at Nagpur University, India. She obtained her Ph. D degree from University of Adelaide, Australia. Her interests are in the areas of urbanisation, migration including labour migration, women's employment, and gender roles and status.

Debapriya Bhattacharya is the Executive Director of the Centre for Policy Dialogue (CPD), Dhaka. He is currently on leave from the Bangladesh Institute of Development Studies (BIDS), where he is a Senior Research Fellow. He did his Masters in Economics and Ph. D in Economics from the Plekhanov Institute of National Economy, Moscow. His current areas of work include reform economics and adjustment policies, industrial competitiveness and technology capability.

Shamsul I Khan teaches International and Asian Studies at the School of International Studies, University of South Australia, Adelaide, and is currently the Director of the Centre for International and Cross-Cultural studies, University of Australia. He was previously Assistant Professor, Department of International Relations, University of Dhaka. His publications include Political Culture, Political Parties, and the Democratic Transition in Bangladesh (with S. Aminul Islam and M. Imdadul Haque).

Nazli Kibria is Assistant Professor of Sociology at Boston University. She obtained her Ph. D from University of Pennsylvania, U.S.A. Her interests are in the areas of globalisation processes and cultural change, especially in the arenas of family, gender relations, and collective and individual identities.

Nasreen Khundker is Associate Professor, Department of Economics, University of Dhaka. She obtained an M Sc, (Econ) degree from the

London School of Economics and Ph. D from Boston University, U.S.A. Her research interests include technology innovations in the informal sector, structural adjustment and reforms, poverty and famines, and NGOs.

Simeen Mahmud is Senior Research Fellow, Bangladesh Institute of Development Studies, Dhaka. She completed her M.A. in statistics at the University of Dhaka in 1974 and joined BIDS as Staff Demographer the same year. She obtained an M.Sc in Medical Demography from the London School of Hygiene and Tropical Medicine in 1976. Her Current research interests include women's status and fertility, female labour use and behaviour, and exploring the influence of development interventions on women's lives.

Mustafizur Rahman is the Research Director at Centre for Policy Dialogue and Professor in the Department of Accounting, University of Dhaka. He did his Ph. D from Moscow State University. He has been a visiting Fellow at Queen Elizabeth House, University of Oxford, and Institute of South-East Asian Studies, Singapore. His principal area of research is in trade policy, competitiveness, regional trading arrangements and impact of globalization on economies of LDCs.

Rehman Sobhan is Chairman, Centre for Policy Dialogue (CPD), has held positions as Professor of Economics at Dhaka University, Member of Bangladesh Planning Commission, Director General, Bangladesh Institute of Development Studies and Member, President's Advisory Council. He has been president of the Bangladesh Economic Association, Member of the UN Committee of Development Planning, Member of the Council of the UN University, Member of the Board of UNRISD, Member of the Executive Committee of the International Economic Association and Member of the SAARC *Group of Eminent* Persons. He is currently Chairman of the Board of Grameen Bank and of the South Asia Centre for Policy Studies. His major publications have been on public enterprise, privatisation, aid and development, the role of the state, rural development and agrarian reform, South Asian co-operation and governance.

Preface

The present publication on Gender Issues has had a long gestation period. It is the outcome of a study initiated by the Centre for Policy Dialogue (CPD) on *Gender Issues on Export Based Industrialisation* in 1996. The work reflected a long standing concern of the Centre for Policy Dialogue with the issue of widening the participation of women in Bangladesh in the development process, a goal which is important for realising social justice as well as enhancing the efficiency of the economy. The two areas where scope for such participation by women in the Bangladesh economy has exponentially expanded over the last decade, are to be found in opportunities for self-employment through access to micro-credit and through entry of women into the wage labour market through the ready-made garments (RMG) sector.

CPD's concern with gender happily coincided with a global programme on a more *Gender Equitable Macro-Economic Agenda* organised by the United Nations Research Institute on Social Development (UNRISD). Over the last decade UNRISD's work on gender has been of some influence in the development discourse. Its attempt to globally address the implications of women participating in the labour market was thus of particular interest to CPD because it provided a broader perspective to the Bangladesh experience. CPD thus joined hands with research teams in Viet Nam, Uganda, Morocco and Jamaica in addressing the implications of women's participation in the market economy.

In the specific context of Bangladesh, the entry of close to 1.5 million women into the labour market through some 2400 RMG enterprises located in the Metropolitan areas of Dhaka and Chittagong, remains as close to a social revolution as Bangladesh has experienced. Within a decade and a half, not even a generation, a million and a half women, mostly unmarried girls in their teens, have transplanted themselves from their villages to work in the RMG factories of

Dhaka and Chittagong. The presence of close to a million women walking to and from their place of residence in the *bustees* of Dhaka to their place of work on the Airport Road, Gulshan, Tejgaon or Mirpur in the early morning and in the late afternoon, often after dark, is a change of seismic significance in the circumstances of the women of Bangladesh. That these women had mostly never stepped out of their villages, that their families were and mostly remain farmers, with no exposure to factory labour, that the traditional work space of rural women was in the homestead where women were hardly visible on the streets of their village let alone on the streets of Dhaka or in the work place, gives us some perspective to the social transformation associated with the arrival of women in the formal labour market of Bangladesh.

A social transformation bringing women into the wage economy may have eventually, taken place in Bangladesh in any case. But the pace of this transformation was accelerated by the emergence of the RMG market in Bangladesh at the beginning of the 1980s. The RMG industry has globally, since the turn of the century attracted and valorised women's work. The spectacle of women working in ill lit, damp tenements in the garment district of New York City is part of the folklore of the US labour movement. The common thread binding women in the RMG sector across the globe and across time appears to be their willingness to work in a low wage industry, without excessive protest at their condition of work, at tasks which demand some manual dexterity, enormous patience and diligence but above all a capacity to work under adverse conditions without undue complaints, because women were persuaded to behave that they had *no better option*.

The RMG sector, has over the years emerged as the quintessential labour-intensive industry where low wages have remained a crucial valuable in establishing the global competitiveness of the industry. Unlike other industries in the textiles sector such as spinning, weaving, dyeing and finishing which require sizeable capital investment, the RMG enterprise requires limited capital to establish a competitive unit, where the value addition largely depends in the dexterity of its labour force. In the specific context of Bangladesh, the entrepreneurial input into the RMG sector associated with marketing, design, even financing of the enterprise, is limited. Thus the entrepreneurial input in all but a handful of enterprises is basically to supervise labour and deliver the endproduct of their labour for shipment to the port. This last task is however far from simple in Bangladesh, given the frequency of politically derived work stoppages during a year. The availability of quotas in the North American market and the GSP facility in the European Union (EU) provided a captive market for Bangladesh's RMG exporters. Such a system of regulated markets has located many of the traditional functions of the RMG entrepreneur into the hands of a class of expatriate buying houses who have intermediated market relations between Bangladesh's RMG entrepreneurs and the North American/EU market. However a new of class of hands-on Bangladeshi RMG entrepreneurs who deal directly with major retail buyers in the overseas market has established its presence through accumulation of market *savvy*, managerial expertise and reinvestable capital. This class is now investing in backward linkages, thereby contributing to the changing role of entrepreneurship in the RMG sector.

As it stands today, the operational part of the RMG sector still depends exclusively on the labour skills of its women workers to assemble the imported yarn and fabrics into a finished garment which can be sold at competitive prices abroad. The skill needed for the job are mostly acquired by the spontaneous learning capacity of our rural women. On the job, little investment is made by the RMG entrepreneurs or the GOB to upgrade these skills either prior to entry into the labour force or during their employment. Bangladesh's success as a RMG exporter depends as much on the contribution of these working women as it does on it new entrepreneurs. Unfortunately the role of these women has tended to be underplayed both in the social recognition accorded to the RMG sector as well as in the distribution of *rewards* from the explosive growth of this sector.

The paper by Debapriya Bhattacharya and Mustafizur Rahman in this volume addresses the global dynamics underlying Bangladesh's RMG sector so as to provide a macro-economic perspective to the growth of women's employment in this sector. This component of the study establishes that the livelihood not just for a large number of women but also for their rural families depends on the dynamics of global trade as determined by trends in the global economy and the competitive regime determined by the World Trade Organisation (WTO). Thus, the extent to which rural women may expect to be absorbed into the organised labour force in Bangladesh will depend on what is happening to the privileged market opportunities opened up for Bangladeshi RMG exporters in USA and North America and in the European Union. This is a market designed through a process of global negotiations where workers have little say. This market, in its present regulatory framework *may expect*, under the provisions of the WTO, to expand upto 2005. After 2005 the regime of regulated market for RMG exports is expected to be dismantled and the future of the RMG sector will be thrown on to the forces of the global market. In such an open trading regime Bangladesh will no longer have privileged access to the EU and North American markets and will have to compete with more mature economies such as China, India, Republic of Korea, Thailand, Indonesia, Mexico and Turkey, as also with new competitors such as Viet Nam and the emerging East European economies. These changes in the global economic order will expose Bangladesh's rural women to relentless competitive pressure which could not only squeeze their already low wages but would make enormous demands on them to raise their productivity. The scope for Bangladesh's RMG sector to remain competitive will have less to do with our women's capacity to work hard or to assimilate new skills but in the managerial skills as well as the incentive and training regime for these workers in place by the RMG owners backed by the GOB.

The capacity of Bangladesh's private sector, again backed by public policies and investment to promote vital backward linkages to the RMG sector, will also be crucial to the fortunes of its women workers. The emerging global trade order thus carries significant opportunities as well as challenges for our women. If Bangladesh can remain competitive in the global market the work opportunities for women in the RMG sector could double, even treble in the next decade and expand further in the spinning and weaving industry. The Grameen Bank — Gano Shastha Kendra (GSK) textile project to *channelise* handwoven *Grameen Check* for sale in the global market employs virtually all women in its newly installed factory premises in Sirajganj district. This indicates that Bangladeshi women can move beyond the RMG sector to work in more complex production facilities.

The other papers in this volume by Simeen Mahmud, Nazli Kibria and Rita Afsar spells out the complex chain of events which moves women from the household into the rural labour market and eventually into the RMG units in Dhaka and Chittagong. These papers establish the capacity of these women to assimilate new skills, to demonstrate enterprise and to depend on complex social networks which bring them out of the village into the factory and helps to sustain them in this unfamiliar environment. These studies as well as research outside this volume by Salma Chaudhuri and Pratima Paul Majumdar of BIDS, highlight the problems of social survival, the physical and emotional stresses at work, the adverse conditions of work and living and the insecurities of life in an adverse working environment. The studies however provide an eloquent testimony to the adaptability of these women, their commitment to their families who depend on their wage labour, their quest for economic independence and human dignity and above all, their resilience in coping with the severe challenges presented by this sea change in their living environment.

All the studies, but particularly the work by S.I. Khan, on Trade Unions in the garment industry, expose the injustice inherent in the working circumstances of these women. It is evident that women have entred the RMG sector because, as was argued a decade ago by Salma Sobhan, Hameeda Hossain and Rowshan Jahan, they had *no better option*. Such a lack of opportunity was exploited by the market and the employers to induct women into an industry where men have remained less inclined to participate in large numbers because they feel that their role as primary family providers may make it impossible for their households to survive on wages offered by the RMG sector. It is thus hypothesised that only women, whose wage earnings are part of a household survival strategy and not unique to household survival, can be presumed to accept the low wages on offer by an RMG sector competing in a global market. The social dynamics underlying women's entry into the labour force is compounded by an inequitable social order in Bangladesh and the weak commitment of the GOB to realise both social as well as gender justice. Over the last two decades the RMG sector has emerged as the lead export of Bangladesh as well as the lead sector in the industrial economy. It accounts for 75 per cent of commodity exports and 75 per cent of the net growth in manufacturing value added, over the last decade. Without the growth of this sector, Bangladesh would go back to a state of high aid dependency and industrial stagnation. Since virtually the entire dynamics of the RMG sector originates in the value added by the labours of its women workers, it is arguable that these women are today the mainstay of the Bangladesh economy. However, there is no reflection of this life sustaining contribution by the RMG workers to the national economy in the allocative regime within their enterprises or in the social investment behaviour of the GOB. This inequitable response to the contribution of these women is both unjust as well as inefficient. The survival of our RMG exports depends on raising the productivity of these women. This productivity increase cannot be expected to come through imposing more physically exhausting work, involving longer hours, on these women. It has to emerge out of investments in skill development, incentives to raise productivity and improvements in the wellbeing of these women so that they will be invested with the physical and motivational capacity to raise their productivity. To both enhance justice and efficacy amongst the working women the following agenda is suggested:

1. Workers in the RMG sector should be given a positive stake in the end results of their labour, which is so crucial to the sustainability of the industry. This stake could be offered in the form of an equity share in the enterprise where they work, which could reach upto a third of the equity holding of the company. This share ownership could be leveraged through credit offered to the workers by the nationalised commercial banks (NCB) in the same way that they finance share purchases by the elite. The ownership of the shares could be made specific to the enterprise so that a worker in the enterprise would have to resell the share to the enterprise if they leave the enterprise which could then be offloaded to new entrants to the workforce in the enterprise. Such a move would serve to

reduce the high rate of worker turnover which characterises the RMG industry and would give a stake to the workers in upgrading the long term competitiveness and profitability of the enterprise. To the extent that workers do have an equity stake in their enterprise they should also be represented on the Board of Management on a pro rata basis to their equity share.

2. Working conditions in all RMG units should be made compatible with the norms of the *Factory Act*. If finances are a problem for RMG owners to make these units compatible with the provision of the Act a special loan, at interest rates subsidised by the budget and/or tax rebates, should be made available to the entrepreneurs. A coalition of NGOs, the BGMEA and Worker's representatives should be invested with the task of overseeing the upgradation of working conditions.
3. In the long run the GOB should develop a series of RMG industrial estates to relocate these industries out of the residential and commercial areas of Dhaka and Chittagong. RMG enterprises should be given special loans to build worker-friendly factories in these new estates.
4. The GOB and BGMEA, backed by grant financing from aid donors should put in place a universal health insurance programme to cover all RMG workers. This programme could involve a contribution from the workers and employers as well as an initial contribution by the GOB which could for 5 years be underwritten by some aid donors. This health scheme should provide a comprehensive system of preventative care, including immunisation, periodic check-ups and measures for curative care through a referral system. Two hospitals dedicated to garment workers served by this scheme could be set up in Chittagong and Dhaka as a joint venture between the BGMEA and GOB.
5. The GOB, in collaboration with the RMG owners should invest in a transport system between the place of work and residence of the workers which would reduce the time and save the energy of women walking two hours a day to and from work.

6. The GOB should post a special security force, largely composed of police women, to provide security both enroute to work as well as in areas of concentration of these garment workers.
7. The GOB should invest in a dedicated housing programme for such working women. GOB should provide land and some share of the funding to property developers to build special housing estates for ownership and/or rent at low cost for the RMG women workers. Home loans for family units could be provided by the GOB to upgrade and expand existing housing units occupied by these workers. A crash programme by the GOB to build working women's hostels in Dhaka and Chittagong could also be initiated as an interim measure.
8. A major investment should be made in upgrading skills. This may include a series of dedicated training centres to train rural women in RMG skills before they come to the city. The RMG owners should be given tax write offs to encourage them to invest in in-house training to upgrade the skills of their own workers. The GOB, in collaboration with BGMEA, may set up a series of advanced training centres to train a generation of workers already employed in the industry to upgrade their skills so they could be equipped to produce high value garments.
9. The role of legitimate trade unions in the RMG sector should be recognised. Trade unions should not have to function as clandestine organisations under perpetual threat from the employers. They should, emerge through a process of inhouse elections, be legitimised as the representatives of the workers and be expected to play a constructive role in furthering the interests of the workers as well as the enterprise. Ideally each enterprise should have one union and these unions could be federated into a TUC of the RMG sector in the same way that the BGMEA represents the owners. As and when workers graduate into equity owners the concept of a union may evolve into that of elected representatives of the workers who as owners will represent them at the Board.
10. Whilst 1.5 million have come out of the villages to work in the cities of Dhaka, a much larger number of such women will

stay in their villages. In the age of the information revolution these women also need to be included into the wage market. This can be done by locating smaller work units of 25-50 workers, in the village areas, which can absorb the women around the area of the enterprise. These units could be supervised through the use of the internet system which could deliver orders as well as such management centres set up by national corporate bodies could be supervised through the internet. The GOB will have to rapidly promote the spread of telelinks to the rural areas in collaboration with private and non-government communication networks designs. The rural units could be supervised from work centres adjacent to the rural areas. This idea remains open for further discussion and elaboration

The future of the RMG sector does not depend exclusively on the workers. The owners also have to equip themselves as entrepreneurs and managers, to upgrade their capacity to operate in an increasingly competitive world. This will involve coalitions of RMG owners, perhaps backed by equity support and dedicated loan financing by the GOB to move downmarket to invest in weaving, spinning and dyeing and finishing units and upmarket to invest in building design and marketing capacity to directly reach the major buyers in Europe and North America, as well as to access new markets in Japan, Australia, Africa and the Middle East. Such financial support by the GOB to the textile/RMG sector may be made conditional on owners offering an equity stake to the workers in these new enterprises.

The above proposals are at best suggestive. They may be expanded and refined by more qualified people than the writer through a process of ongoing dialogue involving the BGMEA, the workers as well as their representatives, NGOs and the GOB. There is scope here for a number of NGOs specialising in RMG affairs, to equip themselves to play an advocacy and intermediary role in collaboration with the trade unions to support the interests of the workers.

This volume is predicated on the belief that the RMG sector is a microcosm of the new area of opportunities opening up for women in Bangladesh to enable them to move out of gender stereotyped work opportunities into the mainstream of a fast growing labour market. The time is long past for persuading these working women that because they have no better option they should be eternally grateful to their employers for giving them a paid job in their RMG enterprise. Our women have shown a tremendous resilience in coming out of the household and joining the organised labour market. This has had an important role to play in empowering women to be aware of their own self-worth. However, it has also proved to the world that our women can be adaptable and disciplined workers who can contribute to the growth of the economy. It is, thus, important for both the government and society to recognise the enterprise of these working women by identifying more creative ways to give them a stake in the development process which can serve to reward and sustain their enterprise.

In bringing this work to fruition the Centre for Policy Dialogue would wish to acknowledge the financial support of UNRISD which underwrote both the research as well as a major international conference convened by CPD at Rajendrapur in November 1996. This gathering brought together researchers, policymakers and international agencies from around the world to share their experiences and knowledge about women who have entered the labour market all over the world. The insights from this conference were enormously beneficial to our researchers.

CPD is particularly grateful to Dharam Ghai, Director, UNRISD and his colleagues Shahra Razavi and Carol Miller from UNRISD for their support to this work. We would like to acknowledge with deep appreciation Dr. Nasreen Khundker, Department of Economics, Dhaka University for her dedicated effort in co-ordinating this study. We would also like to once again register our appreciation for the highly professional work of the contributors to this volume, Dr. Debapriya Bhattacharya and Dr. Mustafizur Rahman of CPD, Ms. Simeen Mahmud and Dr. Rita Afsar of BIDS, Dr. Nazli Kibria of Boston University and Dr. S.I. Khan of the Department of International Relations, Dhaka University. Without their research effort this volume could not have seen the light of day. The support services invested by Iqbal Hossain and word processing services of Mr. M.A. Quddus are also acknowledged.

Dhaka, October 2000 *Professor Rehman Sobhan*

Chapter 1

INDUSTRIALISATION, EXPORT PROMOTION AND THE CHANGING PATTERN OF WOMEN'S EMPLOYMENT IN BANGLADESH: AN OVERVIEW

Nasreen Khundker

1.1 INTRODUCTION

It is undoubtedly true that women have emerged as an important constituency globally, and women's issues are gaining importance in the development discourse. Within the national context however, policy makers are yet to gain a proper handle on the issue of integrating gender concerns into the development planning process. This stems as much from an inadequate understanding of women's role in the economy and their disadvantaged status, as to a lack of will. Yet, most changes in macro policies have a powerful impact in changing the context of women's lives, in both their productive and reproductive roles.

The point of departure of this study are the developments in the macroeconomic environment in Bangladesh over the last two decades and the concomitant changes in the pattern of women's employment. *It analyses the gender issues and concerns arising out of both the increased participation of women in the labour market and the changed nature of this participation.*[1] A brief review is also

[1] A comparison of trends in participation rates is difficult due to frequent changes in definition in the Labour Force Survey. Despite this, the macro data nevertheless supports the conclusion of higher participation rates of women, especially since the mid-1980s.

given of state policies towards women and that of important actors such as Non-government organisations (NGOs), to see the type of interventions which have been significant in shaping the lives of women. The overall aim of the research is a more informed policy initiative in addressing the needs of women and realising the goal of gender equity.

1.2 CHANGES IN THE MACRO-ECONOMIC SETTING AND THE MAIN RESEARCH QUESTIONS

The Macro Setting

Since the early '80s, there have been important changes in the macroeconomic policy environment in Bangladesh, in the form of greater export-orientation of the economy, liberalisation of trade, and an expanded role for the private sector. While the overall impact on growth and poverty of these policy changes have been modest, there has been more pronounced sectoral shifts in resource allocation, the most significant of which has been the fast growth of the export-based but domestically-owned *ready-made garments* (RMG) industry, mostly located in urban areas. *This has had far-reaching consequences for women, in defining for the first time their entry into formal sector employment on an unprecedented scale*, since seventy per cent or more of the 1.5 m. labour force in this industry now consists of women workers. Employment of women is also increasing at a fast pace in the special export processing zones of the country and in a ratio which outnumbers the employment of men by two and a half. Secondly, this has resulted in increased mobility for women, especially young women, through processes of rural-urban migration, and a transition from the private to the male-dominated public sphere. Third, this has brought women into a new set of relations with employers and with each other as employees, in an urban setting.

These developments are also important in considering future trends in the economy, with its continued focus on the export sector, particularly in attracting investments to the EPZs. Utilisation of female labour is therefore likely to continue to increase in the foreseeable future, given the lower wage costs of women and their comparative advantage in light manufacturing activities. This of course presupposes that the present success with exports is sustained in the ensuing years and a rapidly changing global environment.

The Research Questions

The processes described above, raises a number of issues, which have been posed as research questions for the study. For instance, how are household labour supply decisions made in sending households in both urban and rural areas? Further, what is the role and attitude of the sending community in this regard? On the obverse side of the coin is the question as to what sort of environment prevails in the host urban community for young female migrant workers, and what sort of conditions have been provided for these young women at their work place. For example, are women able to mobilise amongst themselves to negotiate for higher wages and better conditions of employment? On the latter question we need to know if the state of industrial relations are favourable to women in the new industries utilising female labour on a large scale.

On the other hand, the sustainability of these trends in women's employment, as the Bangladesh economy further integrates into the world economy, depends to a large measure on adjustments made at the enterprise level to changing global market configurations, and the way in which these affect women. Are these future trends favourable to women?

While the focus is on industrial employment, the study also analyses the changes in the rural labour market for women, particularly the impact of participation in various NGO programmes. This is felt to be important given that NGOs in Bangladesh have followed a distinctive approach in mobilising rural women and providing them with organisational support, increasing their accessibility to credit and other inputs. It is also true that participation of women in the export sector needs to be understood in the context of overall macro trends in terms of women's participation in the economy, for which an analysis of both rural and urban labour markets is an essential prerequisite.

Changes in the macro policy environment, following the logic of the market place, and changes in the international division of labour, as well as various interventions such as that by NGOs, have thus led to a situation where trends in the female labour market have superseded the objective of State policy and the planning machinery to "mainstream" women into development activities. As a result, the policy imperatives *vis-à-vis* women have changed substantially. The study therefore briefly evaluates the State policy as regards women and the allocation of public expenditures to benefit women, particularly in the area of skill development and diversification, which will influence their capacity to integrate into the evolving national and global markets.

The present study thus fills an important gap in the literature in the context of Bangladesh, particularly in terms of the functioning of the female labour market, the findings of which can not only inform policy makers but also enrich the theoretical discourse on gender issues.

1.3 DISCUSSION OF THE MAIN RESEARCH FINDINGS

The study consists of a set of 6 papers which explore the dynamics of the female labour market and helps us to understand the situation of women in Bangladesh.

This review paper explains the objective of the study, the main research questions, and discusses the key findings. It also gives a conceptual framework for interpreting the results of the study, as well as summarising the recommendations which follow from the individual papers.

The paper by Simeen Mahmud on *The Labour Use of Women in Rural Bangladesh* takes an overview of the rural labour market for women and the forces which have been important in marking the transition for women into market-based activities, as well as the changed nature of household production, particularly as a result of NGO interventions. She then supports her findings by a micro study of four purposively selected villages, drawn from different areas of Bangladesh.

The paper finds that between 1984/85 and 1990/91, 33 per cent of the incremental increase in total employment was due to an increase in women's employment, while 59 per cent of this incremental increase in employment in the rural areas was due to women. During this period rural women in total rural employed population also rose from 9 per cent to 13 per cent. *Thus while the labour force participation of women has been increasing faster than that of men, it is a phenomenon which is not simply confined to urban areas.*

The paper contains some very important findings, based on both secondary source data and the village surveys. For instance, (a) the gender gap in human capital has not only affected the nature of women's participation in wage work, but also their participation in NGO programmes. The paper discusses several ways in which membership in NGO programmes, particularly the organisation of women into groups, have led to greater empowerment of women. These are greater mobility, increased political awareness, greater contribution to family incomes, and an increase in labour supply, as well as higher returns to labour compared to the prevailing wage rate for women in rural areas. However, the basic structural problem remains that due to lower endowment in terms of human capital, women are confined to low return activities, even within such programmes as livestock and poultry, as well as in small-scale manufacturing and trading activities. Second, the paper points out the lower opportunity cost of self-employment compared to wage employment, given the greater involvement of women in household maintenance and expenditure-saving activities, which defines the preference pattern for married women in particular, for self-employment. Third, *in terms of individual characteristics, participation is higher in the age group 20-49 years, and for those with no schooling and more than six years of schooling. Participation rates are also higher at lower income levels. Finally, an important finding is that in the village where women's participation in wage work is highest, wage rates are adversely lower.*

The last two points underscore the dominant effect of push factors, particularly poverty, in determining the involvement of rural women in wage work. It may be pointed out that a significant part of the wage employment is created by state-sponsored *Food for Work* programmes such as earth-cutting, road maintenance, afforestation, etc. This type of employment is largely residual and defines a floor in terms of wages. They therefore attract the poorest women whose opportunity cost for labour is lowest both for household production and the labour market. The findings on the relationship between education level and labour force participation on the other hand points to the existence of a non-linear relationship, which explains the type of work undertaken by women, and the importance of higher levels of human capital formation, in changing the nature and extent of demand for female labour.

The strong set of policy implications which follow from the paper is for the State to take the initiative to overcome the structural constraints women face in terms of lower attainment of skills and education, and to put greater emphasis on creation of more productive employment opportunities. In the case of wage work, this suggests greater investment in rural areas and adoption of industrial re-location policies. For self-employment, as suggested by the paper, technology interventions, skill upgrading and marketing co-operatives, are important policy initiatives which can facilitate the transition to participation of women in higher value-added activities.

The paper by Nazli Kibria on *Becoming A Garments Worker: The Mobilisation of Women into the Garments Factories of Bangladesh*, makes a significant contribution to understanding household labour supply decisions and also the overall economic and social context in which such decisions are made.

The study is based on in-depth interviews with 70 garments workers in sending households located in Dhaka and various rural parts of Bangladesh, mostly in the unskilled category of helpers and operatives, though other skill grades were also included. The study is also unique in that it traces migrant workers to their rural households to understand the context in which the migration decision is made.

The findings from this research on worker profiles corroborates results derived from earlier studies (Majumdar 1991)[2] and also by Rita Afsar as part of this study that most workers were never married, followed by the separated/abandoned/divorced category. On average, they had primary school level education. A significant

[2] Majumdar, P.P. and S. Chaudhury (1991); *The Socio-Economic Condition of Women Workers in the Bangladesh Garments Industry*. Bangladesh Institute of Development Studies, Dhaka, Bangladesh.

proportion of the workforce were also recent migrants from rural areas.

The findings on worker profile thus support the hypothesis of a segmented labour market, within which context entry into formal employment for women is defined. It similarly underscores the importance of rural-urban linkages in analysing labour market processes in Bangladesh.

The paper makes the point that the decision on labour supply is made as members of households where the dynamics of both co-operation and conflict play a role. Three sets of reasons explain the entry into garments work, the most important of which was family survival in households which found it difficult to meet subsistence needs. The contribution from the womens' earnings from factory work was thus very important in meeting household expenses. The absence of a male earner was also a common characteristic of these households. *An interesting finding which has important policy implications is that the opportunity for formal employment not only allowed occupational mobility from low paying wage employment such as domestic service or brick-breaking, earth-cutting etc., but also an intergenerational/familial one*, where the mother or the sister of the worker was involved in a low-paid occupation. Thus wages in garments factories, while low, should be viewed as relative to wages in the informal sector, where most women are employed. Similarly, measures such as the *Harkins Bill*, restricting entry of young workers into formal employment, may deter inter-generational upward mobility.

The history of entry into garments work analysed by *Kibria* also brings out the widespread uncertainty, insecurity and crisis of survival prevalent in Bangladesh society today, which is faced by family members of poor households in different ways. In rural areas, this extends to threats and harassment of young women. In such situations, household conflict, fear of a failed marriage, etc. were instrumental in compelling such women to seek outside employment. Incidentally, the insecurity faced by women in terms of rape and harassment is now similarly pervasive in urban areas.

While poverty and push factors were important, other motivating factors included the prospect for better-off households to enhance their earning capacity, and the desire for financial independence by some women. It should also be noted that factory work was seen to be an improvement in status by many workers, and held expectations of extending the horizons of their experience. Other members of the household viewed the new work opportunity as a way of accumulating dowry, which frequently meant an increase in the future earning potential of the women and ability to choose from an extended pool of marriage partners. Households were thus seen to adopt a long run maximising strategy with respect to work opportunities of young daughters, where in the initial stages, considerable investments were made to secure employment and supplement the earnings of the wage workers. Households/families also acted as a critical safety net to these working women during periods of crisis due to employment lay-offs.

Community attitudes, particularly in rural areas, however were not always favourable to the more independent life style and deportment of garment workers, though the community was seen to mediate the process of entry into factory employment by providing information and linkages with employers.

What the paper thus highlights is the prevalence of considerable tension, both at the level of the household, and at the level of society, faced by new female entrants into formal employment, and a struggle to establish the right to work, outside the confines of the home.

While Kibria looks at the mobilisation of women workers into the garments industry, Rita Afsar's paper is a more general study on the *Gender Dimension of Labour Migration into the Formal Manufacturing Sector of Dhaka City and its Sociological Implications*. The paper is based on a sample survey of 213 (107 female and 106 male) workers drawn from the garments, pharmaceutical, electronics and food processing industries. Five factories were selected from garments and one each from the other industries. The sample was further stratified by gender and age, and a quota sampling method was used to select workers from different skill categories, namely, helper/unskilled worker, operator/skilled worker, and supervisor/technical/managerial category. While garments is predominantly a female dominated industry, the other industries in her sample also show substantial female employment. Her paper therefore provides a basis of comparison amongst a more diversified range of industries.

Rita Afsar's study leads to a number of important findings as to the worker profile and background of female workers in formal manufacturing employment in Dhaka city, their status in the workplace and urban society, as well as the functioning of the urban labour market from a gender perspective.

Thus it is clear from the study that *processes of rural-urban migration continue to be an important factor in understanding the labour market and macro-economic trends*. In her final sample, 27 per cent of workers were identified as recent migrants having migrated between 1991-1996, while 46 per cent had migrated between 1980-1990. Non-migrants, born outside Dhaka city and having migrated prior to 1980, accounted for only 17 per cent of the sampled workers (both male and female). Given our interest in female workers, it is seen that 3/4 of garments workers and 2/5 of female workers in the other three industries had migrated directly to their present job or had come to town in search for work. Interestingly, Afsar also finds that on an average female garments factory workers came from poorer households owning 1.3 acres of land as opposed to 2.0 acres for males in the same factory, and 2.3 acres for females in other manufacturing units. This is evidence that the garments industry attracts women from the poorest rural households. Half of the women workers were also students at the time of migration, though the average level of schooling was only 2.5 and 3.3 years for garments and other workers respectively, prior to migration. Women migrant workers were also on average younger than their male counterparts at time of migration, 13 years in garments, and 18 in other manufacturing units, compared to 15 and 20 respectively for males. The proportion of currently unmarried or divorced/separated women, or widows was also high, 61.5 per cent amongst female garments workers, and 33.3 per cent in other manufacturing units. It is however noteworthy that a little over one-third of the women were in fact married.

Thus the overall impression one gets is one of entry into formal sector employment particularly garments, of very young women workers with some formal schooling and from disadvantaged rural backgrounds. Such employment also seems to widen the range of options for divorced/separated women and widows. However married women are also employed in the industry though it is unclear if they got married prior to or subsequent to entry into wage employment. *Afsar* also draws other implications from her study such as the effect of deferred marriage on population growth, and the effect of remittances, mainly used for family maintenance and education of siblings, for purposes of strengthening the human resource base of the sending families. In terms of earnings, the study finds a 25 per cent gender gap in wages for garments workers and 10 per cent for workers in the other manufacturing industries. She also finds a higher gender gap in wages at the technical/managerial level compared to production workers, but this is largely due to the peculiarities of the sample, since a quota sampling method by matching age was used for production workers, but not for the technical/managerial category.

It may be mentioned that Afsar's findings on the relative wage gap in garments and the other three industries in her sample roughly corresponds to those computed from the aggregate *Census of Manufacturing Industries* data.[3] This data also shows an increase in the male-female wage gap in recent years, partly due to the inclusion of smaller units in the census.

Afsar's paper also shows that there is substantial difference in earnings between unskilled and skilled workers and workers at the supervisor/technical/managerial level. Thus the average wage of a (female) skilled worker is found to be 136 per cent higher than that of an unskilled worker, while the average wages of a supervisor/manager is 82 per cent higher than that of a skilled production worker. *There is also substantial difference in earnings between garments workers and workers in other manufacturing industries, the latter being much higher at all skill grades*. However, the average age and education level in these industries are also significantly higher compared to garments factories. On the other hand, workers in the garments sector work much longer hours, and 40 per cent of workers are found to earn less than prevailing the minimum wage of Tk. 950, though such wages are higher than that of housemaids or compared to the average rural wage.

---

[3] See Table 1.

Afsar's findings thus support the hypothesis that while the export led garments sector has demonstrated a phenomenal increase in employment of women, conditions in this industry typify the case of a dual labour market[4] with high turnover rates for workers, lower wages, high degree of casualisation, but easier entry. The market is also segmented by age, marital status and education. A few other findings from Afsar's study are worth mentioning. For instance, she finds a high degree of group solidarity between female workers which helps them overcome the hardships of urban life, especially when no public or factory support is provided in terms of housing or transport. These workers move to and from work in groups and live in housing arrangements with other co-workers or with family members resident in the city. Married workers also rely on family support for child care. *Thus social networks are the most important factor in enabling women workers to sustain themselves in the urban labour market.* Such networks are similarly important in terms of mediating entry of these women into formal sector employment.

A similar degree of "informality" dictates the process of bargaining and its outcomes at the workplace, given the lack of unionisation, especially in the garments sector. Unions are actively discouraged by employers, but 50 per cent of the sampled garments workers in Afsar's study bargained for paid leave and 60 per cent for higher wages, mainly through help of their factory supervisors. The bargaining outcomes were in general favourable. There was again some difference between garments and the other industries in Afsar's sample. Since working conditions and salary structures were more "formal" in these other units, workers confined their bargains to paid leave. One-third of women in the sample of garment workers also experienced salary cuts due to sick leave. This latter finding is significant in that it points to poor working conditions in this industry, and the considerable hardships faced by women.

The paper by *S.I. Khan* on *Gender Issues and the Ready-made Garment Industry in Bangladesh: The Trade Union Context* also highlights this struggle for women but in a different sphere, that of

---

[4] See for instance Doeringer, P.B. and M.J. Piore, *Internal Labour Markets and Manpower Analysis*, M.E. Sharpe, Inc., 1985.

the work place. The paper makes an important contribution in enquiring into the state of industrial relations in the dominant export industry in Bangladesh, which is also characterised by private ownership. While trade unions are prevalent in the public sector and function in close association with political parties, thus exercising considerable clout, what *Khan's* paper documents is the underdeveloped state of trade unionism in the garments industry, which may typify the situation in the private sector in general, particularly in the "new" export industries. Unionisation incidentally, is completely banned in the export processing zones of the country, though this is currently under review.

The research for this paper is based on in-depth interviews with office-bearers of the federations and unit unions in the RMG sector, owners, officials of the *Labour Directorate* and dispute resolution machinery of the State, and with labour leaders.

Khan's paper finds that a very few garments workers were able to form their federations themselves but relied on the help of activists from outside. Yet, workers depended on the help of labour *federations* in getting legal redress, organising labour movements, settling labour-management disputes, and during lay-offs. Some of the factors identified by the paper for lack of success in forming independent unions by workers include high labour turnover in enterprises, low levels of education, the financially disadvantaged condition of the workers etc. Employers were also found to actively discourage trade unionism, sometimes resorting to illegal practices such as unfair dismissal, harassment of workers using hired musclemen, and preventing registration of trade unions by influencing officials in the *Labour Directorate*. Interestingly, cultural traits and patrimonial attitudes of employers towards workers, fear of militancy, are also stated by the paper as reasons as to why more healthy industrial relations have not prevailed in this sector. Several lapses in the state machinery including the lengthy time involved in adjudication, and the backlog of cases in the Labour Courts, the insignificant penalty for non-compliance of labour laws, are similarly pointed out. The outcome from such evasions of the law include the deprivation of female workers from maternity and other benefits, weekly holidays, as well as poor working conditions in many enterprises.

The paper strongly argues in favour of greater worker participation in management for an improvement in industrial relations, as laid down in the *Industrial Relations Ordinance of 1969*, institutional changes, and the need for State regulation.

The paper by *Debapriya Bhattacharya* and *Mustafizur Rahman* on Female Employment under Export-propelled Industrialisation: Prospect for Internalising Global Opportunities in Bangladesh's Apparel Sector is different in that it looks at the future sustainability of the trend in terms of female employment in the export industries in Bangladesh, particularly in the garments and textiles sector, which has absorbed most of the female labour force and has continued potential to do so. In fact, the paper looks at the long term viability of the sector itself.

The main conclusion of the paper is that the type of firm level adjustments needed for the garments industry to withstand competition following changes in the global environment including a phasing out of the Multi-fibre Arrangement and an end to preferential treatment to Bangladeshi exports in certain (EC) markets, may lead to some *substitution of male for female labour*.

This is especially likely since most women are still employed as operatives or helpers, in the low skills — low wage segment of the industry. As the demand for more skilled labour increases in the industry with technology upgradation, and as firms rely more on product diversification and greater value-addition rather than wage competitiveness to survive in the international market, women may lose out in various ways. Thus established gender norms and biases could discriminate against women in terms of selection for on the job training and hiring. This of course raises the question as to what extent factory employment of women has been able to diminish such gender biases.

The paper also gives data to show that over a fairly long period (1980-1997), the increase in real wages has been highest for skilled workers (40 per cent), compared to a modest 20 per cent rise for trainees and only 14 per cent for semi-skilled grades. These trends in wage rates thus strengthen the point that the gains for women in the longer term will very much depend on skill upgradation.

Two sets of recommendations follow from the paper. The first, it may be stated, is an *externality* argument to subsidies the training costs of female labour. Given the nature of the industry with a large number of competitive firms, such a subsidy may be necessary, since workers have the option to leave and join other units on completion of training. However, other recommendations to retain the female share of employment in this industry such as de-emphasising maternity benefits (to keep the costs of hiring male and female labour at par) is debatable. This will directly affect the welfare of women workers. The same relates to promoting labour market flexibility, if it means discouraging unionisation.

1.4 CONCLUSIONS AND AN INTERPRETIVE FRAMEWORK

What the set of papers included in this study thus highlight is a close link between global forces of competition, the type of macroeconomic policies pursued, and outcomes for women. All these have been powerful forces in changing the nature and extent of women's participation in the economy, propelling more women into wage work. Two other forces which need to be considered are the role of NGOs and that of the state.

Interventions by NGOs have for instance been instrumental in changing the nature of household production, inducing a transition to market-based activities for many women. This is brought out by Simeen Mahmud's paper, but is also reflected by the vast amount of resources channelled to women particularly in rural areas in the last two decades through NGO credit programmes, as a result of which more women are now involved in self employment. NGO programmes have also had an important impact in terms of raising the awareness of women on health and social issues, increasing their political participation, and involvement in various socio-cultural activities.

A review of state policies on the other hand indicates that in terms of the development budget, the flow of resources going to women have been minimal. Thus development expenditures on *Women's Affairs* (under the Annual Development Programme) was less than one per cent of development expenditures in the social sectors in most years during 1980/81 to 1994/95.[5] Women specific

[5] See Table 2 for a break-down of these expenditures.

development expenditures[6] in the other social sectors have also been small in comparison to the total expenditures in those sectors, except for some particular years in health and family planning, due to construction of several infrastructural projects.

Besides budgetary allocations, the various plan documents also give an insight as to the conceptualisation of gender issues in the development planning process. The earlier plan documents while emphasising the mainstreaming of women into development activities, simultaneously delineated separate spheres for men and women in terms of the nature of women's participation in the economy. The same approach and emphasis was carried through to the Third Five Year Plan. This changed somewhat in the Fourth Plan (1990-95), which envisaged a more diversified participation of women in the economy and outlined steps to close the gender gap, which was most effective in increasing female school enrolment rates. While some progress has thus been made, the issues for the future are better implementation of the plans, improved governance and a better conceptualisation of the women's agenda in terms of both efficiency and equity.

By focusing on changes in the macroeconomic policy environment in Bangladesh and concomitant changes in the labour market, the study therefore makes an important contribution. It shows that macroeconomic processes are not "gender neutral", but have different implications for men and women. Thus certain types of industrial processes incorporate a higher demand for female labour, based largely on an economic rationale, but which is also culturally determined, to the extent that these jobs are perceived to be "female jobs". On the other hand, worker profiles in these *feminised* sectors show that the labour market for women is segmented by age, education, marital status etc., so that while entry into these sectors are easier for women, it is not completely free of all barriers. Globalisation has thus not been able to prevent "crowding in" effects which not only reduces wages in the particular sectors but

[6] Women specific development expenditures refer to projects specifically targeted towards women. or towards women & children. found to be important in sectors education. health & family planning. youth and sports. social welfare. and rural development and institutions.

also throughout the economy, by reducing the opportunity costs of female labour.[7]

A further feature of the female labour market in Bangladesh is the *segregation of tasks*, which to a significant extent accounts for the observed *average* gender differential in wages in an industry or enterprise, even though such a wage gap may be narrow or non-existent for a particular skill category. Again, globalisation has not been able to solve this problem, calling for interventionist measures by the State.

Women's ability to respond to macro economic demand factors, whether in the labour or product markets are however dependent on *micro* processes, at the level of the household and that of enterprises, and at the level of society (the **meso** level).

As both *Kibria* and *Afsar* point out, the community plays an important role in mediating the process of entry of women into formal sector employment and their absorption into the urban labour market, by providing information and linkages.

Community attitudes however remain ambivalent to female workers in both the rural and urban setting. This is heightened by the general instability and crisis which prevails at the societal level. Social attitudes thus continue to exert an important influence in determining the status and position of women in the transition. As *Afsar's* study concludes, family and kinship net works provide a much more solid basis of support in this regard, especially when no public or factory-based support services are available such as transport, housing or child care.

On the other hand, both the labour supply decision and the outcomes in terms of women's status, position and welfare, are critically determined within the household. Here, as discussed by *Kibria* the dynamics of co-operation and conflict, the betterment of the household as well as that of the women herself and a long-run maximisation or survival strategy underlie the labour supply decisions of young women workers. Gender relations no doubt play a role (Kabeer 1995),[8] as

[7] See Mazumdar, D. (1983) "Segmented Labour Markets in LDCs". *American Economic Review*, Vol. 73, No. 2.

[8] Kabeer (1995). Necessary, sufficient or irrelevant? Women, wages and intra-household power relations in urban Bangladesh. IDS working paper no. 25. Institute of Development Studies, Sussex.

does other forms of inequality within the household. The latter case is typified by women's participation in household-based market activities, where the significant gender gap in human capital limits the type of activities in which women invest[9]. Also, the non-linearities that *Mahmud* finds between participation rates and schooling (higher for no schooling and more than six years of schooling) clearly indicate that higher levels of human capital formation improves woman's chances of finding work. Given that poverty and lower educational attainments are correlates, push factors drive poorer and less educated women from the rural areas into wage work, including that provided by state sponsored programmes.

Gender differences at the enterprise level on the other hand not only relate to wages and benefits, which reflect differences in educational attainments or prior experience, but also to the nature of *bargains and outcomes*. The two papers by *Afsar* and *Khan* focus on these processes at the workplace. Thus *Afsar's* paper finds that more women face salary cuts due to sick leave and also women tend to bargain via supervisors. On the other hand, the high turnover rates amongst female garments workers appear to reflect their search for a better deal, by utilising their experience accumulated by working in different factories. *Khan's* paper, which focuses on the state of trade unionism in the ready-made garments sector, clearly show that the efficacy of state regulatory mechanisms, lack of a tripartite structure for dealing with labour issues, remain serious constraints on improving the working conditions of women in the export based ready-made garments sector. Here too however, women have shown considerable initiative in mobilising themselves and joining federations, as well as in articulating their demands.

What the study thus illustrates is that macroeconomic policies, influenced by globalisation, resulting in sectoral shifts in resource allocation, have significantly affected the outcomes for women. In the case of Bangladesh, this has opened the doors for women's employment in the formal sector and has significantly increased female

---

[9] Thus from inception to December '94, 33.4 per cent of the total number of Grameen Bank loans were utilised in livestock and fisheries, 22.9 per cent in agriculture and forestry, 22 per cent in processing and manufacturing, 14.7 per cent in trading, 3.8 per cent in shopkeeping, 1.29 per cent in collective enterprises, 1.09 per cent in peddling and 0.9 per cent in services (GB 1995).

migration. It has also made women more "visible" in the male dominated public space.

The study however shows that these changes are circumscribed by the disadvantages women face both within the household and in the wider socio-economic context, perpetuating gender segregation in the labour market and in enterprises. *It nevertheless underscores the significant strides made by women in responding to the new challenges faced by them, their capacity to learn and undertake new roles, and negotiate bargains in their favour both within the household and outside.*

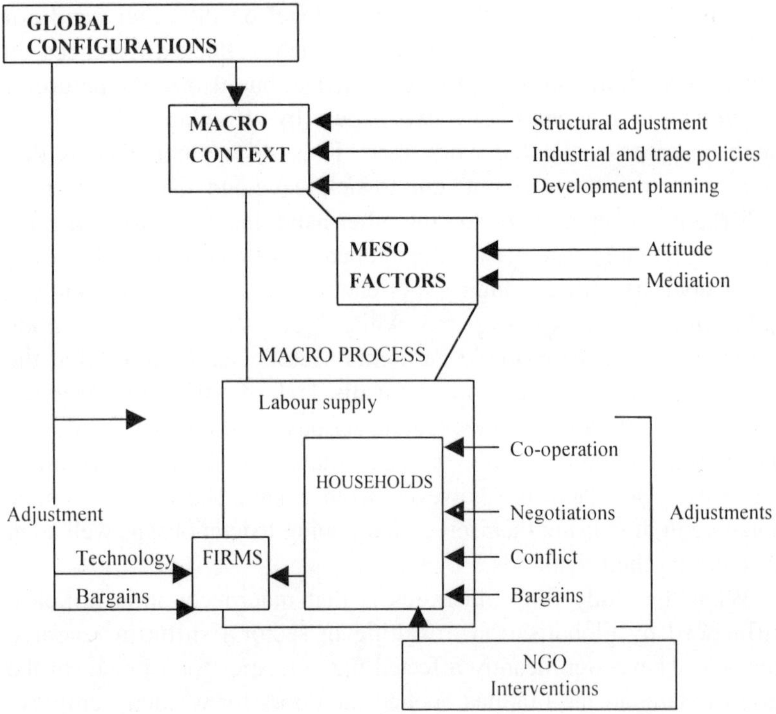

Fig. 1.1: The Pattern of Women's Employment and Outcomes: Key Influences

In sum, while the global context has been important in defining the entry into formal sector employment for women in Bangladesh, this has been governed by traditional inequalities at the micro, meso and macro levels. These different levels of analysis are therefore needed to understand the outcomes for women, both positive and negative, as well as the scope for corrective action. (See Fig. 1.1). Moreover, the women's capacity for bargaining and negotiation are important determinants of the labour supply decision and working conditions. Group solidarity, social and kinship networks, are factors which have been used by women to sustain themselves in the urban labour market.

The study similarly underscores the importance of interventionist measures by NGOs and the state in influencing such outcomes in favour of women. The former has been most effective in the sphere of self-employment, while the scope of the latter is incorporated in budgetary allocations and the planning process. Moreover, the role of the state in developing an appropriate regulatory framework and creating the enabling conditions for women's participation in the labour force, cannot be overemphasised.

It is also worth mentioning that an appropriate framework for addressing gender issues in the macroeconomic agenda, requires that this agenda itself should incorporate equality in its various dimensions including gender, as an objective, and not simply focus on macro-economic growth and efficiency.

1.5 POLICY RECOMMENDATIONS

The study leads to some specific policy recommendations. These are outlined below:

i. to increase the efficiency of female workers by reducing the gender gap in education and training.

ii. to introduce schemes for technology upgradation in market-based-activities within the household.

iii. to enhance women's spatial and occupational mobility by ensuring security both at the workplace and at the societal level and through investment in housing and improved communications for women in the urban labour market.

iv. to ensure greater budgetary allocations for women in key sectors such as education and health, especially to remove labour market segmentation, but also to improve the health status of working women.

v. for the state to take measures for improving the institutional set-up affecting labour in the female dominated industries. This includes enforcement of labour laws, particularly where these relate to women, through strengthening the Labour Directorate, improving the functioning of labour courts and encouraging a tripartite arrangement to settle labour issues.

vi. to initiate measures at the enterprise level so that employers, through state support, can introduce health and training schemes for workers and

vii. for the state to counter attitudinal biases against women, especially working women, through media coverage, and through appropriate modifications in the curriculum content.

viii. a similar initiative by the state to remove the barriers to women's employment in a much wider range of industries and occupations, including affirmative action in the sphere of public employment.

The ultimate goal should be to reduce gender inequality and improve the efficiency of women workers. The latter is an imperative in achieving economic growth and efficiency, given that women constitute a rapidly increasing part of the incremental labour force in both rural and urban areas.

TABLE 1.1

Average Female Wage as % of Average Male Wage for all Employees

Ind.	Industry Name	85-86	87-88	88-89	89-90	90-91	91-92
311*	Food mfg.	93.95	98.6	63.33	54.10	39.61	47.97
3119	Rice Milling	105.63	52.44	79.31	71.89	51.14	65.55
3126	Tea & Coffee Processing	66.19	66.45	58.38	73.57	79.06	61.19
3127	Tea & Coffee Blending	–	–	78.22	79.06	–	–
3143	Bidies	–	–	57.56	55.29	90.13	51.01
3211	Cotton Textile	90.37	76.14	68.82	67.04	95.0	78.81
321*	Textile mfg.	80.43	68.36	81.33	45.21	83.1	61.69
3216	Handloom Textiles	52.29	78.66	79.24	93.53	57.96	89.25
3225	Cordage, Rope & Twine	–	80.7	60.77	84.46	74.51	61.1
322*	Textile mfg.	65.02	64.28	59.92	61.96	51.11	40.76
3231	Ready-made Garments	77.79	72.77	73.16	74.00	70.69	70.29
323*	Wearing Apparel	77.79	72.77	73.16	74.02	70.69	70.29
324*	Leather & its Products	–	41.64	91.92	74.74	82.82	76.69
327*	Embroidery of Textile Goods	–	–	–	32.92	16.09	55.79
3318	Bamboo & Cane Products	–	–	61.03	57.25	55.88	84.47
331*	Wood & Cork Products	93.31	93.67	25.29	27.15	29.24	40.42
3511	Allopathic & Medicines	112.68	77.59	85.85	91.82	84.32	95.79
351*	Drugs & Pharmaceuticals	112.49	79.59	85.48	91.46	85.4	95.77
3524	Fertiliser mfg.	134.38	126.0	181.11	35.90	451.22	362.08
3535	Matches mfg.	81.01	99.1	86.77	111.28	83.72	65.58

(Contd.)

(Continued)

Ind.	Industry Name	85-86	87-88	88-89	89-90	90-91	91-92
353*	Other Chemical Products	79.4	99.67	84.72	108.46	115.47	83.59
3611	Earthenware	–	–	90.24	81.90	–	–
361*	Pottery & Chinaware	62.15	55.24	67.38	63.01	62.6	109.43
3691	Bricks, Tiles & Clay Products	–	–	76.07	62.69	86.67	104.02
369*	Non-Metallic Mineral Products	143.28	151.21	63.83	163.11	76.2	123.8
3847	Electronic Components	–	–	–	68.63	71.77	97.08
384*	Electrical Machinery	106.54	97.01	191.18	127.48	202.04	104.77
291*	Decorative Handicrafts	–	–	33.89	64.47	60.5	225.25
	% in all industries	**70.8**	**54.10**	**51.05**	**45.36**	**48.26**	**51.55**

Source: *Computed from Census of Manufacturing Industries, various years, BBS.

TABLE 1.2

Percentage Distribution of Development Expenditure in the Ministry of Women's Affairs

Sector	RADP 1980/81	RADP 1985/86	RADP 1987/88	RADP 1988/89	RADP 1989/90	RADP 1990/91	RADP 1991/92	RADP 1992/93	RADP 1993/94	RADP 1994/95
1. Training	33.50	44.57	43.77	48.52	51.59	35.86	27.86	33.14	30.35	15.30
2. Employment & IncomeGenerating Activities-	3.43	7.01	4.47	3.73	3.96	8.69	32.84	33.75	19.65	36.57
3. Socio-economic Development	53.09	28.62	39.45	29.97	33.31	11.28	4.88	2.70	19.41	18.29
4. Awareness	1.19	–	–	2.97	1.83	9.32	6.00	5.86	4.11	2.30
5. Rehabilitation	2.33	–	–	–	–	2.39	–	–	–	–
6. Hostels & Residence	0.83	11.86	–	–	0.47	–	–	–	–	–
7. Child Care	5.64	7.94	12.30	14.62	8.83	5.43	9.43	9.11	8.49	19.13
8. Technical Assistance Project	–	–	–	0.19	–	27.01	18.99	15.45	18.00	8.42
Total	**100.00**	**100.00**	**100.00**	**100.00**	**100.00**	**100.00**	**100.00**	**100.00**	**100.00**	**100.00**

Note: RADP = Revised Annual Development Plan.

Source: Various issues of *Demands for Grants & Appropriations (Development)*, Ministry of Finance, GOB.

Chapter 2

THE LABOUR USE OF WOMEN IN RURAL BANGLADESH

Simeen Mahmud

2.1 INTRODUCTION

Within the broad framework for integrating gender into the macro-economic development policy of Bangladesh the need to integrate gender concerns from the perspective of rural women cannot be overemphasised. This is particularly crucial in view of the widely held notion that since rural women remain largely outside the purview of the visible cash economy, being primarily functional in the domestic and the informal economies, they are beyond the jurisdiction of macro policy formulation. There are a couple of country-wide programmes, however, in which women feature quite prominently. The first of these is the national family planning programme that has one of the most extensive field level infrastructures in rural areas to provide women contraceptive services at the doorstep. The more recent attempt to bring women under the purview of policy has been rural development programmes that support women's income earning employment through the provision of micro credit. Both these major policy thrusts have been driven by broader macro economic imperatives (the control of population growth rate and the reduction in poverty levels) rather than the need to incorporate gender concerns into macro policy. Understandably, these policies have not been informed by knowledge or experience about issues of gender equity, efficiency or empowerment.

Very recently urban women have received some policy attention at the macro level, particularly in industry, more by default than by choice. This has occurred as a result of the unprecedented entrance of women workers into the formal urban labour market due to employers' preferences for hiring women in the export based garment manufacturing industry, but again more from concerns about growth in labour productivity and exports rather than from a gender perspective. Hence there is some limited knowledge about changes in the level, pattern and nature of employment for women in urban manufacturing (Bhattacharya 1994).

Considerably less is known about the nature of women's paid work in rural areas although visible changes have also been reported in terms of employment level and sectoral pattern. In fact, the vast majority of women workers in the garment manufacturing industry originate in the rural areas and rural women's entrepreneurial role has expanded significantly in the recent past. Given that labour force participation of rural women is bound to rise in the near future (as will be elaborated later), these developments bear implications for the identification of new and more remunerative opportunities for women's productive employment in the rural areas.

Gender Roles and Women's Labour Use

Of particular policy concern is the fact that women continue to play a marginal role in the visible non-domestic economy relative to men, especially with regard to participation in the labour market, and even when they do it is usually under more harsh conditions compared to men. An understanding of the situation is often hampered by the dominant view that women in Bangladesh are trapped, on the one hand, by inflexible cultural traditions that value their confinement within the home and, on the other, by increasing poverty that pushes them into the harsh outside world for survival. In other words, women are viewed as having no economic agency of their own, being compelled to participate in development programmes or in the labour market by their destitute status or at the expense of their social prestige as a result of breaking with the cultural practice of *purdah*.

What is little acknowledged is the fact that, largely irrespective of class, socio-economic institutions (of marriage, family formation, inheritance and the labour and product markets) enforce a rigid gender role differentiation, which dictates the economic roles of both women and men and gives rise to gender specific production spheres. Thus, women perform multiple economic roles which produce goods and services that save expenditure[1], while men perform economic roles which produce goods and services that have market value. Moreover, women's economic activity takes place at much lower levels of technology compared to men's economic activity. The implications of both gender specific economic roles and women's lower level of technology adoption compared to men are that women have relatively less labour time available than men for non-domestic production and are less able than men to invest in market valued human resource acquisition.

The consequence on women's labour use is clearly visible in the time use patterns of women and men in rural areas (Table 2.1). Unlike men, women use the major proportion of their working time for expenditure saving household production, and this general pattern has persisted over time. Patterns of gender specific time-use reveal that in rural areas ever-married women spend upto 85 per cent of labour time in household production and only 15 per cent in paid employment, while for ever-married men these figures are 4 per cent and 96 per cent respectively (Amin 1994). There is an observed socio-economic class effect on women's labour time spent in income-earning work. In land poor households, and to a greater extent in households where there is no male earner, women spend relatively less time in household production and more time in income earning compared to women in landed or non-poor households. A small income effect is also evident for men.

In reality, decisions influencing women's and men's labour use forms part of the broader household agenda to meet consumption needs through the most efficient allocation of resources and labour. For women, more than men, the allocation of labour between home and market production is also shaped in response to existing local opportunities for female employment, including the demand for

---

[1] In Bangladesh these generally include household maintenance, food processing and preservation, care of children and the elderly, health care provision, self-provisioning activities and unpaid work on family enterprises.

TABLE 2.1
Daily Hours of Work in Income-earning and Home Production in Rural Areas by Gender

Year		Income Earning		Home Production		All Work	
		Women	Men	Women	Men	Women	Men
1977	Mymensingh	1.16	7.40	6.68	1.29	8.29	8.33
1980	Comilla	3.90	5.90	5.60	0.90	9.50	6.80
1991	Rajshahi	1.53	6.75	6.25	0.64	7.78	7.39

Source: Cain 1978; Khuda 1980; and Amin 1994.

female wage labour which is usually more limited than the demand for male wage labour. Hence women's participation in non-domestic employment is unlikely to be entirely driven either by women's destitute status or by the need to uphold the cultural practice of women's seclusion, but is more likely to be a rational response to existing supply and demand forces.

The Need for "Gendering" Development Policy

As such female labour use is directly and indirectly affected by the developments in the national and local economies and by the macro-economic policy agenda. However, in Bangladesh incorporating "gender" into the process of policy formulation for economic development continues to be an elusive goal. Since the early 1980s successive five year plans have all articulated the government's commitment to enhance women's role in the process of economic development by bringing them into the mainstream of the development arena. Despite the fact that national statistics are increasingly being collected on a gender disaggregated basis, a ministry and a directorate of women affairs have been in operation since 1978 and 1984 respectively, WID Focal Points have been established in 31 line ministries and agencies to ensure the reflection of the government's WID concerns in their programmes, and a strong local WID advocacy movement outside the government has emerged, but gender concerns continue to be marginalised and are yet to enter mainstream development policy and programmes.

Conventional development policy consists of bringing together resources, technology and expertise to raise incomes and enhance employment opportunities for the resource poor. Thus, mainstream development projects that emphasise income generation and employment creation within the public domain automatically exclude most women needing incomes. Alternately, special projects that emphasise homebased income and employment generation based on women's traditional skills marginalise women with respect to the non-domestic economy since productivity is low and incomes are meagre.

The reality is that, whether consciously or otherwise, women face both exclusion and marginalisation in the overall process of economic development. Hence, there is an urgent need to recognise women as a distinct constituency in development policy and planning in the sense of direct economic agents and consumers rather than marginal actors and indirect beneficiaries. There is also a need to recognise the gender perspective on development which is that gender differentiated economic roles and experiences require that development interventions are gender sensitive rather than gender neutral.

2.2 FEMALE LABOUR MOBILITY IN THE RURAL AREAS

Shifts in the economic resource bases of households and the persistence of widespread poverty has different consequences on the labour mobility of women and men. One of the ways in which this happens is through the gender differentiated effect on labour use. With regard to women's labour mobility, the allocation of women's labour time is affected to a greater extent in poor households.

Since traditionally women's economic activity has been largely homebased[2] rather than market based, women's labour mobility will be assessed in terms of movement from the household to the non-household economy. The labour mobility of women between home production and market production is constrained both by supply and by demand restrictions. The major supply constraint has been gender differentiated responsibility for household production and gender specific access to human capital. The major demand constraint on women's mobility has been the segmented and sex segregated nature

---

[2] These activities have included child care, household maintenance, food and crop processing, animal husbandry, homestead horticulture, and rural manufacturing including handloom products.

of the labour market. Especially among the poor, for whom female labour supply is relatively more elastic, the real constraint to movement is no doubt inadequate demand for the level of skills currently on offer by the women.

The most comprehensive information on women's employment is available from official statistics collected by the Bangladesh Bureau of Statistics (BBS) under the aegis of the population censuses and nation-wide labour force surveys. Censuses or complete population enumerations are undertaken every 10 years and the latest available is for 1991. Labour Force Surveys (LFS), conducted since 1980, are nationally representative household sample surveys[3] undertaken more frequently, but tend to be irregular, with the most recent conducted (during writing of this paper) in 1990/91. Hence, even though aggregate trend comparisons are possible, these have to stop at 1991 since more recent data are not available.

The Nature of Female Labour use in Rural Areas

Women's movement into the labour market is indicated by the labour force participation rate[4] (LFPR). Official statistics indicate that women participate in the labour market at significantly lower rates than men, but that the female LFPR has been growing at a faster pace than the male LFPR (Table 2.2). In rural areas women's LFPR doubled between 1984/85 and 1990/91 whereas male LFPR remained almost unchanged. In urban areas the LFPR appears to have increased only marginally, but since the growth of the urban population is much greater the absolute increase in labour force is substantial. Between 1984/85 and 1990/91 33 per cent of the incremental increase in total employment was due to increase in women's employment; in rural areas 59 per cent of the increase in employment came from female entrants into the labour force. During this period the share of rural women in total rural employed population also rose from 9 per cent to 13 per cent.

---

[3] The 1990/91 survey covered 9000 sample households selected from 240 rural and 120 primary sampling units.

[4] The LFPR is calculated as the number of persons economically active divided by the number of persons aged 10 years or more expressed as per cent. Persons of age 10 years and above who are either employed (paid or unpaid) for 15 hours or more during the reference week or unemployed and looking for work are defined as economically active.

TABLE 2.2

Labour Force Participation Rates by Gender and Residence

Year	Rural		Urban	
	Female	Male	Female	Male
1974 Census	5.8	73.7	4.0	80.0
1981 Census	5.0	79.0	6.8	74.8
1984-85 LFS	7.7	78.8	12.1	78.8
1989 LFS	7.3	82.5	29.0	72.7
1990-91 LFS	14.4	80.0	12.7	76.2

Source: Population Census and Labour Force Surveys conducted by the Bangladesh Bureau of Statistics.

Clearly, rural women have been allocating an increasing proportion of labour time to market based economic activity (relative to home based economic activity) since the late 1980s, at a pace that is growing much faster than that of men's. If this trend in employment growth has continued then aggregate female LFPR in rural areas could be as high as 20 per cent at present. The crucial question in terms of poor women's well-being is whether this movement has been largely supply driven or demand induced or both.

Implications for Women's Well-being

Although it is not always possible to distinguish whether women's movement into the labour market has resulted from the "demand pull" or the "supply push", the implications for women's well-being can be very different in the two cases[5]. Some insights may be obtained by looking at the quality of employment in terms of the sectoral patterns and status in employment.

In 1990/91 (the latest year for which information is available) the most important sector for rural women's market activity was manufacturing (in household based units) followed by agriculture. Since 1984/85 the personal/community service and the household sectors[6]

[5] The excess movement of women into the labour market can lower the supply price of female labour and dampen wages due to the influence of "crowding", while genuine demand for female labour can actually reduce the gender wage gap.

[6] The household sector is a concept used in Labour Force Surveys but is not adequately defined.

have been declining while agriculture and manufacturing sectors have been gaining in importance. Thus, rural women have been able to move into potentially more productive areas of work. Women's greater participation in agricultural activities is accompanied by a narrowing of the gender gap in wages to the extent that average wages are only 14 per cent lower for women compared to men. However, in agriculture women's increased activity has come about mainly from livestock rearing which has relatively lower returns compared to other household based activities, while in manufacturing it is not clear whether there has been a movement from less productive activities (like coir rope and mat making) to more productive ones (tailoring and dairy products).

A gender comparison of occupation in employment indicates that employed women and men in rural areas are equally likely to be professional, administrative or clerical workers, suggesting that access to formal and semi-formal sector employment may be easier than believed for women who have some education. There also appears to be a slight rise in the share of white and blue collar occupations for women but not for men. Women are more likely than men to be service workers and production workers (where the activity usually takes place inside the home), but less likely to be sales workers, reflecting no doubt the persisting public/private divide in gender specific production spheres.

The share of wage employment (including casual labour) in total employment declined slightly from 39 per cent in 1984/85 to 37 per cent in 1990/91, while the share of unpaid workers increased from 18 per cent to 24 per cent and the share of self employment (including employer) remained the same. While the share of wage employment remained the same for employed men its importance declined from 64 per cent to 36 per cent for employed women.

In terms of status in employment (Table 2.3) it appears that during this period of 8 years there has been a shift in women's status in employment from employee to unpaid worker. The share of unpaid work among employed women more than doubled in rural areas (but was similar in urban areas), and the share of self employment increased in all areas. Women were also twice as likely to be self employed or even employers, while the proportion of day labourers

TABLE 2.3

Status in Employment in Rural Areas (%)

	1990-91		1983-84	
	Male	Female	Male	Female
Employer	21	9	–	–
Self employed	19	23	43	17
Unpaid worker	25	38	18	13
Employee	11	14	10	52
Day labourer	24	15	31	17
Other	4	2	<1	<1
All statuses	**100**	**100**	**100**	**100**

Note: Figures may not add to 100 due to rounding.

Source: LFS 1990/91 and 1983-84.

TABLE 2.4

Occupational Distribution of Employed Population in Rural Areas by Gender (per cent)

	1990-91		1983-84	
	Women	Men	Women	Men
Proof/tech/adm./ Clerical worker	8	5	4	4
Sales worker	3	11	5	9
Service worker	12	2	43	3
Agriculture worker	55	67	11	72
Prod/transport Worker	21	14	32	12
Not defined	1	1	2	1
All occupations	**100**	**100**	**100**	**100**

Note: Figures may not add to 100 due to rounding.

Source: Computed from LFS 1990/91 and 1983/84.

remained unchanged. While the increase in the proportion of self employed and employer is a favourable change, the shift in employment status from employee to unpaid worker may not be such a positive trend.

Gender comparisons of status in employment reveal that in 1990/91 only 9 per cent of employed women were employers or own account workers compared to 21 per cent of employed men; 23 per cent of women and 19 per cent of men were self employed; and 38 per cent of women and 25 per cent of men were unpaid workers. In the agriculture sector women were overwhelmingly employed as unpaid workers (over 90 per cent),, but in non-agricultural activities women found employment as employees (41 per cent) or were self employed (39 per cent). Among employed men 33 per cent were unpaid workers in agricultural activities, and 32 per cent and 48 per cent were employees and self-employed respectively in non-agricultural activities. For men the share of self employment was almost the same while the share of unpaid work increased but not to the same extent as for women. Thus, the shifts in status in employment were less prominent for men.

The Role of the Rural Non-farm Sector in Employment

The potential importance of the rural non-farm (RNF) sector in generating rural income and employment is supported by the fact that during the 1980s the non-agriculture sectors, including construction, services and manufacturing, grew at a faster rate than agriculture[7] and absorbed the incremental increase in the total labour force, which went primarily into small manufacturing, trading and transport services. An assessment of the quantitative share of this sector in the overall rural labour force was made using census and LFS data for the period 1981 to 1991 (Mahmud 1996). In spite of problems of comparability due to data limitations it was concluded that the non-agricultural share of the rural labour force has been increasing steadily over this period and constituted about 38 per cent of total employed persons in the rural areas in 1991 (Table 2.5).

---

[7] The growth performance of the different sectors reveal that between 1981 and 1994 agriculture grew at the annual rate of 2.15 per cent, manufacturing at 3.99 per cent, construction at 6.30 per cent and services at 5.31 per cent, whie overall GDP growth was at 3.93 per cent per annum. Between 1990 and 1994 the growth in agriculture slowed down to 1.58 per cent while manufacturing growth increased to 6.71 per cent. Given this growth scenario the share of the agriculture sector in overall growth declined from 44 per cent in 1980/81 to 35 per cent in 1993/94, while the share of manufacturing remained almost stationary at around 11 per cent. The share of the service sector in GDP registered an increase from 41 per cent to 48 per cent, accounting for 60 per cent of the incremental growth in GDP between 1984 and 1994. By comparison only 12 per cent of the incremental increase in the GDP took place in the manufacturing sector.

TABLE 2.5

Proportion of Rural Population Employed and the Share of Non-agricultural Sectors in Employed Population, 1981-1991

	Population Census		Labour Force Survey		
	1981	1991	83-84	84-85	90-91
Per cent of rural population employed					
Both sexes	25.8	25.9	28.9	29.3	31.8
Male	49.5	49.7	52.3	53.2	53.3
Female	2.5	3.6	4.8	5.0	8.8
Share of non-agricultural sectors in employed population (%)					
Both sexes	29.3 (32.6)	33.9 (37.9)	34.3	34.4	38.6
Male	27.2	30.9 (34.9)	28.5	29.4	35.1
Female	67.3	76.1 (77.8)	89.5	88.8	61.3

Note: Figures within parentheses corresponding to census estimates show the estimates adjusted for including semi-urban (non-municipal) areas within rural areas.

Source: Mahmud 1996.

TABLE 2.6

Coverage of Rural Women and Men by Selected Rural Development Programmes

Name of programme	Villages covered	Households covered	Groups		Members	
			Number	% F	Number	% F
BRDB 1995	418[1]	–	13350	–	709789[2]	–
BRAC 1995	26940	–	44656	92	1500000	–
RDRS 1995	5015	260000	12500	56	–	–
ASA 1996	8640	–	25824	99	500445	–
GB 1994	34913	–	412145	94	2013130	–
Proshika 1995	6778	841773	47758	54	262669	–

Source: Annual Reports and personal communication

Note: 1. Refers to thanas covered

2. In the RPCP programme 80% members were women.

Between 1981 and 1991 the employed population in agriculture grew by 1.36 per cent per annum compared to 4.16 per cent per annum for the employed population in non-agriculture, 2.53 per cent per annum for the total labour force and 2.17 per cent per annum growth for the population as a whole. The share of non-agriculture in the total rural employed population rose from 29 per cent to 34 per cent. The rise in the share of non-agriculture was even higher for the rural female employed population compared to that of employed rural men. However, according to LFS data the proportion of rural women employed in the non-agricultural sector appears to have declined during the last 5 years. This is confirmed by the relative expansion in agricultural occupations for women in the rural areas, but is not supported by census data.

The fact that the RNF labour force is estimated to have grown at a considerably faster pace than the overall rural labour force suggests the increasing diversification of the rural economy. If labour force participation among women is higher in households that have non-agricultural occupations, then the implications for women's labour use is a possible increase in women's labour supply for market work since 1991.

2.3 IMPACT OF DEVELOPMENT INTERVENTIONS ON FEMALE EMPLOYMENT IN RURAL AREAS

It is commonly assumed that programmes for employment creation will be able to reduce rural unemployment which is believed to be widespread in rural Bangladesh, especially among women. The argument is that such interventions, especially targeted credit programmes and skills training programmes, will influence both the demand for labour by raising the productivity of self employed labour and inducing the demand for wage labour, and the supply of labour by increasing access to resources and human capital.

Coverage of Rural Women and Men

The magnitude of coverage of resource poor women and men by rural development programmes is quite impressive, and has increased dramatically in the recent years. In 1994 the Grameen Bank alone operated in over 34 thousand villages nationwide, accounting for nearly half of all villages in Bangladesh, while the coverage of BRAC, the largest NGO, extended to nearly 30,000 villages (see Table 3.1). Institutional support for employment generation has been largely provided by GO and NGO programmes for poverty alleviation, and the main mechanism for input delivery has been through the process of group formation and mobilisation for collective action at the village level. Groups are typically organised initially around savings activities, and later around income-generating activities that are undertaken either individually or collectively with small amounts of collateral-free credit provided by these organisations. The evidence indicates that the coverage of rural women is far greater relative to the coverage of rural men, and this is visibly so for the two largest NGOs (BRAC and ASA) and the Grameen Bank, for which women constituted over 90 per cent of membership in 1994/95.

The Role of Group Membership in Enhancing Women's Capabilities

Particularly for women, membership in these groups provide them with the first, and often only, non-kin support system through which they are able to gain knowledge and information, access productive and managerial skills, achieve financial discipline, and get peer support for social action. In addition, group membership significantly increases women's physical mobility and interaction in the "public" or the non-domestic economy. Research has indicated that group membership has visible influence on women's role in household decisions[8]. These

[8] This is evident from several studies that investigate the influence of programme participation on women's status. Women in households that had received a Grameen Bank loan through a male member had the least participation in decision-making, while women who were active Grameen Bank members and had taken a loan had the greatest role (Rahman 1986). Women loanees of credit programmes that did not organise women's groups were found to have lower mobility and a weaker role in household non-traditional decisions than loanees of programmes that mobilised women into groups (Mahmud 1994). Women's relative control over monetary decisions or incomes from credit based activities was, however, less likely to be influenced by group membership. Male family members, especially husbands, were found to be more involved than women loanees in buying inputs and deciding how much to sell and at what price (Ahmed *et al.* 1990). Involvement in credit programmes increases women's mobility, their ability to make purchases and major household decisions and their legal and political awareness (Hashemi *et al.* 1996). In the case of female irrigation groups women were able to retain control over the sale of irrigation water only when groups had strong internal cohesion (Van Koppen and Mahmud 1995). Exploitative class relationships were also better tackled by group

experiences suggest that institutional support to women in the form of group mobilisation can meet both the practical and the strategic needs of women and enhances their functional capabilities within the non-domestic economy.

Impact on Employment Opportunities and Labour Force Participation

Most studies, whether based on qualitative methods or on conventional village surveys, that attempt to assess the impact of development programmes on women's lives have direct or indirect evidence of a positive effect of membership or programme placement on the opportunities for women's paid employment.

A 1990 evaluation of two programmes for rural women, the Socio-economic Development Project for Women (SEDPW) run by the Directorate of Women Affairs and the Shaptagram Nari Swanirvar Parishad (SNSP) an NGO, studied the impact of programme interventions in six villages on indicators of household economic situation, one of which was the perception of women survey respondents regarding opportunities for female employment (Asaduzzaman and Akhter 1990). The comparison was between target group (TG) programme members and TG non-members from both programme and non-programme villages. The survey found that 53 per cent of programme members compared to 41 per cent of non-members in the non-programme villages believed that there was an increase in work opportunities. On the other hand, 47 per cent of non-members in the programme villages also thought work opportunities had increased. In other words, members perceived an increase in employment opportunities more commonly than non-members in the non-programme villages, while among non-members in programme villages this perception was almost the same as that of the members.

However, a comparison of the actual levels of participation in paid employment was not reported so that the magnitude of direct impact on women's work opportunities or labour force participation was not known. There was also no information on the type of

---

mobilisation since elite women had a smaller chance of dominating group decisions and activities.

opportunities available or the returns to labour. Some insights are obtained by examining the type of inputs received by members which showed that 14 per cent of SNSP members and 16 per cent of SEDPW members received either vocational training, employment in earth work or other employment. Hence, only a small proportion of women members actually received programme inputs that would lead to increased employment.

A study on Grameen Bank (GB) and Bangladesh Rural Advancement Committee (BRAC) based on ethnographic research and a sample survey conducted in six villages in 1992 examined the impact of credit on women's contribution to family support, which was indicated if "part or all of the family expenses were met through their own independent earnings" (Hashemi *et al.* 1996). It was recognised that although all women who received credit gained access to additional resources, not all of them succeeded in using the loan to generate independent incomes. It was reported that 72 per cent of GB members and 40 per cent of BRAC members made direct contributions to family income compared to 27 per cent of non-members in GB villages and 20 per cent of non-members in the non-programme villages. The odds ratio[9] of contributing to family support from women's own independent earnings was nearly 7 times greater for GB members and 2 times greater for BRAC members relative to a comparison group (women residing in a non-programme village but eligible to join either BRAC or GB) after adjusting for education level, relative wealth, age, surviving children, and geographic location.

In other words, membership in these two development programmes, and especially in GB, positively influenced women's participation in independent paid employment through effective utilisation of and control over their loans. As with other studies the degree of impact on women's labour supply was not evident. Case studies revealed that members earned an average annual cash income of Tk 12600 which ranged from 5 per cent to 25 per cent of household income in different villages. However, since the hours of

[9] The odds ratio is defined as the probability of contributing to family support relative to the probability of not contributing.

employment for women was not reported the returns to women's labour could not be measured.

A more recent comparative study of three micro credit programmes[10] in rural areas did attempt to estimate the impact of programmes on the employment of women generally and on the employment of members. The study concluded that programmes had been generally successful in expanding self-employment opportunities (Rahman and Khandker 1995). Labour force participation rates for members and non-member women were calculated (Table 2.7), and found to be higher than the rates reported in official Labour Force Surveys. In particular, participation rates were higher among members than among target group (TG) non-members in both programme and non-programme areas. Thus, both the level of overall employment as well as the level of self employment was raised in programme villages.

TABLE 2.7

Labour Force Participation Rate by Programme Participation Status (total Observations = 6335)

Programme Participation status	Labour Force Participation Rate (LFPR)	
	Male	Female
A. Grameen Bank Villages		
Participants	91.33	68.32
Non-participants	94.15	54.97
Non-target group	89.33	49.69
Total	**92.24**	**57.87**
B. BRAC Village		
Participants	90.82	51.18
Non-participants	86.38	42.93
Non-target group	83.08	35.48
Total	**86.57**	**45.31**
C. BRDB Village		
Participants	93.05	64.51
Non-participants	95.15	56.45
Non-target group	87.56	46.53
Total	**90.86**	**53.71**

(Contd.)

[10] The programmes were the Grameen Bank, Bangladesh Rural Development Board's RD-12 Project (BRDB) and BRAC.

(Continued)

Programme Participation status	Labour Force Participation Rate (LFPR)	
	Male	Female
D. Non-program/Village		
Target group	93.55	62.97
Non-target group	92.31	45.83
Total	**92.90**	**54.27**
Whole Sample	**90.41**	**52.63**

Source: Rahman and Khandker 1995.

There was also a visible programme placement effect in that TG non-members had a higher probability of self employment than similar non-members in non-programme villages. In fact it appeared that programme placement was likely to benefit women more than men. However, the probability of wage employment was consistently lower among members compared to TG non-members in all areas suggesting that programmes may encourage members to withdraw from wage work.

Impact on Women's Employment Hours and Time Use

Very few impact evaluation studies report differences in employed hour and time use between members and non-members which could then be linked to programme membership. Such differences were reported in the study by Rahman and Khandker (1995). It was found that women members spent more or less similar hours of total work per month (65, 46 and 46 respectively for GB, BRAC and BRDB members) compared to TG non-members (56) in the non-programme villages (the differences were not statistically significant). However, members were found to supply fewer hours per month to wage employment than TG non-members, which was believed to push up the wage rates in the programme villages. The higher wage rates in the programme villages were thus a boon for non-member households that sold labour, increasing their hours of wage employment and the returns from wage labour. Not only that, self employed workers also increased their hours of work since they substituted their own labour for hired labour because of the rise in the wage rate. Hence, programme placement appeared to increase labour supply for both women and men in all households irrespective of programme membership, especially in Grameen Bank villages.

Average employment per worker, both female and male, was much larger in programme than in non-programme areas. The largest differences (14 per cent and 39 per cent respectively for male and female wokers) were found in the GB villages. Less marked differences were observed in the other programme areas. In all cases the increase in average employment was much higher for women than men.

Impact on Returns to Labour and Productivity

The estimation of the rate of return to labour for economic activities of rural households is difficult because of labour market characteristics in rural areas. Inspite of these problems[11], hourly average return to self employment was calculated and it was found that the average return to self employment is higher than the wage rate, except for livestock rearing (Rahman and Khandker 1995). Thus, targeted credit programme placement improves the overall productivity of agricultural and non-agricultural self employed activity, and both member and non-member TG households benefit through induced village-level impacts.

What is disturbing, however, is that for programme member households the hourly return to self employment sharply declines as the proportion of female labour used increases. This pattern is evident for livestock rearing, crop agriculture and non-agricultural activities, and the return is lowest for livestock rearing. The low return to self employment for households with a higher proportion of female labour use is partly due to women's greater involvement in the low return livestock activity. Thus, the low productivity of female labour, commonly cited as a reason for the lack of demand for female labour, arises because women, even with institutional support, are unable to participate in higher return non-agricultural activities to the same extent as men.

---

[11] These labour market characteristics are identified as a large seasonal labour surplus, a segmented labour market with a large gender gap in the wage rate, limited opportunities for female wage employment and a preference for self employment (Rahman and Khandker 1995).

2.4 FEMALE LABOUR USE IN RURAL AREAS: EVIDENCE FROM VILLAGE SURVEYS

The Survey Methodology

In order to gain greater insight into the demand and supply forces that drive women's labour use decisions a household survey was conducted in four villages during May to July 1996. The methodology consisted of a total enumeration of all households in the village. The instrument used for data collection was a structured labour force type of questionnaire, but including detailed information on household income during the last year (three seasons) from different sources such as crop agriculture, non-crop agriculture, family enterprises, remittance and wage work. The villages were purposively selected to give some geographical diversity and to represent the differential contexts under which female employment takes place in rural Bangladesh. There is, however, no illusion at attempting to achieve national representation.

The four villages were located in the *thanas* of Kishoreganj, Satkhira, Rajbari and Bogra. The latter two villages had significant NGO interventions and activity, compared to the two other villages. The Bogra village was primarily agricultural with high adoption of modern agricultural practices. The Rajbari village was selected because of women's involvement in silk worm rearing, while the Satkhira village was selected because of women's involvement as wage labour in shrimp production, both of which have potential for linking up with export based industry. The village in Kishoreganj was selected because of its proximity to the capital city and reported high rates of out migration. The average number of households per village was 306 and a total of 1226 households were covered by the survey.

Household and Population Profiles

Household profiles by village are shown in Table 2.8. In terms of demographic characteristics of households (mean size of household, the proportion of household members under 10 years of age, mean age of the head and the proportion of households that were female headed) all the four village appear more or less similar. In terms of

TABLE 2.8

Socio-economic Characteristics of Households in 4 Villages of Bangladesh, 1996

Household Characteristics Number of Households	Kishoregonj 282	Satkhira 323	Rajbari 302	Bogra 319
1. Mean size of HH	4.95	4.79	5.15	4.27
2. % HH members under 10	35	29	30	29
3. Mean age of head (years)	41	42	43	40
4. % female head	9	7	5	11
5. Schooling level of head (%)				
No schooling	67	44	59	65
1-5 years	19	35	21	21
6+ years	14	21	20	14
6. Mean homestead land (dec.)	9	12	15	6
7. % female earner[1] HH	8	23	2	10
8. % labour selling HH	41	63	41	41
9. % Non-farm HH	53	63	61	39
10. % NGO member HH	21	15	39	59

Note: 1. At least one female member earns a cash income.

Source: Four Village Survey 1996.

economic characteristics of households the villages are more differentiated. The major household occupation is agriculture in Bogra, trade/service in Kishoreganj and Rajbari, but sale of non-agricultural labour in Satkhira. The proportion of female-earner households ranges from 2 per cent in Rajbari to 23 per cent in Satkhira. The proportion of non-farm households is relatively low in Bogra while the proportion of NGO member households is the highest at 59 per cent compared to the other villages. The proportion of labour selling households is the highest in Satkhira at 63 per cent compared to 41 per cent in the other villages. The size of the homestead (which may be taken as an indicator of the quality of life) is the highest in Rajbari at 15 decimals, but less than half that size in Bogra.

Table 2.9 shows the average level of annual household income by source, average land owned and operated by households and the average value of non-land assets of households for the four villages. Households in Kishoreganj appear to be wealthiest both with respect to annual income and with respect to asset ownership,

TABLE 2.9

Household Income and Asset Level and Sources of Household Income in 4 Villages, 1996

	Kishoregonj		Satkhira		Rajbari		Bogra	
	Taka	%	Taka	%	Taka	%	Taka	%
Number of Households	282		323		302		319	
Total annual income	**47405**	**100**	**30676**	**100**	**41526**	**100**	**32776**	**100**
Agricultural income	8845	19	6309	20	9005	22	12313	37
Non-agricultural income	27190	57	8869	29	20022	48	11561	35
Remittance	2229	5	1138	4	1478	3	2155	7
Wage income	8795	19	14362	47	11020	27	6747	21
Total Asset Value	**11544**	**100**	**4613**	**100**	**9369**	**100**	**6359**	**100**
Liquid Asset	7976	69	2737	59	4169	44	3544	56
Livestock asset	3568	31	1876	41	5200	56	2815	44
Mean own land (decimal)	51	–	64	–	90	–	61	–
Mean operated land (dec.)	59	–	46	–	61	–	53	–
Main source of H income	**Trade/service**		**Non-agricultural**		**Trade/Service**		**Agriculture**	

Source: 4 Village Survey 1996.

while households in Satkhira are the poorest. Average annual household income is 35 per cent higher in Kishoreganj compared to Satkhira. Household income sources are also most diversified in Kishoreganj with 57 per cent of household income arising from non-agricultural sources and only 19 per cent from agriculture. The next most diversified village area is Rajbari. In that respect Bogra remains the most traditional in relation to occupation structure with agricultural income contributing the highest share in household income. In Satkhira the diversification is manifested in the form of a significantly higher share of wage income in total household income. Mean value of remittance is highest in Kishoreganj possibly reflecting the relatively high out migration from the area.

In spite of occupational diversification, however, income distribution was the most unequal in Kishoreganj with the lowest 20 per cent of households earning 4.01 per cent of income and the upper 10 per cent of households earning 49 per cent of the village income. The next most skewed income distribution was in Rajbari, while income distribution was slightly better and similar in Satkhira and Bogra[12].

The average ownership of land and livestock assets is the highest in Rajbari, while the average size of operated land is fairly similar across villages, except in Satkhira where it is somewhat smaller compared to the other villages. The share of liquid assets in total assets is the highest in Kishoreganj, no doubt reflecting the dominance of trade and service occupations.

Population characteristics of the four villages are presented in Table 2.10. The total population covered is 5850 persons with a sex ratio of 104. The demographic dependency ratio[13] indicates that two economically active persons, on average, have one inactive person dependent on. The population under 10 is about 30 per cent generally, with a slightly higher proportion in Kishoreganj where the dependency ratio is also higher. In all villages women are much more likely than men to be divorced or separated and less likely to be unmarried. The most commonly reported occupation (according to respondents' perception) for women is household work in all the four surveyed villages. For men trade/service occupations tend to be the most common in all villages except Bogra, where agriculture is the most commonly reported occupation. In Satkhira non-agricultural labour selling is also a common occupation for men.

Levels of human capital are assessed by examining literacy levels (ability to read and write a letter), years of formal schooling and skills training received. On all these counts men in Satkhira appear to have a higher level of human capital compared to men in other villages. The level of human capital at the aggregate is lower for women compared to men in all villages, although among women themselves women in Satkhira and Bogra fare the worst. Thus, the gender gap in terms of aggregate human capital level is most pronounced in Satkhira. A point to note is that while women

[12] In Rajbari, Satkhira and Gabtoli the bottom 20 per cent of households earn respectively 6.3 per cent, 8.6 per cent and 7.1 per cent, while the top 10 per cent of households earn respectively 39.4 per cent, 27.4 per cent and 23.6 per cent of total village income.

[13] The demographic dependency ratio is defined as the number of persons aged under 10 years and over 65 years divided by the number of persons aged between 10 and 64 years or the economically active population.

TABLE 2.10

Socio-economic Characteristics of the Population of 4 Villages in Bangladesh, 1996

	Kishoregonj	Satkhira	Rajbari	Bogra
Total Persons	**1388**	**1546**	**1554**	**1362**
Male	703	782	802	698
Female	685	764	752	664
Sex ratio	103	102	107	105
Population under 10 (%)	34.5	31.1	29.7	29.0
male	32.7	27.3	27.0	28.9
female				
Dependency ratio	57.9	47.2	49.4	45.2
Read and write letter (10+)				
male	47	62	57	49
female	40	37	44	36
Marital status (10+)				
Unmarried male	59	56	60	58
female	50	47	50	48
Currently mar male	40	43	40	41
female	44	44	44	45
div./separated male	0.8	0.8	1.0	1.4
female	5.8	9.2	6.6	7.4
Major occupation				
male	trade/serv trade/serv	non-ag lab	trade/serv	Agriculture
female	hh work	hh work	hh work	hh work
Education level (10+)				
no schooling male	49	33	43	44
female	56	58	55	60
1-5 years male	32	45	36	37
female	34	33	34	32
6+ years male	19	22	21	19
female	10	9	12	9
NGO membership (10+)				
male	0.4	2.1	6.5	1.6
female	13.8	7.2	22.1	38.8
Training received (10+)				
male	2.6	5.5	2.3	1.0
female	0.5	1.1	7.4	0.6

Source: 4 Village Survey 1996.

generally are more likely than men to be members of NGO programmes in all the villages, they are far less likely to have received any skills training.

The Economic Context of Women's Non-domestic Labour: The Supply and Demand Factors

It is a common belief that Bangladesh has surplus labour, and estimates of underemployment as high as 26 per cent (World Bank 1994) are not unusual. Female labour, particularly, is seen as being much more underutilised than male labour. Under the circumstances of such "involuntary" under — and unemployment the factors affecting labour supply decisions have hardly received much attention.

Because of gender roles women's labour supply decisions, unlike men's, are based not on the simple choice between wage employment, self employment and leisure[14], but also has to take into account the opportunity cost of labour for market work which includes the marginal utility of household production, among other things. The opportunity cost of labour for women varies depending upon women's household situation (women from landed households spend more labour time in home production than women from land-poor households), and can be high enough to prevent women from supplying labour for market work even if income is needed. Other supply barriers which raise the direct cost of women's market work consist of their lack of resources and capital, their lack of information and their lack of access to technology and marketable skills, all of which lower the marginal return from both wage and self employment. Despite the fact that female labour may be underutilised, it is important, therefore, to identify the supply factors that influence female labour use.

With regard to income earning work self employment is the preferred form of labour use among women because it has a lower opportunity cost for women compared to wage employment (because it can be combined with household production and can be

[14] This choice consists of equating the marginal return from wage employment (the wage rate) with the utility of the marginal revenue product of self employment and the marginal utility of leisure.

undertaken within the home) and may even carry more prestige than wage employment. But only a small proportion of women, compared to men, actually report involvement in paid self employment or avail of new opportunities for self employment provided by development programmes. In supplying labour for wage work the opportunity cost can be very different depending upon the class and life-cycle characteristics of women. Thus, married women with families are less likely to engage in wage work compared to women without large families to look after, such as women household heads or women in sub-nuclear households whilst better-off women are less likely than resource poor women to engage in wage work.

Women's relatively lower access to productive resources (capital, skills, technology) are determined to some extent by household socio-economic class, although this type of deprivation generally cuts across class. The gender of the household head is also of importance in women's labour supply decisions since women's direct access to cash income is limited by the fact that most self employment activities are mediated by male family members and women are often unable to retain control over cash earnings and wages. Hence, the household factors which are thought to influence women's labour supply are the main household occupation, household income level and the sex of the household head. Besides individual human capital variables such as age and skill level are also likely to influence female labour supply decisions. In the absence of a more direct measure of the opportunity cost of women's non-domestic labour (the wage rate is an underestimate given the low market demand for the skills that women posses) marital status is taken to indicate the magnitude of this opportunity cost.

The level of women's employment is also influenced by factors which determine the demand for labour. In the case of self employment the very low marginal product of labour restricts the full utilisation of family labour in most family enterprises. This is more crucial for female compared to male self employment since women are less able than men to acquire productive skills, both traditionally and through development interventions. There is evidence that the provision of micro credit make it possible to expand the demand for self employment among women members and induce demand for female wage labour for non-members. A more diversified resource and income base generates demand for female labour in both self and wage employment, while a more skewed income and land distribution generates demand for female wage labour.

The Level of Female Employment

In this study female employment level is estimated by the labour force participation rate (LFPR) according to three definitions of economic activity. The official definition used in the BBS labour force surveys is equivalent to 94 eight-hour days in the last year. This is designated as LFPR1. The extended definition (LFPR2) defines economic activity as work for pay or profit or unpaid work for at least 50 days during the last year. The most extended definition (LFPR3) defines economic activity as work at any time during the last year, irrespective of the amount of time spent.

LFPRs according to all three definitions are presented in Table 2.11 disaggregated by a number of household characteristics. LFPR3, which indicates the overall extent of women's involvement in income earning work, shows the vast extent (over 60 per cent) of rural women's participation in income producing activity although the intensity of work at the individual level in terms of labour days per year may be quite small. Labour force participation according to the conventional definition (LFPR1) indicates that actual participation in the rural areas has increased from the levels of 1991. The reasons for this increase, as well as the differences by location, may lie in nature of the labour supply and demand factors at the household and village levels.

Labour Supply Factors

In order to identify the most important labour suppy factors disaggregated comparisons of labour force participation, using only the conventional definition, i.e., LFPR1, are made. In general, female employment is most common in households where the main income source is labour selling, both agricultural and non-agricultural irrespective of location, followed by trade and service households. Women belonging to farming and business households are the least

TABLE 2.11

Labour Force Participation Rates for Women (usual definition) According to Socio-economic Status of Households in 4 Villages, 1996

Household Socio-economic Status indicators	Kishoregonj		Satkhira		Rajbari		Bogra	
	N	LFPR	N	LFPR	N	LFPR	N	LFPR
All Households								
LFPR1	436	7	529	21	506	16	471	16
LFPR2	436	14	529	29	506	–	471	–
LFPR3	436	47	529	64	506	63	471	61
Main HH Income								
Agriculture	100	3	86	16	81	11	155	15
Agriculture labour	55	4	86	42	108	16	30	33
Trade/service	140	11	146	20	184	18	83	13
Non-agriculturer	76	9	152	18	71	24	98	21
labour business	65	5	63	6	62	8	105	10
Sex of head								
Male	402	6	495	17	485	16	420	14
Female	34	18	34	71	17	24	51	33
Household Income								
< 10000 taka	30	20	4	–	20	22	22	36
10001-20000	104	3	157	9	97	133	133	21
20001-30000	85	5	149	21	133	95	95	12
3000+	217	8	219	22	256	221	221	13

Source: 4 Village Survey 1996.

TABLE 2.12

Labour Force Participation Rate for Women (usual definition) by Individual Characteristics, 1996

Individual Characteristics	Kishoregonj		Satkhira		Rajbari		Bogra	
	N	LFPR	N	LFPR	N	LFPR	N	LFPR
All Women	436	7	529	21	506	16	471	16
Age (in years)								
Under 20	119	2	149	21	162	1	140	1
20-49	274	9	302	23	267	26	274	24
50+	43	9	73	12	77	13	55	16

(Contd.)

(Continued)

Individual Characteristics	Kishoregonj		Satkhira		Rajbari		Bogra	
	N	LFPR	N	LFPR	N	LFPR	N	LFPR
Marginal Status								
Unmarried	97	2	121	21	132	0	126	1
Married	299	7	338	15	324	23	298	19
Divorce/separated	40	20	70	50	50	12	47	38
Schooling								
No schooling	257	7	316	25	275	20	295	22
1-5 years	122	3	163	15	159	9	127	3
6+ years	56	14	9	12	72	17	45	16

Source: 4 Village Survey 1996.

likely to be employed. In all areas, especially in Satkhira, women in female-headed households are more likely to be employed compared to women in male-headed households. By income level the pattern is clearly rising participation with declining household income.

Individual characteristics which determine the level of human capital is also expected to influence labour supply for income earning work. Women in the active age group, i.e., between 20 and 49 years, are the most likely to engage in income earning work. Women with no schooling and women who have completed 6 or more years of schooling are also more likely to participate in income earning work than women with 1-5 years of schooling. Divorced or separated women have a higher participation rate than married or unmarried women in three villages. Unmarried women are the least likely to work except in Satkhira where their participation rate is higher than that of married women. Obviously, village level work opportunities vary according to women's life-cycle stage.

Thus, in rural areas household features that induce female labour supply for income earning work are labour selling or trade/service households, female headship and low household income. Individual features that facilitate female labour supply are an active working age, schooling above the primary level and the lack of male earning members. The lack of male earning member may also be interpreted as contributing to a more active role by women in making decisions on their own participation in income earning work.

Labour Demand Factors

Community level factors that influence the demand for labour are identified by relating women's labour force participation to village characteristics (Table 2.13). That women's participation in rural areas varies according to location suggests the impact of labour demand factors on female labour use. By all definitions LFPR for women is the lowest in Kishoreganj and the highest (three times higher) in Satkhira. Kishoreganj appears to have a lower employment level among women while Satkhira appears to have a higher level compared to the national average for the rural areas.

TABLE 2.13

The Relationship Between Labour Force Participation Rates of Women and Aggregate Village Characteristics, 1996

Characteristics of Village	Kishoregonj	Satkhira	Rajbari	Bogra
1. % village income from non-ag. Sources	57	29	48	35
2. % non-farm HH	53	63	61	39
3. % labour selling HH	41	63	41	41
4. Income distribution	highly unequal	Less unequal	moderately unequal	less unequal
5. NGO activity	low	Low	moderate	high
6. % head with some schooling	33	54	41	35
LFPR 1	7	21	16	16
LFPR 3	47	64	63	61

Source: 4 village survey 1996.

We have seen that although average household income level is higher in Kishoreganj and incomes are most diversified, the distribution of income is the least equitable. In Satkhira average household income is lower but the income distribution is less skewed. It appears, therefore, that the demand for female labour and opportunities for self employment may be linked to the nature of village level income distribution. Also it appears that a high level of male wage labour may induce the demand for female wage labour. The aggregate level of NGO activity is also likely to induce greater female participation in income earning work, but mostly through provision of credit rather than skills training. The proportion of female headship at the village level is not necessarily linked to greater female participation.

The Nature of Female Employment

The nature of women's employment in terms of main occupation (reported), type of employment, hours/days of work/employment and wages earned are shown in Table 2.14. On an aggregate level (pooling data for all villages) 41 per cent of employed women are wage employed and 59 per cent are self employed, so that self employment is slightly more common among working women. A small per cent of women who report self employment as the first activity also engage in wage employment as a second income earning activity. The most common occupation (first activity) for women is homestead agriculture (48 per cent) which includes poultry and animal rearing. The next most common occupation is wage labour (32 per cent), followed by manufacturing, processing and trading activities which occupy 20 per cent of employed women. In wage employment women worked an average of 205 days during the last year and 42 hours in the last week, compared to 164 days and 27 hours in self employment. The large variations by area suggest the impact of demand factors on women's employment.

The annual average wage income is Taka 7822 for wage employed women and Taka 1105 for self employed women who engage in wage employment as a second activity. The implied daily wage income displays marked variation by area and is estimated at taka 63, 34, 57 and 35 respectively in the four villages. The implied wage rate is the lowest in Satkhira where wage work is more common compared to the other areas. The implied daily wage rate is double in Kishoreganj and also visibly higher in Rajbari where women's wage work is far less common. This could be an indication of the crowding effect pushing down the supply price of labour.

Gender comparisons reveal that men are generally employed for more days per year in both self employment (251 days) and wage employment (283 days) than women, and they also tend to work more hours per week. The gender difference in total days of work and total hours is more pronounced in the case of self employment,

TABLE 2.14
Nature of Employment for Rural Women Working for at Least 94 Days Last Year, 1996

	Kishoregonj	Satkhira	Rajbari	Bogra
No. of women	30	110	81	76
Main occupation (%)				
Wage labour	23(7)	62(68)	1(1)	26(20)
Trade/service	27(8)	7(8)	6(5)	16(12)
Homebased agr.	40(12)	31(34)	65(53)	58(44)
Manuf/processing	10(3)	–	27(22)	–
Type of employment (%)				
Self employed	63(19)	30(33)	80(65)	63(48)
Wage employed	37(11)	68(75)	10(8)	37(28)
Unpaid worker	–	2(2)	10(8)	–
Employed days last year				
Self employed	197	172	151	160
Wage employed	228	195	246	205
Employed hours last week				
Self employed	29	29	27	25
Wage employed	34	46	36	34
Annual wage income (taka)				
Self employed	3553	2609	0	720
Wage employed	14356	6681	11760	7186
Implied daily wage rate	63	34	49	35

Source: 4 village survey 1996.

confirming that the conditions of employment are more flexible for women in self employment than in wage employment. This may be one reason for women's preference for self employment over wage employment. The implied daily wage rate for men is remarkably unvaried by area (between taka 55 and 57), and is 40 per cent higher in Satkhira and 14 per cent higher in Rajbari compared to the implied daily wage rate for women, but is actually lower in Kishoreganj.

Thus, the micro evidence indicates that women are most likely to be self employed in homebased agricultural activities that includes livestock rearing, an activity that is often undertaken with the support of NGO credit. Wage employed women work more days per year and more hours per week than self employed women in all areas. Women are more likely to be wage employed when the household itself depends mainly on labour selling for income. Women are more likely to be self employed when the household depends on agriculture and business occupations for income, and women's wage employment is relatively more common in households where the main income source is trading or service. Women's earnings from wage employment are depressed compared to men's earnings both because they are employed for fewer days per year and because they have a lower level of earnings.

2.5 DISCUSSION AND POLICY IMPLICATIONS

It is evident that clearly, women have been responding to changes in labour processes in the rural areas. These changes have been in response to both policy initiatives (rural credit, garments export) and developments in the macro (village) and micro (household) economies. However, the evidence indicates that despite some expansion in the aggregate level of employment, women in agricultural households continue to be locked into low productive homestead agricultural activities such as livestock rearing. This type of employment, although having a lower opportunity cost, is not very favourable for women either in terms of returns to labour or in terms of women's increased mobility and participation in the public domain. Women's employment in non-agricultural activity or in wage work is more evident in those households that are engaged in trading, services or professions or in labour selling households. This type of employment is to be more favourable for women in terms of the potential for higher returns and other positive externalities such as women's increased mobility and control over their earnings, but is likely to have an adverse effect in terms of women's total work burdens and leisure.

In all cases, however, women's lack of access to productive resources (despite some expansion in access to credit) and their low level of human capital (because of limited access to both formal schooling and to less formal skills training) compared to men raises the more direct costs of women's labour by limiting the demand for women's labour and by depressing earnings and incomes, especially relative to men. The demand for women's labour and its returns are also low because of several well identified phenomena that affect rural non-agricultural activity, especially rural manufacturing, more generally. These "domestic hurdles" include underdeveloped local and urban markets that do not demand consistently high standards of quality, the lack of exposure to a modern market environment, the lack of infra-structure particularly electricity, low investment in equipment and technology and in extension services for human capital development, the absence of marketing and information networks, and of course inadequate levels of institutional finance (Yusuf and Kumar 1995).

For women who will prefer self employment in homebased agriculture[15], and the numbers are likely to be significant since a large proportion of rural households will remain primarily agricultural households, the challenge is to increase the returns to labour and productivity levels, and to enhance women's control over earnings to ensure savings and reinvestment. This requires the provision of effective extension services for upgrading technology, the provision of support services for marketing and ensuring women's control through the formation of cooperatives or savings and credit groups, equipping them to move into high value agricultural products and expanding markets by providing for value addition to women's primary labour activity through linking up with agro-processing for the manufacture of agricultural and dairy products. The other option is suggested by the experience of women's collective enterprises in crop production activities through land leasing or share cropping arrangements using hired male labour. This type of activity is more rewarding to women both in terms of returns to labour and in terms of control over incomes. However, it is limited by the local availability of agricultural land under general conditions of land scarcity.

For women who are able and willing to take up non-agricultural employment[16] and wage employment, and the numbers are likely to swell with the increasing diversification in rural incomes, the challenge

[15]This is because in agricultural households the existing demands on women's time for home production pushes up the opportunity cost of women's labour so that they prefer homebased self employment even if returns are low.

[16]In non-agricultural households the opportunity cost of women's labour is likely to be less allowing women to allocate time for higher return activities especially in trading and manufacturing and in wage labour.

for policy is to expand the demand for female labour in non-agricultural activity in both self employment and wage employment. The demand for women's labour in non-agricultural activity could be given a boost by conscious industrial re-location and sub-contracting of economic activity from the urban to the rural areas, by making available larger amounts of institutional credit for financing new rural based enterprises and by improving the infrastructure for linking rural and urban markets. At the same time attempts should be made to forward link rural to urban and even foreign markets, by effective upgrading of equipment and skills, and by exploring and targeting "niche" export markets that are more profitable but also riskier. All these imply certain sunk costs that must be borne, part of which must be shared by exporters and industrial entrepreneurs. Here NGOs can play a critical role in intermediating links between poor rural producers and the national as well as global market.

This brings us to the critical question of what should be the appropriate approach to integrating gender into the macro policy agenda in Bangladesh — equity, efficiency or empowerment. The fact that women are lagging behind men in terms of employment opportunities and returns to labour necessitates that equity considerations must feature prominently in development planning. The fact that women are locked into low productivity activities both in the domestic sphere as well as in the public sphere, and the fact that investments in raising women's productivity have greater positive externalities than investments in raising men's productivity indicates that efficiency considerations cannot be brushed aside in the context of scarce resources. Finally, since development cannot be an end in itself, the empowerment of women that leads to their greater control over resources and incomes and enhances their role in the household decision making agenda must form an integral part of all development activity.

References

Ahmed, Z *et al.* 1990: "Gender Differences and the Role of Women in Households: The Case of Female Loanees of BRAC", Research and Evaluation Division, BRAC.

Amin, S 1994: "The poverty-purdah trap in rural Bangladesh", paper presented at the IUSSP Seminar on *Women, Poverty and Demographic Change*, Oaxaca, Mexico, October 1994.

Asaduzzaman, M and F Akhter 1990: "Evaluation of Poverty Alleviation Programmes for Women", EPAP Project, BIDS.

BBS 1994: "Report on the Labour Force Survey, 1990-91", Bangladesh Bureau of Statistics, GOB.

BBS 1995: "Women and Men in Bangladesh: Facts and Figures, 1970-1990", Bangladesh Bureau of Statistics, GOB.

Cain, M *et al* 1979: "Class, Patriarchy and Women's Work in Bangladesh", *Population and Development Review*, Volume 5, No 4.

DWA 1995: "Inventory of sectoral programmes on women in development, 1995", Department of Women Affairs, MWCA, GOB.

Hashemi, S M, S R Schuler and A P Riley 1996: "Rural Credit Programs and Women's Empowerment in Bangladesh", *World Development*, Vol.24, No.4.

Khuda 1980: "Time Allocation Among People in Rural Bangladesh", DERAP Publications No 101, Bergen, Christian Michelson Institute.

Koppen, B van and S Mahmud 1995: "Women and Water Pumps in Bangladesh", Intermediate Technology Publications, 1996.

Mahmud, S 1994: "The Impact of Women's Employment Programmes on Fertility Regulation in Bangladesh", forthcoming *The Bangladesh Development Studies*, Vol.22, Nos.2&3.

Mahmud, W 1996: "Macro-evidence: the Push-pull Debate Reconsidered", paper presented at the BIDS-World Bank seminar on *Stimulating Growth Through Rural Non-farm Activities*, July 1996.

Majumdar, P and S Mahmud 1994: "Barriers to women's employment in urban Bangladesh", Bangladesh Institute of Development Studies.

Rahman, R I 1986: "Impact of Grameen on the Situation of Poor Rural Women", Bangladesh Institute of Development Studies.

Rahman, R I 1996: "Impact of Credit for Rural Poor: An Evaluation of Palli Karma Shahayak Foundation's Credit Programme", BIDS Research Report, No.143.

Rahman, R I and S R Khandker 1995: "Role of Targeted Credit Programs in Promoting Employment and Productivity of the Poor in Bangladesh", paper presented at the BIDS-World Bank workshop on *Credit Programs for the Poor*, March 1995.

The Fourth Five Year Plan 1990-1995: Ministry of Planning, GOB.

The Third Five Year Plan 1985-1990: Ministry of Planning, GOB.

Yusuf, S and P Kumar 1995: "Non-farm Development: Comparative Experience and Bangladesh's Prospects" background paper for the Rural Non-farm Project of the World Bank.

Chapter 3

BECOMING A GARMENTS WORKER: THE MOBILISATION OF WOMEN INTO THE GARMENT FACTORIES OF BANGLADESH

Nazli Kibria

In Bangladesh, relatively low rates of women's participation in wage employment have traditionally been understood as a reflection of cultural factors unfavourable to such participation.[1] Recent developments, however, challenge the notion that women in Bangladesh, whether due to cultural or other factors, are disinclined to enter the wage labour market. Since the 1980s, an export-based garment industry has mushroomed in Bangladesh. Perhaps the most notable feature of this industry is its heavy use of women workers; an estimated 70-80% of those employed in the industry are women (Majumdar and Chaudhuri 1994).

The rapid development of the garments sector, along with its mobilisation of women workers, has made it a popular issue of concern among a wide variety of groups in Bangladesh, including policymakers, activists and scholars. Despite this attention, many basic questions about the industry's workers remain unanswered, hampering the effective assessment of the impact of macro-policies on the sector. This paper looks at the factors and processes that

---

[1] For a review and critique of how culture is emphasised as an explanatory factor in discussions of women in Bangladesh see Kabeer (1991) and White (1992).

underlie the mobilisation of women into the garments labour force. How and why do women come to seek and enter into jobs in garment factories? The materials for this paper are drawn from a qualitative study, based on 70 in-depth interviews with women garment workers and their households in Dhaka and various rural parts of Bangladesh.

The garments sector in Bangladesh has helped to create a new group of women industrial workers in the country. Studies indicate that many of the women who work in the industry have had no prior wagework experience (Bangladesh Manufacturers and Exporters Association; Majumdar and Chaudhuri 1994).[2] In explaining this development, employer preference and global tradition are clearly important points to consider. In export production factories around the world, women have emerged as preferred workers; employers often cite the lower costs, and the docility and nimbleness of women in comparison to men (Elson and Pearson; Lim). However, a full understanding of the movement of women into the garment factories of Bangladesh requires us to consider not only the "pull" but also the "push" factors that underlie this trend. What has driven or enabled women to respond positively to the expanded job opportunities?

Analyses of women's entry into wage employment in Bangladesh often emphasise the role played by extreme poverty and the related dynamic of male unemployment and desertion in driving women into the wage labour market. Since the 1970s, growing numbers of rural women in Bangladesh have sought wage employment in the areas of agricultural labour, as well as earth-cutting, brick-breaking, construction and road maintenance. Mahmud (1992) notes that two groups of women have been particularly likely to engage in these jobs: women in low-income male-headed households and women heads of household. Thus impoverishment and the absence of a male breadwinner are two characteristics of the wage-seeking women. An emphasis on these "push" factors is in many ways consonant with the notion that cultural barriers have been critical in deterring women's wage employment. That is, it is only under the tremendous pressures of extreme poverty that woman violate cultural proscriptions against

---

[2] Majumdar and Chaudhuri (1994) note that 49.1% of the workers surveyed had been unemployed/at home prior to working in garments, and 23.9% had been students.

women's involvement in paid employment, particularly in jobs that require them to be in male-dominated public spaces.

To what extent are extreme poverty and male absent family structures behind the movement of women into the garments industry.

Available studies of women garment workers in Bangladesh suggest that while these are relevant factors, they are not sufficient explanations for the movement. Kabeer's (1995) work points to the complexity and diversity of the economic motivations of women garment workers. She asserts that while for some the job is a matter of basic survival, for others it is a way of improving their standard of living, or of earning money for personal accumulation and expenditure. While not exploring the issue of economic or other motivations *per se*, the findings of Majumdar and Chaudhuri's (1994) survey study also affirm the diversity of women garment workers. Diversity in socioeconomic background is suggested by the levels of household income reported by the workers as well as the range of occupations of household members.[3] While only an approximate indicator of the presence of a male breadwinner, the survey's findings on marital status also show women garment workers to be a variable group in terms of this characteristic.[4] These findings suggest that poverty and the absence of a male breadwinner are not adequate or complete explanations of why women enter into garments work. One of the goals of this paper is to explore the conditions and motivations that underlie entry into garments work without blurring the lines of diversity among women.

In what follows I describe the methods of this study and provide some basic information on the sociodemographic characteristics of the sample. Following this, I analyse women's accounts of how and why they entered into garments work, paying particular attention to the context of the household in these accounts. The final section of

---

[3] As far as household incomes, 15.3% reported 1000 taka and below, 27.7% between 1000-2000, 29.9% between 2000-3000, 20.9% between 3000-5000, and 7.5% over 5000. The occupations of household members included typist/clerk, garments work, labourer (Majumdar and Chaudhuri 1994).

[4] Majumdar and Chaudhuri (1994:29) report 38.6% of their respondents to be married, 54% unmarried, 2.1% widowed, 3.5% divorced and 1.9% abandoned.

the paper is an analysis of the role played by the community in mediating the process of becoming a garments worker.

3.1 RESEARCH AND A BRIEF PROFILE OF THE WORKERS

This paper is based on interviews with women garments workers and their households. All of the interviews for the study were guided by an open-ended questionnaire. Most of the interviews were tape-recorded, and interview tapes were later transcribed.

Seventy in-depth interviews were conducted with women garments workers, defined as those currently or recently (within the past 2 months) employed in export-oriented garment factories. The sample of women workers was generated through "snowball" sampling techniques. We began by visiting three garments factories located in different parts of Dhaka city. During these visits we located garment workers willing to participate in the study. We then visited these workers in their homes and conducted interviews with them. During these visits to the homes of the workers we recruited additional respondents for the study. That is, we located other garments workers in the neighbourhood and enlisted their participation in the study. The final sample of garments workers that resulted, while not randomly generated, included women from a range of neighbourhoods and factories.

In the second phase of the study we conducted 30 household case-studies. That is, we visited the family homes of garments workers and interviewed family members. Twenty two of these case studies were conducted in the rural areas of Bangladesh, including the districts of Comilla, Gazipur, Kishoreganj, Mymensingh and Sirajganj. Eight were conducted in the family homes of garments workers located in Dhaka city. The selection of the household case-studies occurred in the following manner. Eight garments workers who were living with their families in Dhaka but who were otherwise a diverse group (in terms of marital status, socioeconomic background, household structure) were selected. For the rural household case-studies, we began by identifying thanas and villages that were important areas of origin among the garments workers interviewed. We then selected 5 rural areas that appeared to vary (as indicated by our interview respondents) in the extent of the flow of women into garments work in the city. Following this, we travelled to the villages of the respondents who originated from these rural areas to conduct household case-studies. On a scale of high to low in terms of the flow of workers, the 5 areas rank as follows: Gazipur, Mymensingh, Sirajganj, Kishoreganj and Comilla. Other rural districts from which some of our interviewees originate but we did not select for intensive case-study include the following: Faridpur, Barisal (high sending areas) and Khulna (low sending area).

The majority of the workers in the sample were between the ages of 15 and 25, with a substantial minority falling below and above this age range (Table 3.1). As shown by Table 3.2, of the 70 women workers, 35 are never-married, 14 are currently married, 19 are separated/abandoned/divorced and 2 are widowed. As far as education, (Table 3.3) 17 women have no formal education, 33 have 2-4 years, 13 have 5-7 years, and 7 have 8 or more years of education. Most of the women are helpers (17) or operators (42), with very few with job titles such as quality inspector, folder, and finisher (Table 3.4). As shown in Table 3.5, most of the women had been involved in garments work for a relatively short period of time, under 4 years. Also of note is that of the 70 women interviewed, 37 had sending family households that were urban, and 33 had sending family households located in rural areas.

To sum up, the collective profile of the workers that emerges is of a young group of women, large numbers of whom are unmarried. On average, they have had some primary level education, although there are both those who have no education and secondary level education. The low numbers of women with more than primary level education may be a reflection of the dominance of operators and helpers in the sample, rather than jobs requiring a higher level of education, such as quality inspector, supervisor.

3.2 BECOMING A GARMENTS WORKER

Garments Work Explanations, Histories and the Household

Three types of explanations were apparent in women's accounts of why they had entered into garments work. In what follows I turn to

TABLE 3.1
Age of Workers

Age	Number of Workers
Below 15	11
15-20	32
21-25	18
26-30	6
30+	3
Total	**70**

TABLE 3.2
Marital Status of Workers

Marital status	Number of Workers
Never-married	35
Married	14
Separated/abandoned	15
Divorced	4
Widowed	2
Total	**70**

TABLE 3.3
Years of Schooling of Workers

Years of schooling	Number of Workers
0	17
1-4	33
5-7	13
8+	7
Total	**70**

TABLE 3.4
Job Post of Workers

Job post	Number of Workers
Helper	17
Operator	42
Folder/Finisher	3
Ironing	2
Quality inspector	6
Total	**70**

TABLE 3.5
Years of Work in Garment Industry

Years of work	Number of Workers
2 or less	21
3-4	32
5-6	11
7+	6
Total:	70

an in-depth analysis of these explanations, and the household conditions and processes that underlie their construction. With few exceptions, women make the decision to enter into garments work as members of a household. The dynamics of garments entry are thus shaped by the particular conditions, resources and constraints that such membership places on the women workers. In looking at how women experience the garments entry process as members of households, I draw on conceptualisations of the household that recognise the reality of both intrahousehold co-operation and conflict (Sen 1990). The vast literature on "household strategies" has brought our attention to the ways in which households co-operatively work or strategise to realise collective goals. This emphasis on co-operation has however not been accompanied by a recognition of the concurrent reality of conflict and division within the household. As feminist scholars have pointed out, these assumptions of democracy, altruism and consensus reflect an idealised view of the household, one in which age and gender do not create basic distinctions in the experience and interests of members (Wolf 1992). An effective consideration of the household in relationship to the garments entry process must take into account the dynamics of both co-operation and conflict that are a part of household life.

In looking at the process by which women enter into the garments industry I pay particular attention to the role of what I call the "sending family household." I use this term to refer to the household unit that the worker identifies with most closely, regardless of whether or not she currently resides with them.[5] To put it another way, the sending family household is the unit that the worker sees as the centre of her family. Thus for an unmarried worker living with other single women in a "mess" in Dhaka, her sending family household may consist of parents and siblings living in the village home. In contrast, for a married woman living with her husband and children in Dhaka, the sending family household is synonymous with the household in which she resides. The sending family household, I suggest, is likely to play a crucial role in the process of garments entry.

"I Entered Garments for my Family's Survival"

The most widespread explanation offered by the informants was that they had entered garments in order to ensure their family's survival. While this was an explanation offered by women of varied marital status, it was largely confined to women who were residing with their sending family households, which were based in Dhaka city.

In consonance with the understanding that garments work was a matter of family survival were the particular areas in which the woman's pay was expended: food, rent, and the repayment of pressing loans incurred by the household. The fact that the woman's pay was absorbed into the household economy for basic needs did not however mean that there were not varied income management practices amongst these women. In some cases the woman's pay was earmarked for a specific purpose such as rent while in others it was absorbed more amorphously into a collective household pot. Some

[5] It is theoretically possible for a worker to not live with her sending family household even when it is located in Dhaka, but this is rare.

women simply handed over their pay to the household head while others spent the money themselves.[6]

In general, the women who talked of their garments work in family survival terms came from sending family households that can be characterised as poor. Notwithstanding the economic variations among them, for all of these households meeting subsistence needs was a difficult task. Virtually all of these households had monetary debts, and few had assets or savings. The most common occupations of adult males in these households was rickshaw pulling and small-scale trading (e.g., selling *pan*, vegetables). However, equally common was the absence of a male wage-earner. Many of the women lived in households in which fathers or husbands were seasonally employed. There were also many cases in which men, due to death, divorce or desertion, were simply not present in the household.

What was the Process of Garments Entry Like for the Women who Identified Family Survival as a Primary Motivating Factor?

Two types of garments work entry histories were recounted. The first was one that related a shift from other types of income-earning activities into garments work. In some cases, the woman herself had moved from a different job into garments, while in others the change had been a intergenerational familial one, with the mother and/or older sister of the worker being involved in another employment sector. But for all of these women, the process of becoming a garments worker was clearly not one that involved negotiating the question of whether or not to have a job. Rather, the issue at hand was that of what type of job to pursue. Among the prior occupations mentioned by the women, in descending order of significance, were domestic service, paid agricultural work (in rural areas), brick-breaking, ground-cutting, home-based sewing, making paper bags, and home tuition of primary school children.[7]

---

[6] While outside the scope of this paper, these different budgetary practices may have different implications for women's power, or the extent to which women derive power from their wagework (see Kabeer 1995).

[7] In this sample, 7 of the women had mothers or older sisters who had worked as domestic servants. Eleven of the women had themselves worked as domestic servants.

The accounts of garments entry related by these women involved "making sense" of or explaining the occupational shift they had undergone. With the exception of the rare cases in which the woman's prior occupation had involved the respectable tasks of sewing at home or home tuition, the entry into garments work was generally seen as a movement of upward mobility. That is, working in garments, for all its many problems, was a better way to make money than what one had done in the past. Of those who had worked in paid jobs before entering garments, domestic service was the most common prior occupation. For Ruma, a 15 year old working as a helper in a garments factory, a positive assessment of the advantages of garments work over domestic service was a vital part of how she came to enter garments work. The household of which Ruma was a member struggled with the costs of food and of repaying spiralling loans. Ruma's father worked periodically in construction jobs while her mother broke bricks and occasionally worked as a cleaning woman (*jhi*):

> When I was young a relative [chachato dadi] brought me to Dhaka and put me in a job, as a live-in domestic in a person's house. At that time my mother and father were not living in Dhaka. So from a very young age I have been working in people's homes. I could not stand it anymore. It's a lot of work, all day and night, and then there are a lot of hassles with people. You are constantly getting scolded, getting hit. So I left [about a year ago] and came to my mother who was living in the bastee [squatter settlement] with my younger brothers and sisters. She [mother] was angry at first but then the people living around us said: "Why do not you send your daughter to garments?" A woman, who is well-respected in our neighbourhood, said to my mother: "Your daughter has been working as a servant for a long time. Give her some relief, let us take her to garments."
>
> My salary now is 400 taka a month, which is more than what I got working as a domestic (100 taka), although they also gave me food. The problem with garments is that sometimes I get the salary and sometimes I do not. Still I think this is better than working in people's homes. If I can become an operator then my salary will be higher and my family will be able to live better. In garments you do not have to work all the time, sometimes you get Fridays off, and sometimes you can finish work at 5 p.m.

Besides occupational shift, another common theme in the garments entry accounts of these woman was the experience of a household crisis which served to propel the woman into employment, perhaps for the first time. Women entered into garments as a way to cope with crisis, perhaps to avert its most disastrous economic consequences. As Rahman (1995) has noted in his work on rural poverty, households in Bangladesh are routinely subject to a variety of crises which make them vulnerable to downward mobility. The household crises mentioned by the women were of various sorts, including financial losses in business, unemployment, illness, death, divorce and abandonment. To take one example, Nargis, a 15 year old sewing machine operator, had begun garments work after her father's small store was burned down and he went into heavy financial debt. The crises mentioned by the respondents included shifts away from the male headed structure of the household, either due to the departure of the male household head, or his inability to work due to illness or unemployment.

The situation of Baby, a sewing machine operator in her late 20s, illustrates the tremendous vulnerability to poverty that is characteristic of female heads of household in Bangladesh (Hamid 1995; Siddiqi 1994). Baby had begun garments work about three years ago, shortly after the second marriage of her husband and his subsequent departure from the household. She lived with and supported her two sons (aged 4 and 6) as well as her elderly parents. Before joining garments, she had done various kinds of odd jobs, including baby-sitting and sewing work at home. Her husband, who had worked as a driver's assistant on a truck, had been the primary breadwinner of the household. Prior to her husband's departure, she had not seriously considered working in garments, being quite busy with her part-time odd jobs and the work of taking care of her young sons. She also mentioned that she had always thought that getting and doing garments work was much easier for young unmarried girls than for a mature married woman like herself. All of these considerations were however pushed aside when the household fell into dire financial straits with the departure of her husband.

The role and attitudes of household members towards the women's entry into garments work reflected the conditions of poverty and crisis in the household. Not surprisingly, there was virtually no household opposition to the women's entry into garments work. In fact, on the contrary, several women spoke of being pressured by family members into taking a garments job, which if possible they would prefer not to do. Given their limited economic resources, it was clearly in the interest of the sending family households to encourage the woman's entry into garments work, since the resulting income was important to their survival. However, household members often interpreted or understood the women's garments work in ways that differed from the framework of family survival offered by the woman herself. These differences highlight the contested character of understandings of the women's garments work within the household. For example, one comment I often heard from male household heads was that 'the woman's income was supplemental to the survival of the household rather than essential to it'. Also advanced was the idea that garments work was in the personal interest of the woman rather than a benefit for the household as a whole. Thus with respect to single women, household members could emphasise that garments work enhanced the marrigeability of the woman. Potential marriage partners would be attracted to her proven ability to generate income and perhaps even to the dowry that she had accumulated through her garments job.[8] In a variety of ways, these interpretations could serve to reduce the significance of the status of the woman as an important income-earner in the household. As I have argued in a previous paper (Kibria 1995), the effects of women's income-earning on family power relations are deeply affected by the meanings that are given to the income.

"I Entered Garments to Improve my Family's Condition and Prospects"

For a relatively small number of the women workers, the entry into garments was explained as a move that had been undertaken to

[8] The idea that the woman's income was being accumulated for her dowry expenses was presented despite the fact that the income of the women in all these cases was being used immediately to pay for living expenses. But the idea that the woman's income was used for a dowry savings pool also reflected the perception that when the family economic situation stabilised, the woman's income would indeed be diverted into such a pool, rather than being used for basic household expenses.

enhance the economic situation of their sending family households. In their accounts of how they had come to work in garments, these women emphasised that it had been a matter of choice rather than necessity; they and their families could and in fact did survive quite well without their income. All of these women were residing with their sending family households. In contrast to the first group that I have described, none of the sending family households in this group were headed by women. Several of the households owned small businesses, while others contained multiple wage-earners or members in skilled and technical occupations (e.g., tailor, driver, typist/clerk). The pay of the woman was spent on luxury expenditures or more frequently, on investments designed to enhance the family's surplus income or financial security. Particularly common was the earmarking of income for the current or future needs of children or younger siblings. Many of the women indicated that their money would be spent to educate family members, or to set them up in business, send them abroad, or get them married. Once again, a variety of household income management practices operated here. In some cases, the woman spent or invested the money herself, while in others, the pay was handled by a household member.

For the women who explained their employment in the framework of "family betterment", accounts of how they had entered garments work almost invariably contained reference to a moment of altruistic realisation. That is, the worker came to recognise that the "sacrifice" of working in garments was one that would enable the household to advance itself socioeconomically. Kin, friends and neighbours played a crucial role in bringing her attention to the financial benefits of garments' work.

While the themes of altruism and sacrifice were prominent in the accounts of these women, there were other, less visible but important elements as well. Tulshi, a garment worker in her late teens, talked of how she had come to the decision to work in garments because of her desire to help her father expand his business. But her motivations for entering garments work also included a desire to expand her range of experience, and to gain a sense of financial independence. In the following, we also get a sense of how the social image of women garments workers may hold certain attractions for young women, representing a certain measure of social independence:

> We own a store, and we can get by quite well with that. But after passing class 8, I decided to find a job in garments. There were some girls I knew who were working in garments. From them I heard about how much money you could make. Because we had a sewing machine at home and I knew how to sew, I knew it would not take me long to become an operator. (Why did not you stay in school?) I thought it would be better to work, make some money for myself. My father would like to expand the store, and with my savings we can do that in the future. To tell you the truth I was not an exceptional student. I did not want to sit around at home, doing nothing. In garments, you can meet different people, learn about new things. I used to see the garments workers on the streets, walking to the factories together. I wanted to see what it was like to live that life.

A sense of insecurity was another element in women's accounts of how they had come to work in garments. We see this in the account of Shilpi, a married sewing machine operator in her mid-20s. According to Shilpi, she had decided to seek a job in garments even though she had never worked in her life and her husband had not wanted her to get a job. She explained her decision to nonetheless enter into garments work in two ways. There was, on the one hand, a desire to work and generate savings that could finance a small business for her husband. But also notable in her account was a deep sense of insecurity about the stability of her marriage, due to the difficulties that she and her husband were experiencing in conceiving a child. The problem of infertility made her fearful that her husband would soon remarry. She had entered garments work partly out of anticipation of this possibility.

The opposition of family members to the decision to enter garments was a common element of the garments work history of these women. Such opposition was articulated in culturally expected ways: the woman's work was contrary to the norms of male/female segregation and respectability, and would thus threaten the reputation and honour of the family. While in some cases the opposition was not persistent or strongly presented, in others it was substantial enough to require much persuasion on the part of the woman. There were lengthy conversations in which women would try to convince family members that working in garments was the right thing to do; relatives and friends could be enlisted by the woman to support her case. Some women, in particular those who were unmarried, spoke not simply of a period of persuasion but actually of entering garments covertly, keeping it secret from the male household head for a period of time.[9] Sharifa's father, for example, as indicated by his account below, found out that his daughter was working in a garments factory one month after she started doing so. After being presented with it as a fait accompli, he came to accept the situation:

> When Sharifa asked me about working in garments, I said no, it is better that you stay at home. It is true that now there are many girls working in garments, many good girls, from respectable families. But still I did not want my daughter to be in that environment; I did not want that she have to work all day. Then I found out that she was working in garments. I was angry, but I didn't try to stop her. If she wants so much to work in garments, then I will not stop her.

The issue of family opposition to garments entry was complicated in several cases by the fact that the decision to enter garments work had itself been triggered by the woman's conflicts with one or more family members, often over the allocation of household economic resources. In one case an informant entered garments work out of a sense of frustration with her father's decision to invest virtually all the household's assets into paying for her older brother to go as a worker to the Middle East. She felt that the heavy investment in her brother's passage abroad would eventually deprive her younger siblings of the chance to continue their education. She felt this way in part because of her assessment that her brother was unlikely to pay the family back with his earnings from abroad.

The dominant explanation of "family betterment" presented by these women was often different from that offered by household members. Household members were more likely to speak of the woman's wagework as an activity that was for her own benefit rather

---

[9] None talked of keeping garments employment a secret from mothers or other older female family members. This is perhaps because men are more likely to be out of the home all day and thus do not miss the absence of the woman worker. It could also be because the opposition comes mainly from men rather than women family members.

than for that of other family members. They spoke of how she could purchase personal luxury items from her wages. And in the case of unmarried women, her wages were to be accumulated and used for her future, perhaps for a marriage dowry.

"I Entered Garments to Take Care of Myself, to Make My Own Way in the World"

The third set of explanations offered for the decision to seek garments employment centred around the idea that this path was a way to financially take care of oneself and build one's own future, thus reducing the burden and responsibility of the family for one's upkeep and well-being. This framework was a prominent one among the 33 young single rural migrant women in the sample. These were women who did not live with their sending family households, which were located in rural areas outside of Dhaka. Some had taken up residence with relatives in the city while most shared living quarters (called "mess") with other unmarried women garment workers.

The economic status of the sending family households of these women, as suggested by an analysis of patterns of land ownership, was poor. The majority (25 out of 33) came from landless or functionally landless households while the remainder came from households that can be categorised as small or medium landowning.[10] An intriguing characteristic concerns the position of the worker within the sending family household. In a large number of cases, the rural migrant garment worker was the eldest sibling of the household.

Poverty and scarcity were common themes in the women's accounts of how they decided to come to the city and work in garments. Part of the decision to enter into garments was an assessment then that such work was better than what was available to them in the village. The rural income-generating opportunities mentioned most often were agricultural wage work (e.g., threshing rice), domestic service, and various types of small-scale self-employment

---

[10] For classifying land ownership categories, I draw on those reported and used by the Analysis of Poverty Trends Project, BIDS as reported by Sen (1995). Landless households are those with less than 0.05 acres, functionally landless are those with 0.05 to 0.49 acres and marginal owners are those with 0.50 to 1.49 acres.

activities, including weaving baskets and mats, raising livestock and growing vegetables. According to the women, the major comparative benefit of garments work was financial, one could make far more money on a regular basis in garments than in other activities in the village. Besides the financial incentives, the nature of garments work and the social image that it holds seemed to hold some attractions over the more traditional forms of income-generation in rural areas. As suggested by the remarks of one respondent from Barisal, garments work was perceived as less physically taxing, particularly in comparison to work in the agricultural sector. Garments work, with its bureaucratic routine, was also seen as new or modern in character:

> What I heard about garments work was that it was easy for girls without much education to find a job. I heard about the pay; the pay is higher than what you can make in the village. There are no jobs (*chakri*) in the village; you can make some money raising chickens or working for other people. Garments work is difficult, but it is easier on the body than cultivating crops, and you get paid every month. Garments work is also good because you go to the office every day, and you learn some new work.

With assessments such as the one above, women came to see entering garments as an effective way to reduce the economic burdens on the household. Often as the eldest sibling of the household they felt a special sense of responsibility for the family's economic well-being. The decision to go to the city and work in garments was seen as one that would alleviate the family's economic burdens in two ways. For one thing, the household would not face the burden of feeding and clothing the woman. But perhaps even more importantly, the burden of arranging and paying for the marriage and dowry expenses of the woman would be alleviated. It is worth emphasising here that the dowry enhancement expected by garments work was not simply a matter of accumulated money that would be paid in cash or goods to the bridegroom. Dowry was also defined as the future earning potential of the woman. Some household members interviewed also mentioned that women garments workers had enhanced dowry in the sense of an expanded pool of marriage partners, due to their exposure to a greater range of persons in the urban environment. We see some of these considerations in the account of Feroza, a seventeen year old garment worker from Kishoreganj. Feroza was the eldest of seven brothers and sisters. Her household had no cultivable land; only the small area on which the family home was located. Her father and uncles worked as agricultural wage labourers:

> There was nothing for me to do in the village. My father talked of giving me in marriage, but it is difficult these days for those who are poor; everyone wants money, a cow, a bed, a watch. How can my father afford these things? In my village there are many girls who work in garments. I thought, if I go and work with them then at least I will be feeding myself. I will not be a burden. And if I can learn the work well, then may be in sometime I can pay for the education of my younger brothers and sisters.

During interviews with the family members of single rural migrant garment workers, the problem of dowry emerged as a critical "push" factor. In the following, a father of a young garment worker, from a village in Mymensingh, talks of how his inability to meet dowry costs shaped his decision to allow his daughter to migrate and enter into garments work. His remarks suggest that the rising costs of a woman's marriage in Bangladesh, a general trend that has been noted by observers (Lindenbaum 1981), may be operating as a "push" factor:

> When I was younger there were families that were rich, there were families that were poor. But no one would consider sending their daughters to work in garments. Your responsibility as a father was to arrange your daughter's marriage. But now for those who are poor, there is no way out. All the marriage proposals that come ask for money or for other things. What can poor people do? It's better that your daughter goes to work in garments rather than stay at home.

Besides poverty and the problem of dowry, accounts of the garments entry process often contained reference to the "push" factors of threats and harassment from family and village members, as well as marital disruptions. Rejina, a 19 year old sewing machine operator, had been working in the garment industry for four years. In her account of how she left her village in Bagerhat to come to Dhaka, both economic scarcity and harassment from a male cousin were important factors. Family members opposed her decision, but ultimately could do little but accept it:

> I am the eldest of 6 children. My father owns a small amount of land, but it is not enough for us to get by well. I left our home to come to Dhaka with my uncle [mama]. (How did your mother and father feel about it?) They were not willing to let me go. But I scared them. I said, if you want peace then you will let me go. And if you do not want peace in this home, then you will stop me. So they did not then stand in my way. It was best for them that I leave. I had a cousin [chachato bhai] who wanted to marry me. He would follow me around wherever I went. I was so scared I had to stay in the house, I could not go to school because of him. He and his parents are very greedy. They wanted him to marry me but they also wanted my father to give them the land that he has in exchange for the marriage. I could not accept that. I could not see my parents and brothers and sisters starve.

Ironically, the problem of sexual harassment, although this time from other sources, continued to plague Rejina after she moved to Dhaka. She, like about one-fourth of the women we interviewed, spoke of experiences of harassment from men in the workplace (co-worker, supervisor) as well as the neighbourhoods in which they lived. Typically the harassment took the form of persistent demands from the man that the woman agree to marry him, coupled with threats and retaliation in the form of unsavoury rumours and gossip about the sexual reputation of the woman.

A number of the rural migrant women had taken the decision to go to the city and work in garments in response to a failed marriage. Quite typical was the account of Hosneara, a garment worker in her late teens from a village in Comilla. After her marriage ceremony, her husband and his family refused to take her home with them unless her family gave them 10,000 taka and several items. Shortly thereafter, the marriage was legally dissolved. About seven months after the incident, Hosneara left her village for the city with a cousin who was already employed in garments. Economic scarcity was not a critical "push" factor in her case; her father owned enough cultivable land to support the family. Hosneara was rather motivated to leave out of a desire to distance herself for a while from the village community as well as to gain some new experiences.

Family tensions and squabbles were sometimes another part of the history of garments entry for these women. Bokul, in her late teens, worked as a quality control inspector in a garments factory. She had left her village home in Comilla after a serious fight with her parents and elder brother. A good and ambitious student, she was told a year before she was to take the S.S.C. (Secondary School Certificate) exam that the household did not have the resources to finance her schooling. Bokul was outraged by this announcement; she felt that the money had been diverted for other purposes. Her anger was so deep that she did not contact her family for almost a year after leaving the village home.

Like the women workers themselves, family members tended to explain the women's garments entry as a course of action that would enable her to take care of herself and to make her own future. However, while the women tended to place these motivations within the larger goal of economically helping the family, household members were more likely to assess the work in individualistic terms, as an activity that brought benefits to the woman. In fact, patterns of economic exchange between the rural migrant workers and their sending family households suggest that at least in the short run, the women's garments work results in few new resources being added to the sending family household economy. Only a few women indicated that they remitted money to the village home, although occasional gifts of money, food and other goods during visits home were common. Given the generally short tenure (under 4 years) of women in the garment industry, it is possible that this pattern is one that shifts as involvement in the industry lengthens.

However, for the rural single migrant women that we interviewed, the dominant flow of resources was in the other direction. Many of the women relied on their families to bear the initial costs of travelling to the city and getting settled with a job and a place to stay. Families typically continued to help out the woman with rice, money and clothes, particularly during the initial stages of her garments career. All unskilled workers who enter the garments industry typically begin in job of helper, the low salaries (average of 400-600 taka a month) of which make it difficult to meet one's own subsistence needs. However, even among women in the more highly paid job of sewing machine operator (average of 1000-1200 before overtime), material assistance from sending family households was not uncommon. Most of the rural migrant women workers indicated that they had little or no money left over from their salary after paying for the costs of food and rent. The sending family household thus operated as a critical safety net. This became quite clearly evident during the national political crisis of 1996, a time when many garment factories closed their doors or stopped payment of salaries to workers. Unable to financially support themselves, a number of women went back to the village home during this time. Thus the garments work of the women cannot be understood in simple terms as a strategy for enhancing the economic resources of the sending family household. As reflected in the understandings of the women and their families, garments work was a way of reducing the costs of maintaining the woman and paying for her marriage. The sending family household operates as an important economic safety net for the women.

3.3 COMMUNITY SUPPORT, OPINION, AND GARMENTS WORK

The process of becoming a garments worker is one that unfolds not only in the context of the household, but also the community in which the household is located. In this section of the paper I discuss some of the ways in which communities mediate the garments work entry process. I define community as the social circles and networks in which the worker and the sending family household are embedded, including kin, friends, neighbours, and village folk. I focus on the sending community, or the community of which the woman is a part before she begins the process of becoming a garments worker.

One of the ways in which the community can affect the garments entry process is by extending practical support for becoming a garments worker. This practical support is of various kinds: information about the availability, salaries, and conditions of garments jobs, assistance in finding a job, coming to Dhaka, and locating a place to stay. For those women based in Dhaka, practical support was generally extensive, reflecting the fact that there are currently few low-income areas in Dhaka where there are not women who are engaged in garments work. Pakhi, in her early to mid teens, had been working as a helper for about 7 months. She, her parents and siblings had migrated from Potoakhali about a year ago, driven by landlessness. After coming to Dhaka, they settled into a *bastee* (squatter settlement) inhabited by people from their area of origin. Pakhi describes how neighbours led her towards garments work:

> After coming to Dhaka my mother and I broke bricks to make money. There were some girls in the bastee working in garments. When they first told us [mother and I] about it, I said, will I be able to do it? I was not sure, because I never had a job [chakri] before. The girls said that I could do the work; you did not need to be educated to work in garments. They said that first I would be a helper and then after I learned the work I could change factories and become an operator. My mother asked the girls to take me to the factory with them. They told me what to say and do during the interview. After going to two factories I found a job.

For rural migrant women workers, the practical support required for successful entry into the garments labour force is necessarily more extensive than that needed by those living with their families in the city. Relatives and fellow village folk who were already involved in the garments business typically provided the rural women with the necessary information and assistance to successfully make the transition into garments work. For obvious reasons, such assistance was most likely in those villages with an established flow of persons into the garments industry. Where such an established flow did not exist, the process of garments entry was necessarily more complex. In a few cases women indicated that they had been recruited by garments factory owners who originated from their village areas. These owners were members of well-known, respected and prosperous families. In other cases of "pioneering" garments work, the process of garments entry began with a trip to Dhaka for purposes other than working in garments. Jahanara, for example, went to the city to visit her uncle (*chacha*). After arriving there, she found out about garments work and decided to try it. In another case, a woman came to Dhaka with the goal of living in her uncle's (*mama*) home and going to school. But soon after her arrival she found her uncle unwilling to pay for her upkeep, a situation that drove her into garments work. Thus in all these cases, the decision to enter garments began only after the worker arrived in the city, where she was exposed to the information and resources necessary to enter into garments work.

The experience of becoming a garments worker is shaped not only by the practical support extended by the community, but also by the community's attitudes and evaluations of the meaning of garments work for women. Virtually all of those interviewed indicated that a layer or segment of community opinion was extremely negative in its view of women's garments work. While such unfavourable ideas were present everywhere, they appeared stronger in areas where the population of garments workers was small rather than extensive. Objections to women's garments work were framed in socioculturally normative ways. That is, women garments workers were sexually loose and immoral, or at least suspected of being so, because they worked with men; they did not respect and obey their family elders. Some other criticisms of the conduct of women garments workers are highlighted by the remarks of the brother-in-law of a garments worker in Comilla. According to him, the negative views reduced the value of unmarried women garments workers within the "marriage market" of the sending community:

> There are many who do not want to marry a girl who has worked in garments. Because the environment is not good. Such a girl will not be attentive to the needs of the household (*shongshari*). We see the girls who come back to visit; they are different. They are not shy in front of people, they know how to talk to outsiders. They speak in good Bengali (*shuddho bangla*). When my sister-in-law comes home, she spends all her time outside the house. She wears *salwar kameez*, not saris. There are some neighbours (*para protibeshi*) who say the girls who work in garments are bad, evil (*shoytan*).

Community perspectives on women's garments work were not however only negative. The women's move into garments work could be justified by the evaluation that it had been taken out of desperation, as a measure of last resort. During a household interview in Mymensingh, a village elder remarked that no one thought badly of the girl since everyone knew why she had left to go and work in garments. The economic difficulties of her family meant that she had little choice but to do so. Thus dire economic or other circumstances (such as a marriage that had failed due to the misdeeds of the man) served to push aside or at least downplay negative judgements about women's migration and factory work. As I have noted in the discussion of the sending family household, in the community too, attitudes towards women's garments work were affected by the problem of dowry. That is, there was recognition among community members of the rising costs and difficulties of marriage for girls. It was acknowledged that families with limited resources would have difficulty arranging the marriage of their girls. In these circumstances, sending the girl to the garments factory was justified, it was an acceptable if not desirable course of action.

3.4 SUMMARY AND CONCLUSIONS

Poverty and the Mobilisation of Women Garments Workers

Among the different groups of women that the garments sector has mobilised are women from poor urban households. For these women, wage employment, whether it is brick-breaking or domestic service, is a necessity. The ability of the garments sector to recruit such women has stemmed from the relative attractions of garments work in comparison to the other types of unskilled employment available to women with low levels of education in urban areas. Besides women from poor urban households, the garments sector has mobilised into its ranks, women who would quite likely not be engaged in wage employment if jobs in garments were not available. For these women, garments work is a way to enhance personal and/or household economic resources. It is also a way to gain a measure of economic and social independence.

Women from rural households constitute an important segment of the garments labour force. In many ways the mobilisation of these women is the most striking, given that it involves not only a movement into the world of industrial wagework, but also into the urban environment. Single rural women who migrate to urban areas alone have traditionally been destitute and impoverished from the lowest socioeconomic strata of rural society. With the development of the garment industry though, we are now seeing the solo migration of rural woman from a more diverse array of socioeconomic backgrounds. While many of the rural migrant women in this study came from landless households, there were also those with some landholdings. More importantly, while economic scarcity was a general condition of the rural sending family household, a number of other "push" conditions and factors operated to provide the critical impetus for the move. In other words, economic scarcity alone does not provide a sufficient picture of how rural women become garments workers. Economic scarcity operates in conjunction with other "push" factors, such as family conflicts, marital breakdown, problems of harassment and uncertain marriage prospects.

Marriage Dynamics and the Mobilisation of Women Garments Workers

The instability and uncertainty of marriage for women is an important dynamic underlying the mobilisation of women into the garments workforce. As I have noted, a significant proportion of the sending family households of the garment workers are female-headed, a condition that is related to the poverty of the households. Also, for some women, the decision to enter into garments work may be triggered by the experience of a failed marriage. A number of these marriages are dissolved immediately or shortly after they commenced, often due to demands for dowry on the part of the bridegroom and his family. In general, the problem of dowry seems to play a critical role in the dynamics of garments work entry among single rural women. Further research and analysis is sorely needed on the issue of dowry inflation, in particular its causes and consequences for women.

In the event that the problem of dowry remains and perhaps even becomes enhanced over time, it is possible that wagework before marriage may become a "normalised" life stage before marriage for a strata of women in Bangladesh. That is, as is the case in some East Asian societies, it will come to be expected that young women work for a few years before marriage. Such a development will be more likely if employment opportunities such as that represented by the garments sector continue to develop. However, the achievement of a state of "normalisation" of young women's garments work requires greater sociocultural acceptance of garments work than is apparent at the present time. Particularly in the rural areas of Bangladesh, women's garments work continues to carry a certain stigma.

Community Networks and the "Pull" of Garments Work

It is perhaps stating the obvious to say that the entry into garments work does not occur in a social vacuum. Information and support from community members is a critical part of the garments entry process. Those who come from communities where garments work is an established course of action are more likely to enjoy the assistance of sending community members in the garments work entry process. The information provided by community networks about garments work is effective in mobilising women because of the distinctive opportunity that garments work represents for women. For many women in both urban and rural households, garments work is financially more lucrative than other available opportunities. But the perceived advantages of garments work cannot simply be understood in financial terms. Garments work has a certain image and status connotations that make it attractive to some women. Garments work was a job (*chakri*) or occupation; it was work that was of more significance and status than informal income-generating activities. Few who actually work in garments factories would claim that these jobs are not taxing or restrictive in many ways. However, the accounts of garments workers suggest that garments work may be seen as less physically strenuous than other available employment opportunities. It has also developed a certain image and reputation that may be attractive to young women. Garments work connotes social and economic independence and more generally, modernity.

The Absorption of Women's Wages into the Household Economy

As far as patterns of wage absorption into the household economy, a clear distinction is apparent between those workers who live with their sending family households and those who do not. For those who reside with their sending family households, wages are more likely to be absorbed into the collective household pot and used to meet household needs in a collective sense. This is not of course to say that conflicts over the control and use of wages are not part of the experiences of these women.

But for those who live apart from their sending family households, the pattern tends to be very different. In general, I found economic remittances to the sending family household to be a limited affair among the rural migrants. This is quite different from the situation noted by studies of "working daughters" in many other societies (Greenhalgh 1988; Harevan 1982; Ong 1987; Tilly and Scott 1978). As I have mentioned, this finding must be interpreted with caution, given the fact that most of the women interviewed has been working in the industry for a short period of time, usually under 4 years. Longitudinal studies that trace the remittances of workers over several years are needed. Nonetheless, I suggest that the absence of a pattern of regular remittances from the worker to her household reflects the attitudinal context in which rural migrant women tend to enter into garments work. An attitude of "she's taking care of herself" was a prevalent one. That is, the woman's entry into garments work is understood to be a means for her to take care of her own needs rather than that of the household. Among garments workers, however, there is a widespread desire and even anticipation of eventually using earnings to help out the family. Perhaps a far more fundamental issue than attitudes is the fact that most of the women who did not live with their sending family households had little left over from their paycheque after paying for their living expenses. In other words, even if they wished to send money home, they did not have the means to do so. Often neglected in current discussions of the garment industry is the point that becoming a garments worker, particularly for those who do not live with their families, requires some financial investment. The job of helper is essentially an informal apprenticeship for the position of sewing machine operator. Those who work as helpers can sustain themselves on their own income only with great difficulty. While the financial situation of women improves when they move into operator positions, most of those interviewed indicated that they had little or no surplus income, or money left over from their paycheque, once basic living costs were paid. Sending family households were thus an important economic resource and safety net for the rural migrant women. Also of note is that marriage continues to represent an important strategy of economic security for women.

Some Policy Implications

The mobilisation of women into the garment industry in Bangladesh reflects the operation of deep-seated and long-term economic and sociocultural shifts. In the coming years we are likely to see important changes in the garment industry, such an increased demand for trained and skilled workers. Given the long-term and structural nature of the "push" factors that lead women to garment factory employment, it is recommended that steps be taken to ease the potential dislocation of women workers as a result of industry changes. Alternative wage employment opportunities as well as training and education programmes can help to minimise the potential dislocation of women garment workers.

Many of the women who enter the garment industry are single rural migrants. Among the major problems faced by these women is that of safe and affordable housing in the city, as well as safe and affordable forms of transportation from the residence to the factory. Policy measures that address these concerns will contribute significantly to the well-being of the garments labour force. A related issue is that of sexual harassment in the workplace. It is recommended that factory managers institute a programme of education and enforcement of regulations against the harassment of workers.

References

Bangladesh Population Census 1991: Analytical Report September 1994, Bangladesh Bureau of Statistics, Ministry of Planning, Government of Bangladesh. Begum, Najmir Nur 1994: *Low-Income Families of Metropolitan Dhaka.* Centre for Family Services, Dhaka.

Chaudhuri, Salma Zohir and Pratima Paul Majumdar 1991: "The Conditions of Garment Workers in Bangladesh: An Appraisal". Bangladesh Institute of Development Studies, Dhaka, Bangladesh.

Cleland, John; James F. Philips; Sajeda Amin; G.M. Kamal 1994: *The Determinants of Reproductive Change in Bangladesh: Success in a Challenging Environment.* The World Bank, Washington D.C.

Greenhalgh, Susan. 1988: "Intergenerational Contacts: Familial Roots of Sexual Stratification in Taiwan". *In A Home Divided: Women and Income in the Third World.* ed. D. Dwyer and J. Bruce. Stanford, CA: Stanford University Press.

Hamid, Shamim 1995: "Female-headed Households" Pp.177-192 in *Rethinking Rural Poverty: Bangladesh as a Case Study.* Dhaka, Bangladesh: University Press Limited.

Harevan, Tamara 1982: *Family Time and Industrial Time.* NY: Cambridge University Press.

Kabeer, Naila 1995: "Necessary, Sufficient or Irrelevant? Women, Wages and Intra-household Power Relations in Urban Bangladesh". Institute of Development Studies, Sussex Working Paper No. 25

Kabeer, Naila 1991: "Cultural Dopes or Rational Fools? Women and Labour Supply in the Bangladesh Garment Industry". *European Journal of Development Research*, 3:133-60.

Khundker, Nasreen 1995: "Gender Issues in Export-based Industrialisation in Bangladesh. Background Paper", Centre for Policy Dialogue, Report No.11, Dhaka.

Kibria, Nazli 1995: Culture, Social Class and Income Control in the Lives of Women Garment Workers in Bangladesh. Gender & Society. Vol.9 No.3 289-309.

Lindenbaum, Shirley 1981: "Implications for Women of Changing Marriage Transactions in Bangladesh". *Studies in Family Planning*, 1:394-401.

Mahbub, A.Q.M. and Hafiza Khatun 1989: "The Urban Poor in Bangladesh". Phase I, Vol. IV Sector Report. Demographics and Social Structure. Centre for Urban Studies, University of Dhaka. For UNICEF.

Mahmud, Simeen 1992: "Women's Work in the Family Economy," Pp.219-231 in *From Crisis to Development: Coping with Disasters in Bangladesh.* eds. Hameeda Hossain, Cole P. Dodge, F.H. Abed.

Majumdar, Pratima Paul and Chaudhuri, Salma Zahir 1994: *Bangladesher Poshak Shilpe Niyojito Nari Sromiker Artha-Shamajik Obosta.* Ekota Publications Ltd. Dhaka.

Majumdar, Pratima Pal and Chaudhuri, Salma Zahir 1992: "Employment and Occupational Mobility among Women in Manufacturing Industries of Dhaka City: Findings from an Employees Survey". Bangladesh Institute of Development Studies.

Majumdar, Pratima Paul; Simeen Mahmud; Rita Afsar 1989: "Squatter Life in the Agargaon Area". Bangladesh Institute of Development Studies.

Mitra, S.N.; M. Nawab Ali; Shahidul Islam; Anne Cross; Tulshi Shah 1994: "Bangladesh Demographic and Health Survey, 1993-94. National Institute of Population and Training" (NIPORT).

Ong, Aihwa 1987: Spirits of Resistance and Capitalist Discipline: Factory Women in Malaysia. Albany, NY: SUNY Press.

Quddus, Md. Abdul; M. Solaiman; and M. Rezaul Karim 1985: "Rural Women in Households in Bangladesh: With a Case-study of 3 Villages in Comilla". Bangladesh Academy of Rural Development, Comilla.

Rahman, Hossain Zillur 1995: "Crisis and Insecurity: The 'Other' Face of Poverty". Pp.113-131 in *Rethinking Rural Poverty: Bangladesh as a Case Study*. eds. H.Z. Rahman and M. Hossain. Dhaka, Bangladesh: University Press Limited.

Safilios-Rothschild, C. and Simeen Mahmud 1989: "Women's Roles in Agriculture Present Trends and Potential for Growth. Agriculture Sector Review". Dhaka: UNDP and UNIFEM.

Sen, Binayak 1995: "Income-earning Environment of the Poor: Aspects of Dislocation, Adjustment and Mobility". Pp.193-220 in *Rethinking Rural Poverty: Bangladesh as a Case Study*. eds. H.Z. Rahman and M. Hossain. Dhaka, Bangladesh: University Press Limited.

Siddiqi, Najma 1994: Family, Work and Dimensions of Poverty. 1:93-102.

Tilly, Louise and Scott, Joan 1978: *Women, Work, and Family*. New York: Holt, Rinehart and Winston.

Wolf, Diane 1990: "Daughters, Decisions and Domination: An Empirical and Conceptual Critique of Household Strategies", *Development and Change*, 21:43-74.

Chapter 4

SOCIOLOGICAL IMPLICATIONS OF FEMALE LABOUR MIGRATION IN BANGLADESH

Rita Afsar

4.1 WOMEN'S INDEPENDENT MIGRATION: COPING WITH THE URBAN LABOUR MARKET AND SOCIETY

Introduction

In recent years we have witnessed an increase in public awareness about women's productive rather than reproductive role in society and women's contribution to development. Nevertheless, the interrelations between migration of female labour and factors/forces that facilitate or constrain women's entry, survival and ability to change their socio-economic situation in the labour market and urban society have received little attention in the policy discourse. Such a neglect is regrettable, not only because female migration is occurring on a scale comparable to that of men in most regions of Asia but because there are interrelations between female migration, the functioning of urban labour markets and society, and women's role and status.

The existing literature suggests that migrant women differ markedly from migrant men in terms of the extent of under-employment and unemployment they face, in their prospects for occupational mobility, in the incomes they earn, in occupations they perform, in their participation in the informal sector and in their tendency to send remittances home (Anker and Hein 1986; Chant 1992; Findley and Williams, 1991; Lopez, Izazola and Gomez de

Leon 1993). Some of these studies (viz. Findley and Williams, 1991; Lopez, Izazola and Gomez de Leon 1993) also note differences in the characteristics between migrant and non-migrant women workers in the labour market. However, it is argued that these differences need to be documented systematically and analysed in terms of processes leading to them (Hugo 1993: 65). Moreover, none of these studies attempt to understand the interactions between women's economic roles and social situation in the urban society.

Historical evidence suggests that the expansion of the manufacturing sector is one of the key elements in the urbanisation and migration process in the developed and many developing countries. In Bangladesh, the sudden and rapid boom of the ready-made garments (RMG) industry in the 1980s generated considerable female employment in the formal export based manufacturing sector. It should be noted that in Bangladesh, the share of women in the total labour force in manufacturing industries was 64 per cent in 1994, compared to 35 per cent in some other developing countries (e.g., Morocco and Jamaica) which experienced a steady rise in manufacturing output.

The average annual growth rate of the female labour force in the industrial sector was 16 per cent in 1990, that is nearly double compared to the 1980s growth rate of 9 per cent (World Bank 1997). According to the Bangladesh Garments Manufacturers and Employers' Association (BGMEA) garments factories alone absorb 1.5 million workers of which 90 per cent are women. Some of the existing surveys (e.g., Zohir and Majumdar 1996; Afsar 1998) on the other hand, found that these factories are composed of nearly two-thirds women and one-third male workers. Hence, it is extremely important to understand the mode of entry of female migrant labourers into the formal manufacturing sector of Bangladesh, their relative strengths as well as weaknesses in the labour market and urban society, compared to both men and non-migrant co-workers.

Objectives of the Study

The study explores the ways and means by which migrant women enter and cope with the demands of the urban labour market and urban society, and how this differs from male and non-migrant workers. In other words, it addresses the following questions:

- Whether there is any difference in the socio-economic characteristics of migrant men and women who enter into the urban labour market, and whether these characteristics also noticeably differ from those of non-migrant men and women.
- Whether there is any difference in the motivation, means and processes through which migrant men and women enter into the labour market.
- Whether migrants receive differential treatment in the labour market and whether their working/living conditions differ in the labour-market and urban community.
- Whether they adopt different ways and means to survive in the urban society and improve their working conditions.

Data and Methods

The study is primarily based on a small-scale sample survey of the migrant labourers of some selected garments factories in Dhaka. However, comparison was also made with a small number of male and female workers of other manufacturing industries namely electronics, pharmaceuticals, and food processing, which also absorb a good number of women workers.

Sampling Methods

As a complete master frame of employees of different skill categories by gender, migration status and age was not available, it was decided to draw a sufficiently large number of samples to select the final respondents for the study. Using quota sampling technique, a minimum of ten and a maximum of 25 respondents, depending on the size of the population, were drawn from each skill category such as skilled and unskilled production workers, and supervisors/managers, to select the final sample for the study. However, in the case of non-availability of the specified quota, all the workers of that category were interviewed[1]. For example, at the technical/managerial level, it

[1] Problems of data collection are discussed in detail in Annex-1.

was difficult to fulfil the minimum quota of ten workers, particularly in the case of women. Excepting Jeacon garments and Haque Brothers Ltd., none of the sample factories have ten women in the technical/managerial category. Bari Apparels have only three women and the remaining factories have five women in this category. All but Bari Apparels have ten or more men in the managerial category and none of the other manufacturing industries in the sample could fulfil the minimum quota in the technical/managerial category for men. In this process, a list of 530 workers, 374 from garments and 156 from other manufacturing industries were prepared through quota sampling methods for the selection of the final sample.

Types of Samples Selected: Categories of Male and Female Workers

An initial census was conducted of the enlisted workers in the factories chosen to create a Master sample frame. A few basic questions, such as, gender, age, current place of residence, place of birth, year of migration, marital status, district of origin, level of education, training, experience, year of joining the factory, previous work experience, etc., were asked to all categories of workers. Table 4.1 describes the sampling process for the study. The workers were stratified by age and gender, and from each quota (e.g. unskilled production worker, skilled production worker and supervisor/manager/technical category), five samples, each for men and women from each of the eight selected factories were drawn as the final sample for the study. In this process, although a minimum number of five samples were drawn from each category of male and female workers, the total derived was 213 and not 240 due to lack of availability of the quota fixed for each category.

It is arguable that the study of women and migration is often best accomplished by comparing women with men, i.e., using gender disaggregated data to the maximum extent possible. Policy makers are more likely to find these data useful and therefore less likely to dismiss results for women only as a "Special Case" (UNINSTRAW, 1994: 43).

In order to examine the validity of the findings and to supplement the present study, the paper also draws heavily from a recent survey

TABLE 4.1

Total Number of Male and Female Workers of the Sample Factories and the Sample Drawn for the Present Study

Name of the Industry	Total No. of Worker*			Samples Listed Using Quota Sampling Method			Final Samples Derived		
	Male	Female	Total	Male	Female	Total	Male	Female	Total
Garments									
Applique Fashion Wear Ltd.	115	164	279	27	25	52	15	15	30
Bari Apparels Ltd.	235	340	575	33	50	83	16	17	33
Florate (Pvt.) Ltd.	80	170	250	30	43	73	15	15	30
Jeacon Garments Ltd.	300	1200	1500	33	45	78	15	15	30
Sparrow Apparels Ltd.	1100	1400	2500	35	53	88	15	15	30
All Garments	1830	3274	5104	158	216	314	76	77	213
Other Manufacturing									
CIBA Geigy Ltd.	43	28	73	18	20	38	10	10	20
Haque Brothers Ltd.	250	300	550	28	44	72	10	10	20
Mehar Industries Ltd.	67	55	122	25	21	46	10	10	20
All other manufacturing Industries	360	383	743	71	85	156	30	30	60

Note: *Statistics provided by the employers of the sample factories.

Source: Sample survey of migrant workers of Dhaka's formal manufacturing sector, 1996.

of 508 randomly selected workers from 14 garments factories of Dhaka city. Although this latter survey was basically directed to address health, particularly reproductive health related problems of the workers, it had also generated some important sociological insights through "Focus Group Discussion" with the workers, their family members, relatives, friends and neighbours from the communities of their current residence. Moreover, being based on a randomly drawn and large sample, it serves as a useful reference for comparison. Henceforth, results obtained from this survey of 508 randomly selected garments factory workers will be referred to as Afsar (1998).

Migrants and Non-Migrants

The broader sample of workers drawn through quota sampling revealed that more than 90 per cent of the workers of the garments factories are migrants. On the other hand, migrants constitute nearly half of the total respondents in the other manufacturing industries. Almost no divergence is found along the gender lines in this regard. "It should be noted that migration is defined using both geographic and temporal criteria. A person who is not born in Dhaka and migrated here between 1980 and 1996 is defined as a migrant." Further, those who migrated between 1991 and 1996 are defined as recent migrants, whereas others (that is, who migrated between 1980 and 1990) are termed long-term migrants. It is assumed that 15 years is sufficient time to adjust to the urban environment. Hence, those who came before 1980, are treated as non-migrants. In this process, about 37 per cent are classified as recent migrants and 46 per cent as long-term migrants, yielding a total of 83 per cent migrants and 17 per cent non-migrants, among the sample respondents finally studied (Table 4.2).

Employers and Types of Sample Factories

Along with workers, employers of the sample factories were also interviewed to get some basic information on the genesis and the gender composition of the sampled factories. Data provided by the employers show the following gender based composition of the sample factories:

- The sample garments factories were established between 1984 and 1994, whereas the other manufacturing units in the sample

TABLE 4.2

Types of Samples Selected for the Present Study by Skill Categories and Migration Status

Types of Workers	Garments				Other Manufacturing			
	%		Numbers		%		Numbers	
	Male	Female	Male	Female	Male	Female	Male	Female
Helper/Unskilled Production Worker	35.5	36.4	27	28	33.3	36.7	10	11
Operator/Skilled Production Worker	32.9	36.4	25	28	10.0	10.0	3	3
Supervisor/Technical/ Managerial Category	31.6	27.3	24	21	56.7	53.4	17	16
All	100.0	100.0	76	77	100.0	100.0	30	30
Non-Migrants	3.9	6.4	3	5	43.3	53.3	13	16
Long-Term Migrant	46.0	48.0	38	37	40.0	46.7	12	14
Recent Migrant	50.0	45.5	35	35	16.7	–	5	–

Source: Sample survey of migrant workers of Dhaka's formal manufacturing sector, 1996.

are much older. With the exception of the sample pharmaceutical industry (CIBA Geigy Ltd.) which was established in 1984, the food processing (Haque Brothers Ltd.) and electronics (Mehar Industries Ltd.) industries were established in the '60s.

- The size of the sample garments factories varies between 250 and 2500 workers. Sparrow Apparels Ltd. in Mirpur is the largest and Florate Private Ltd. in Tejgaon is the smallest among the selected garments factories. The size of workers in these two factories are 2500 and 250 respectively. Jeacon Garments Ltd. in Gulshan is the next largest with 1500 employees. The remaining two, Bari Apparels Ltd. in Mirpur and Applique Fashion Wear Ltd. in Mohammadpur are medium-sized factories hiring between 300 and 600 employees.
- As regards the other manufacturing industries, excepting the food processing industry (Haque Brothers Ltd.), which employs 530 workers, both pharmaceuticals and electronics are small units consisting of 75 and 122 employees respectively.
- In general the share of women workers, with some variation, is almost double that of men in the sample garments factories. For example, both in the largest and smallest factories, women constitute 80 and 70 per cent respectively of all workers. In the remaining factories, there are three women for every two male workers. Gender composition is more male biased in the other sample manufacturing units. There are three men for every two women in pharmaceuticals. In the remaining two factories, it is more balanced, that is four men for every five women in electronics and vice-a-versa in food processing.

The above discussion suggests that the growth of RMG in the mid '80s and early '90s led to expanded employment opportunities for women compared to men in the RMG sector. During the sampling stage, it was also observed that women workers predominated in the unskilled compared to skilled category in both RMG and other manufacturing industries, while men still dominated at the managerial level. According to the employers, women are preferred over men as both unskilled and skilled operators mainly because:

- Female labour is less costly compared to that of men.
- They are more docile, loyal and law-abiding in nature compared to men.
- They are also more hard working and sincere than their male counterparts.
- They have less contacts, exposure and bargaining power compared to male workers.

The perception of employers at least reveals that women workers are preferred not exclusively as a cost-cutting strategy. Their performance, sincerity and law-abiding nature is also valued by the employers. It also suggests that women workers are in a more disadvantageous position compared to their male counterparts in terms of wages and bargaining power. Male migration is a more established phenomenon in South Asia in general and Bangladesh in particular and mechanisms have evolved over the years to facilitate migration. As independent female migration is a relatively recent phenomenon, less is known about the process which facilitates female migration and settlement in urban areas. The study therefore looks at the motives, conditions and characteristics of migrants and explores whether these differ significantly by gender.

4.2 GROWTH OF THE RMG SECTOR AND WOMENS' INDEPENDENT MIGRATION

Introduction

The growth of export oriented manufacturing has led to expansion of employment opportunities for unskilled women in metropolitan cities of South-Eastern Asia. Bangladesh also witnessed rapid growth of export oriented manufacturing which contributes to two-thirds of the country's total foreign exchange earnings. Bangladesh's export earnings from RMG rose to US $ 976.98 million in 1991 and 2488.50 in 1995 (BGMEA, 1996). Expansion of employment opportunities for unskilled women in the '90s can be substantiated by the author's own findings from three different studies. In 1991/92, a randomly selected survey of slum dwellers in four wards of Dhaka city indicated that the proportion of women involved in RMG industries was found to be well below 10 per cent (Afsar 1995). However, a recent slum census by Afsar in 1996, revealed that about one-fifth of women of active age are found to be working in garments factories (Afsar 1995). Moreover, in some *thanas* such as Mirpur and Mohammadpur (where there is concentration of RMG factories), the proportion of women garments workers increases to a quarter (e.g., in Mirpur) or one-third (e.g., in Mohammadpur). The survey clearly points to an expansion of female employment in the RMG industries, particularly among the rural poor. Moreover, in their study on garments factory workers in 1990, Zohir and Majumdar (1998) found that migrants constituted three-quarters of the total workers and there were more males (83 per cent) than female migrant workers (69 per cent). The present study on the other hand shows that the proportion of migrant workers in garments factories has increased to 95 per cent and no gender based differential is found in this regard. The results of the author's recent survey (Afsar 1998) shows that migrants constituted 90 per cent of the total workers. It also reveals that the proportion of migrant workers who entered employment in recent years (between 1991 and 1996) has been more than double, between 60 and 64 per cent, compared to those who left early between 1981 and 1990, where between 31 and 28 per cent respectively, were female workers. It suggests greater labour migration in recent years, more particularly of young women workers entering the urban market.

The sex-ratio of Dhaka city dwellers over the years is becoming more balanced from 150 in 1961 to 105 in 1993/94 and this endorses the increase in women's independent migration in recent years (BBS, 1995: 44, Twin *et al.*, 1996). This has happened mainly as a direct response to the growth of export oriented labour intensive manufacturing employment, mainly in the RMG sector.

The slum census mentioned above revealed a more balanced sex ratio (96) in the year 1996, which reduces further to 65 for populations belonging to the 15 to 35 years age group (Afsar 1996). However, existing evidence suggests that the overall sex ratio of the slum and squatter settlements is generally balanced (e.g., Majumdar *et al.*

1995; Thwin 1996). What is important to note here is that the population balance is tilting more and more towards women for the population between 15 and 34 years. In 1991, the sex ratio obtained for that group was 103, which reduced to 79 in 1993 and finally to 65 in 1996 (Afsar 1995; Thwin *et al.* 1993). Nearly four out of every five unskilled production workers are recent migrants, who live mostly in slum and squatter settlements and constitute a third of the female workforce in those factories (Afsar 1998).

Reasons for Female Migration

In order to examine the factors which facilitate or constrain female labour migration, the reason for migration was used as one of the major indicators[2]. This is however supplemented by some important characteristics of migrants and the condition of their households at the time of migration or at the place of origin, which often mediates the process of migration decision making significantly. These include age, level of education, occupation, size of cultivable land owned by the household of the migrant, etc.

As with their male counterparts, female workers in garments factories came to the city pre-dominantly in search of work in both RMG and other manufacturing units. Nearly three-quarters of women and men came for work related reasons (Table 4.3). Although two-fifths of women migrants from other manufacturing industries came for economic reasons, a quarter of them were associational migrants who accompanied their husbands to Dhaka. A global review of reasons for women's migration by the UN Secretariat (1993) along with some recent studies show that:

- A significant proportions of women migrate for economic reasons (including migration for education, which leads to securing better employment opportunities later)
- World-wide, more women migrate for family than economic reasons including to accompany other family members or spouse and to get married.

---

2 Often reason for migration is taken as a preliminary indicator of migration decision making. Although useful, it can be subjective and suffer from ex-post rationalisation over time and hence has low response validity.

TABLE 4.3

Distribution of Sample Migrant Workers by Reason for Migration and Some of the Pre-migration Characteristics

Reason for Migration	Garment Industries				Other Manufacturing Industries			
	Male		Female		Male		Female	
	No.	(%)	No.	(%)	No.	(%)	No.	(%)
To avail the Present job	25	34.2	27	37.5	6	35.3	2	14.3
Job search	31	42.5	27	37.5	8	47.1	4	28.6
Marriage/Family migration	–	–	5	6.9	–	–	4	28.6
Education	9	12.3	7	9.7	3	17.6	3	21.4
Others	8	11.0	6	8.3	–	–	1	7.1
All	73	100.0	72	100.0	17	100.0	14	100.0
Age-Group								
<10	10	13.7	8	11.1	–	–	1	7.1
10-19	51	69.9	56	77.8	9	52.9	8	57.1
20-29	12	16.4	8	11.1	8	47.1	3	21.4
30-39	–	–	–	–	–	–	2	14.3
Average age (years)	–	15.1	–	13.2	–	20.4	–	18.3
Level of education								
No education	12	16.4	21	29.2	1	5.9	3	21.4
Primary	24	32.9	23	31.9	1	5.9	4	28.6
Secondary	13	17.8	10	13.9	1	5.9	–	–
High school +	24	32.9	18	25.0	14	82.3	7	50.0
Average education	–	3.0	–	2.5	–	3.9	–	3.3
Land holding								
No land	19	26.0	33	45.8	5	29.4	6	42.9
< 1 Acre	20	27.4	24	33.3	4	23.5	3	21.4
1-2.5	20	27.4	13	18.1	3	17.6	2	14.3
2.51-5.00	10	13.7	1	13.9	3	17.6	1	7.1
5.01+	4	5.5	1	13.9	2	11.8	2	14.3

Source: Sample survey of migrant workers of Dhaka's formal manufacturing sector, 1996.

While the findings of the present study departs significantly from the above pattern, it is consistent with the findings from Bangkok Metropolis (Phongpaichi 1993). In Bangkok, female migration occurred as a direct response to the demand for cheap labour for the export-oriented manufacturing industries. Our findings for instance show that nearly two out of every five garments factory workers, irrespective of gender, came directly for their present job. In contrast, in other manufacturing units, those who migrated directly for the present job constituted one-third of the male and one-fifth of the female workers. Results from the author's more recent survey also show that a little over three-quarters of recent migrants, as opposed to 36 per cent of the long-term female workers, came for employment related reasons. Although employment related reasons always loom large in the case of male migration, it has increased significantly in the '90s (90 per cent) compared to 1980s (68 per cent) (Afsar 1998). It confirms our earlier contention that greater employment opportunities in Dhaka city, led to more migration of both male and female workers in recent years, but particularly for women.

To obtain a better understanding from the otherwise subjective data (reasons for migration), cross-classifications were made by marital status and age at migration. Nearly three-quarters of women respondents from garments factories migrated for work related reasons, whether married or unmarried. Divorced and widowed workers came exclusively for this purpose. Excepting married women, none were associational migrants in the case of sample workers from garments factories. Further, migration for education related reasons were substantially higher (2.5 times) for unmarried female garments factory workers. Although nearly two-fifths of the women respondents from other manufacturing industries migrated for work-related reason, the number increases substantially (two-thirds) for unmarried workers. In other manufacturing units, those who migrated in search of a job reduces to two-fifths in the case of married migrants. A third of married women here migrated for associational reasons and a quarter for higher studies.

The response pattern on the reasons for migration by female workers from other manufacturing units appears to be logical. An unmarried woman worker from those units is on average younger

(27 years old) and better educated (4.7 years schooling), compared to a married woman worker who is 33 years old and has 3.6 years of schooling. In the case of female garments factory workers on the other hand, while the unmarried women are younger by eight years, compared to their married female colleagues the latter had slightly more education, 3.0 years of schooling as opposed to 2.3 years of the former (Table 4.4).

There may also be some inconsistencies in reporting pre-migration and current marital status by the respondents. Table 4.5 presents cross-tabulation by current and pre-migration marital status, using data from Afsar 1998. It shows that five per cent of female respondents, who declared themselves married prior to migration, reported themselves to be currently unmarried at the time of interview. If those respondents are added to the percentage of those who declared themselves to be abandoned by their spouse, the share of women claiming to be formerly married would increase to 14 percent. Compared to their pre-migration situation, the percentage of those female respondents who reported the incidence of broken marriages after migration, has increased four-fold. Clearly, there is a greater threat of marital instability in urban compared to rural areas. During elaborate discussion with women workers from EFCOT factory in Uttara, Columbia and Sparrow factories in Mohakhali and Mirpur respectively, some workers complained that marital instability is one of the important reasons as to why young women work in garments factories. The spread of the garments factories in Dhaka city is both a bane and boon to them. It has generated opportunities for poor young women from rural areas to earn cash income, but it is this income, which entices both married and unmarried young men towards them. On the other hand, women abandoned by their husbands in this process, are economically less vulnerable now that they have an opportunity to earn cash income.

A large number of migrants originate from the central and south-eastern districts of Dhaka, Mymensingh, Faridpur, Barisal and Comilla, districts characterised by highly disproportionate land-man ratios. Four out of every five and two out of every three female workers respectively from garments and other manufacturing units were functionally landless. Nearly half of the male workers, irrespective

TABLE 4.4

Distribution of Respondents by Marital Status, Average Age and Education

Respondents	Male				Female			
	No.	(%)	Average Age	Average Education	No.	(%)	Average Age	Average Education
Garments								
Currently married	20	26.3	27.9	3.2	29	37.7	24.9	3.2
Currently unmarried	56	73.7	18.7	2.9	40	51.9	17.3	2.3
Divorced/separated	–	–	–	–	7	9.1	22.0	2.4
Widow	–	–	–	–	1	1.3	30.0	3.0
All	76	100.	21.9	2.9	77	100.0	20.7	2.6
Others								
Currently married	17	56.7	35.2	3.5	20	66.7	32.6	3.7
Currently unmarried	13	43.3	27.0	4.3	6	20.0	27.0	4.8
Divorced/separated	–	–	–	–	3	10.0	30.7	1.3
Widow	–	–	–	–	1	3.3	45.0	3.0
All	30	100.	31.8	3.8	30	100.0	31.7	3.6

Source: Sample survey of migrant workers of Dhaka's formal manufacturing sector, 1996.

TABLE 4.5

Distribution of Migrant Workers by Pre and Post Migration Marital Status

Marital Status Prior to Migration to Dhaka	Married		Unmarried		Widow/Divorced/ Deserted	Total	
	Male (%)	Female (%)	Male (%)	Female (%)	Female (%)	Male (No.)	Female (No.)
Married (%)	15.4	40.4	–	2.8	54.3	2	97
Unmarried (%)	84.6	58.4	100	97.2	17.4	70	278
Widow/divorced/ Deserted (%)	–	1.2	–	–	28.3	–	15
All (No.)	13	166	59	178	46	72	390

Source: Afsar, 1998.

of type of industries, were functionally landless. Although women workers in general come from landless families, female garments factory workers appear to be more disadvantaged in this regard. On an average they have 1.3 acres of land as opposed to 2.0 acres for their male counterparts in the same factory and 2.3 acres for female counterparts from other manufacturing units.

Yet, it is difficult to describe women's migration exclusively as a push phenomenon because a large number of the workers (nearly half) were students at the time of migration. In Bangladesh, education is positively correlated with the income of the households. In the same study mentioned above (Afsar 1998), the author found that nearly nine out of ten female workers from landless households, either had no education, or did not complete primary school. On the other hand, between two-fifths and half of the female workers in the sample had secondary level education. They belonged to small and large landholding families. The female migrants from garments and other manufacturing factories had on average 2.5 and 3.3 years of schooling respectively. The corresponding figures for their male counterparts were 3.0 and 3.9 years respectively. The evidence, thus, indicates that a combined effect of demand pull and push factors, facilitated by social networks, can serve to explain the motivations of female migrant workers. A consistent pattern of migration from the Central and South-Eastern districts points to a strong history of migration and highlights the role of social networks in this process.

Importance of Information and the Role of Social Networks in the Process of Labour Migration

A large majority of respondents reported having acquaintances in Dhaka city who helped them in the process of migration and settlement. Ninety per cent of female garments factory workers, compared to four-fifths of their male colleagues in the same industry or female counterparts in other manufacturing industries, had family members and relatives living in Dhaka city prior to migration. Friends and neighbours, and employers as well as their agents, were helpful in the process of migration. They assisted migration by providing shelter and helped in searching for a job.

Most of the respondents, ranging from between three-fifths and nearly three-quarters of men and women respectively, also on arrival in Dhaka obtained shelter at the homes of their relatives and acquaintances. Responses recorded on this account do not vary much if we factor for duration of migration or by type of factories, garments or non-garments. The other major type of support they received at the urban end relates to procurement of a job and job related information. Variations in this connection are observed along gender lines, duration of migration, and types of factories. In the case of RMG workers, the proportion of both male and female respondents respectively who received such help increased substantially over the years, by 32 and 20 percentage points between 1981-1990 and 1991-1996 (Table 4.6). More female (40 per cent) as well as male (35 per cent) respondents received such help in the case of non-garments factories.

Independent migration by women and men in Bangladesh should not be seen as a phenomenon occurring outside the context of the family. Elsewhere (Afsar 1995) the author observed that migration is a family based strategy for income maximisation and poverty alleviation. Hence, in the Bangladeshi context, whether migration is independent or associational is determined mainly by the motive for migration. If the purpose of migration is to avail of employment opportunities in the city, the transfer or change of a job, maximising income gains and minimising the family's poverty or seeking education, it can be considered as independent migration. If on the other hand, a person migrates to stay with other family members and or due to migration of the entire family, where the individual members do not necessarily have any specific motivation for migration, then it can be classified as 'associational' migration. Therefore, for purposes of classification, whether the migrants are accompanied by somebody or not, is of prime importance. For example, Table 4.7 drawn from Afsar 1998 shows that less than a tenth of the total migrants, 28 per cent male, and 3 per cent female, came alone to Dhaka city.

All the remaining respondents, irrespective of gender, came to Dhaka city accompanied by their most immediate family members or other relatives, and a few came with their spouses. Nonetheless, nearly nine and eight out of ten male and female migrants

TABLE 4.6

Distribution of Respondents and Types of Help Received after Migration from the Kin Members and Acquaintances who Lived in Dhaka

Respondents Category	Shelter	Help to get Job	Job related Information	Monetary Help	Job & Shelter	Those Who Received Help from Acquaintances (No.)	(%)
Garments							
Male	58.9	33.9	12.5	12.5	33.9	57	95.0
Female	72.7	20.0	16.4	7.3	21.8	55	91.7
Long-term Migrant							
Male	72.0	20.0	8.0	4.0	20.0	25	96.1
Female	70.8	12.5	12.5	8.3	20.8	24	88.9
Recent Migrant							
Male	56.0	45.2	16.1	19.3	45.2	31	93.9
Female	74.2	25.8	19.3	6.4	22.6	31	93.9
Non-Garments*							
Migrant male	71.4	14.3	9.5	23.8	28.6	21	70.0
Migrant female	60.0	20.0	20.0	26.7	33.3	15	50.0

Note: *As only five male respondents were classified as recent migrants, it was decided to present data from other manufacturing units as one category. Data presented here denote multiple responses.

Source: Sample survey of migrant workers of Dhaka's formal manufacturing sector, 1996.

TABLE 4.7

Distribution of Respondents by Gender, Migration Status and Sources who Accompanied them to Dhaka

Marital Status Prior to Migration to Dhaka	Long-Term Migrant (%)		Recent Migrant (%)		Total (No.)	
	Male	Female	Male	Female	Male	Female
Self (%)	12.0	1.7	36.1	4.0	20	13
Spouse (%)	8.0	12.7	–	18.4	2	65
Son (%)	52.0	–	–	0.7	–	2
Parents (%)	20.0	47.4	21.3	23.2	23	119
Siblings (%)	4.0	20.3	21.3	20.6	15	80
Kin-members (%)	–	15.3	10.7	28.0	6	94
In law (%)	–	2.6	2.1	4.0	2	14
Servant (%)	–	–	2.1	–	1	–
Friend (%)	–	–	6.4	–	3	–
Neighbour (%)	–	–	–	1.1	–	3
All (No.)	25	118	47	272	72	390

Source: Afsar, 1998.

respectively came with a specific purpose, related to their own betterment or the upliftment of their families. It is interesting to observe that the propensity to come to Dhaka with parents has declined substantially over the years and this is true for both male and female migrants. Compared to nearly half of the long-term migrants, who were accompanied by their parents to Dhaka city, less than a quarter of the recent migrants were thus accompanied. Recent female migrants on the other hand, demonstrated a greater propensity to migrate with kin members and friends/neighbours, as opposed to their long-term migrant counterparts. Whether accompanied by parents or siblings or relatives and friends, women workers generally migrate with somebody they know well. The propensity to migrate alone has increased among the recent male migrant workers. Nonetheless, given the fact that more than nine out of ten migrant workers came with somebody to Dhaka city, this suggests the importance of social networks in the labour migration process in Bangladesh.

Searching for a Job

Employed female migrants of the sample garments factories reported that they relied mainly on friends and neighbours (a quarter), employer's agent (one-fifth), own initiative (one-third) and family members/relatives (18 per cent) to help them secure a job (Table 4.8). Employed male migrants also depended on the same sources, but a relatively higher proportion of them (one-third) showed a greater tendency to rely on employers and their agents and this is also true for the male workers of the other manufacturing industries in the sample. Greater mobility and more work experience (two years, on an average) of men, compared to women (one year, on an average), might have provided them with greater accessibility to employers or their agents, compared to their women counterparts. In their search for work, women employed in other manufacturing industries on the other hand, depended more on family members and relatives, friends and neighbours, compared to their male colleagues. However, in those industries, both men and women (nearly a quarter of the total of each category) depended on newspaper advertisements for their jobs. In contrast, in the RMG sector, those who depended on formal sources such as newspapers were only a few (7 per cent) for job

TABLE 4.8

Distribution of Sample Respondents by Sources who Help to Secure/Seek the Present Job

Sources	Garment Industries				Other Manufacturing Industries			
	Male		Female		Male		Female	
	No.	(%)	No.	(%)	No.	(%)	No.	(%)
Family members/ Relatives	14	19.2	13	18.1	2	11.8	4	28.6
Neighbours/friends	14	19.2	16	22.2	1	5.90	3	21.4
Employers/employers agent	23	31.5	14	19.4	5	29.4	3	21.4
Newspaper/other Advertisement	4	5.5	6	8.3	5	29.4	3	21.4
Self	18	24.7	23	31.9	4	23.5	1	7.1
All	73	100.0	72	100	17	100	14	100

Source: Sample survey of migrant workers of Dhaka's formal manufacturing sector, 1996.

information. Table 4.8 suggests that women's entry into formal manufacturing industries, particularly garments factories, still remains largely dependent on informal sources of information and social networks. The role of information and social networks as important determinants of migration is amply demonstrated in a number of studies in Bangladesh (Afsar 1995; Majumdar *et al.* 1995) and elsewhere (Lansing and Mueller 1971; Caldwell, 1969; Hugo 1978; Skeldon, 1990).

A study of small garment workshops in a low-rent district of Bangkok showed that virtually all workers were women under 20, mostly recruited among friends and relatives of the owner or from the owner's village. Such an informal system of recruitment ensures loyalty and docility. This is also true for Bangladesh. The President of BGMEA told the author that migrants from rural areas are preferred by the employers over local female workers of Dhaka, because the latter have greater expectations, mobility and bargaining power, compared to the former. Table 4.9 reveals that nearly half of the migrant workers from garments and two-thirds from the other manufacturing units, had contacts with an employers' agent prior to migration. Also nearly half of the recent female migrants from garments factories were relatives of those agents, compared to a-fifth and two-fifths of their long-term migrant male and female counterparts. It thus suggests that recruitment from friends and relatives of employers' agents is increasing for female garments factory workers.

On the other hand, securing employment through known sources might be considered safer by parents of the female workers. In many cases, respondents, who migrated for the present job, also had information about the nature of the work and wages. In this regard, the non-migrants (who are born in Dhaka and also who migrated prior to 1980), had greater access to such information than migrants (Table 4.10). Being in Dhaka for a long time, they could easily acquire such information through network and formal sources. As the majority of women workers (53 per cent) from other manufacturing units belong to this category, they have a stronger information base than other categories of workers in the sample. Thus three out of every four women workers in other manufacturing industries had knowledge about the nature of the work and wages. On the other

TABLE 4.9

Distribution of Workers by the Types of Connection they had with Employer's Agent Prior to Migration (% distribution)

	Blood Connection	Friend/ Neighbour	District/village Acquaintances	Other	All Who Knew Employer's Agent Prior to Migration (No.)	All Who Knew Employer's Agent Prior to Migration (%)
Garments						
All						
Male	30.8	25.6	23.1	20.5	39	53.4
Female	43.2	24.3	10.8	27.0	37	51.4
Long-term Migrant						
Male	22.2	22.2	27.8	27.8	18	51.4
Female	40.0	33.3	13.3	13.3	15	40.5
Recent Migrant						
Male	38.1	28.6	19.0	14.3	21	56.8
Female	45.4	18.2	–	36.4	22	62.9
Other Manufacturing Units						
Migrant male*	45.5	27.3	9.1	18.2	11	64.7
Migrant female*	30.0	10.0	30.0	30.0	10	71.4

Note: *As only five male respondents were classified as recent migrants, it was decided to present data from other manufacturing units as one category. Data presented here denote multiple responses.

Source: Sample survey of migrant workers of Dhaka's formal manufacturing sector, 1996.

TABLE 4.10

Percentage Distribution of the Sample Respondents who had Information about the Nature of the Present job and Wage by Migration Status

Reason for Migration	Had information about the nature of the present job			Had information about the wage		
	No.	(%)	All (No.)	No.	(%)	All (No.)
Garment's Factory						
Migration Status						
Non-Migrant						
Male	2	66.7	3	2	66.7	3
Female	4	80.0	5	3	60.0	5
Long- Term Migrant						
Male	20	57.1	35	20	57.1	35
Female	13	35.1	37	12	32.4	37
Recent Migrant						
Male	19	50.0	38	18	47.4	38
Female	17	48.6	35	16	45.7	35
All						
Male	41	53.9	76	40	52.6	76
Female	34	44.2	77	31	40.3	77
Other Manufacturing						
Non-Migrant						
Male	9	69.2	13	9	69.2	13
Female	13	81.2	16	12	75.0	16

(Contd.)

(Continued)

Reason for Migration	Had information about the nature of the present job			Had information about the wage		
	No.	(%)	All (No.)	No.	(%)	All (No.)
Long- Term Migrant						
Male	7	58.3	12	6	50.0	12
Female	9	64.3	14	10	71.4	14
Recent Migrant						
Male	1	20.0	5	1	20.0	5
All						
Male	17	56.7	30	16	53.3	30
Female	22	73.3	30	22	73.3	30

Source: Sample survey of migrant workers of Dhaka's formal manufacturing sector, 1996.

hand, it is found that half of the recent female migrant workers from garments factories were similarly informed about wages and working conditions compared to their long-term migrant colleagues, only one-third of whom had such prior information (Table 4.10). This is consistent with Peterson *et al.*'s (1988) proposition that recent migrants have better information regarding their jobs than long-term migrants. However, for male workers, this did not change by duration of migration. Increased access to information by female workers suggests wider and stronger networking among recent migrant female workers from garments factories, compared to their long-term migrant sisters. Particularly, the role of social networks in supplying job related information to migrant workers can be considered to be an important determinant of labour migration. The role of social networks in the migration and settlement process is amply documented in a huge body of migration literature (Ritchey 1976; Gore 1971; Hugo 1978, 1981; Majumdar *et al.*, 1995; Afsar 1995). Elsewhere the author has also argued that location of a friend or relative at the place of destination is one of the pre-conditions for migration (Afsar 1995), which equally hold in the case of women's independent migration to the RMG sector.

Of those female workers from garments factories, who migrated in search of work, half of them directly came to Dhaka for the present job compared to two-fifths for their male counterparts. This is even lower in the case of female workers from other manufacturing units (Table 4.3).

Other studies (Zohir and Majumdar 1996) show that the waiting period for getting a job in the garments factories was less than a week for nearly three-fifths of female workers and half of male workers in their sample. Therefore, it appears that the risks involved in migration for job search is minimised with the help of effective and reliable social networks.

4.3 PROFILES OF THE SAMPLE WORKERS

Demographic and Social Characteristics

One major change over the past decade has been the increasing proportion of young women with low levels of educational attainment migrating from the rural areas. The increasing importance of RMG industries in absorbing young and literate or semi-literate women can be observed from the present study. For example, almost all women (96 per cent) from garments factories in the sample had migrated between 1980-1995, half of whom had migrated between 1990-95, and half between 1980-1990. In contrast, none of the women in the sample of other manufacturing units migrated between 1990 and 1995 (Table 4.2). The proportion of those who migrated between 1980-1990 and 1990-1995 were 54 per cent and 46 per cent respectively. Employed migrants of both sexes tended to be young, but women were considerably younger. At the time of migration, a woman worker was on average at least two years younger than her male counterpart. The average age of a female worker from garments and other manufacturing industries was 13 and 18 years respectively at the time of migration, as opposed to 15 and 20 years for their male counterparts (Table 4.3). This is despite the fact that the sample was drawn by matching age. Nevertheless, cross-classification of age by year of migration shows that a recent migrant worker from a garments factory is 17 years old on an average, as opposed to 19 years for their male colleagues (Table 4.11). Although currently a migrant woman working in other manufacturing industries is 29 years old on an average, yet she is two years younger than a male migrant from the same industries. Moreover, a migrant female worker from a garments factory is least educated, compared to either her male or female counterparts from the same or other manufacturing industries respectively (Table 4.3).

The above discussion shows clearly that garments factories are generating employment for younger women. It is also important to examine if entry into formal manufacturing leads to delayed marriage. Delayed marriage itself is considered to be an important step in controlling population growth. The majority of women workers (52 per cent) from garments factories are currently unmarried, compared to nearly three-quarters of their male counterparts from the same and one fifth of female counterparts from other manufacturing industries (Table 4.4). Nearly a tenth of the women workers from garments factories or otherwise were reported to be divorced/separated and widows whilst none of the male workers

TABLE 4.11

Distribution of Respondents by Monthly Wages, Skills Category, Migration Status and Some More Socio-demographic Characteristics

Categories of Workers	Number		Average Wage/ Month (in Tk.)		Average Work Hours/day		Average Experience (Yrs.)		Average Age (in years)		Average Education	
	G*.	O**	G*.	O**.	G*.	O**.	G*.	O**.	G*.	O**.	G*.	O**.
Unskilled Production												
Male	28	11	709.0	1524.0	10.9	6.9	0.8	1.7	16.6	28.9	2.4	3.1
Female	28	12	580.4	1547.4	10.3	4.8	0.6	3.6	16.6	32.4	1.8	2.7
			(0.82)	(1.02)								
Skilled Production												
Male	25	10	1570.0	3539.3	11.1	4.4	2.6	8.9	21.1	33.3	2.6	4.2
Female	28	9	1370.2	3612.2	10.8	4.1	2.1	8.7	21.3	34.7	2.4	4.2
			(0.87)	(1.02)								
Supervisor/Technical/Managers												
Male	23	9	3421.7	5369.0	6.2	8.2	2.9	14.4	26.6	33.1	4.0	4.3
Female	21	9	2493.2	4468.2	8.6	5.5	2.0	0.6	25.5	27.7	3.9	4.3
			(0.73)	(0.83)								
All												
Male	76	30	1813.2	3349.2	9.6	6.5	1.5	2.8	21.1	31.6	3.0	3.8
Female	77	30	1389.3	3043.1	10.0	4.8	1.2	1.4	20.7	31.6	2.6	3.6
			(0.77)	(0.91)								
Non-Migrant												
Male	3	13	1700.0	3474.6	7.8	4.8	3.0	6.3	19.3	35.3	3.0	3.7
Female	5	16	2380.0	3428.1	8.4	3.8	2.9	3.5	23.6	33.9	3.4	4.0
			(1.4)	(0.99)								

(Contd.)

(Continued)

Categories of Workers	Number		Average Wage/ Month (in Tk.)		Average Work Hours/day		Average Experience (Yrs.)		Average Age (in years)		Average Education	
	G*.	O**	G*.	O**.	G*.	O**.	G*.	O**.	G*.	O**.	G*.	O**.
Long- Term												
Male Migrant	35	12	2522.9	4030.4	8.1	6.0	2.7	5.3	23.8	30.6	3.1	4.2
Female Migrant	37	14	1838.6	2603.1	9.5	5.9	1.9	7.1	23.4	29.1	2.8	3.3
			(0.73)	(0.65)								
Recent												
Male migrant	38	5	1168.4	1388.2	11.0	11.8	1.6	1.1	18.8	24.6	2.8	3.4
Female migrant	35	–	772.8	–	10.8	–	0.9	–	17.4	–	2.3	–
			(0.66)									

Notes: *Sample Garments Industries; **Other Manufacturing Industries. Figures in parentheses are the ratio of female earnings to male earnings: (Female Earnings/Male Earnings).

Source: Sample survey of migrant workers of Dhaka's formal manufacturing sector, 1996.

were either divorced/separated or widowed irrespective of the type of industries. The magnitude of the divorced/widowed, marital status of both the female and male workers is found to be almost the reverse of the general urban pattern. It should be mentioned that, whilst Bangladesh Bureau of Statistics (BBS) reports on the magnitude of the *never married* men and women, in the present study unmarried refers to *currently* unmarried workers. A currently *unmarried* person may not necessarily belong to the *never married* category. During field work, it was observed that due to cultural inhibitions, women workers often tried to hide the incidence of divorce/desertion. Male workers too are not immune from such inhibitions and consequently no man has admitted to be either a divorcee or a widower. Interestingly, marital status of the respondents of other manufacturing industries show a striking similarity with the urban pattern, unlike those of their counterparts from the garments factories (Table 4.12). This may be explained by the predominance of non-migrant and long-term migrants among respondents from other manufacturing units.

Two out of every five currently unmarried garments factory worker wanted to defer their marriage until they saved enough money. However one can observe a marked gender gap in this regard. The majority of men (56 per cent) as opposed to one-seventh of women workers from garments factories wanted to defer their marriage for the above reason. The bulk of the female garments factory workers (three-quarters) on the contrary, were waiting for their parents to find a suitable partner for them. The corresponding figures for their male counterparts are 38 and 15 per cent respectively from garments and other manufacturing industries. However, the response pattern of female workers from other manufacturing industries is quite similar to that of their counterparts in the garments industries. The relevant question at this stage of first generational migration of young women workers, is not whether they defer marriage to generate some more savings or surrender to their parent's wishes. Rather, given the employment opportunities available to young girls, the question of a suitable groom is taken into consideration in arranging marriage for girls with low levels of education from largely landless families. In rural areas, a girl from a poorer household is often

TABLE 4.12

Distribution of the Sample Respondents by Age and Marital Status and a Comparison with Urban Bangladesh

Age Group	Sample Respondents								Urban Bangladesh***		
	Currently Married		Currently Un-married		Divorced/ Widowed		All (No.)		Currently Married	Never Married	Divorced/ Widowed
	G*	O**	G*	O**	G*	O**	G*	O**			
10-14											
Male	–	–	100.0	–	–	–	6	–	0.5	99.5	0.0
Female	–	–	100.0	–	–	–	10	–	2.1	97.8	0.1
15-19											
Male	–	–	100.0	–	–	–	27	–	3.6	96.4	0.0
Female	17.4	50.0	78.3	–	4.3	50.0	23.0	2	37.9	60.9	1.2
20-24											
Male	17.4	–	82.6	100.0	–	–	23.0	2	21.4	78.5	0.1
Female	34.8	–	43.5	–	21.7	–	23	–	79.4	18.0	2.6
25-49											
Male	80.0	60.0	20.0	39.3	–	–	20	28	85.0	14.7	0.3
Female	81.0	67.9	9.5	21.4	9.5	10.7	21	28	90.6	2.1	7.3
50+											
Male	–	–	–	–	–	–	–	–	96.5	0.9	2.6
Female	–	–	–	–	–	–	–	–	55.8	0.9	43.3
All											
Male	34.2	56.7	65.8	43.3	–	–	76	30	54.0	45.5	0.5
Female	37.7	66.7	51.9	20.0	10.4	13.3	77	30	61.0	30.6	8.4

Note: *Sample Garments Industries; **Other Manufacturing Industries; ***BBS, 1995:9, BBS data do not provide absolute population size.

Source: Sample survey of migrant workers of Dhaka's formal manufacturing sector, 1996.

considered to be a burden and is married off as soon as possible. The average age of a female garments factory worker is 17 years. Bangladesh Demographic and Health Survey data (1994) reveals that about 60 per cent of Bangladeshi women were married by the time they were 15. It also shows that urban women marry later than their rural counterparts, with an overall difference of more than one year in the median age at marriage among women aged between 20 and 49 (15.4 vs. 14.3 respectively) (Mitra *et al.* 1994: '74-75). Hence, the employment opportunities generated by the RMG sector for the young migrant rural women appears to demonstrate a potential for fertility reduction.

In order to examine whether work opportunities in garments factories leads to fertility reduction of the young and eligible women garments factory workers, comparison was made with the Bangladesh Demographic and Health Survey (BDHS) data (Mitra *et al.* 1998) and studies on garments factory workers (Chaudhury and Majumdar 1996 and Afsar 1998). Table 4.13A shows that whereas *ever married* women of reproductive age have 2.4 children on an average in Bangladesh, the average number of children reduces significantly for the current garments factory workers (0.8) and their predecessors (1.2). Similarly, the proportion of ever-married women of eligible age, who do not have children, was nearly a quarter in 1993/94, when the same figure for garments factory workers was 40 per cent. For the same group,of garments factory workers, those who do not have children further increases to nearly 52 per cent in 1998. At the peak of child bearing age (20-29), when between 80-94 per cent of the ever-married women in Bangladesh have two living children on an average, between 82 and 57 per cent of garments factory workers do not have any children. Of those in child bearing age nearly eight out of ten women garments workers do not have children. Currently married women of reproductive age working in garments factories have remarkably lower numbers of children (1.7) and incidence of child bearing (nearly two-fifths) than Bangladeshi women in general (with the respective figures of 2.8 children and 90 per cent women having children) (Table 4.13B).

Therefore, data presented in Table 4.13A and 4.13.B, clearly suggest that married garments factory workers at present are controlling

TABLE 4.13A

Child Bearing by Ever-married Women Workers

Age Group	Average No. of Children per Worker/Women			% of Women with No Children		
	BDHS data Mitra *et al.*, 1994	Chaudhury & Majumdar 1996	Afsar 1998	Mitra *et al.*, 1994	Chaudhury & Majumdar, 1996	Afsar 1998
< 15	–	0.0	0.0	0	100.0	100.0
15-19	0.3	0.2	0.1	72.6	77.4	90.0
20-24	1.4	0.9	0.6	22.3	41.7	57.0
25-29	2.5	1.7	1.2	6.0	11.4	32.0
30-34	3.3	1.3	1.3	3.8	27.3	19.2
35+	4.7	2.7	2.2	1.9	14.3	12.5
All ages	2.4	1.2	0.8	23.4	38.8	51.9

Source: Mitra *et al.*, 1994; Chaudhury and Majumdar 1996 and Afsar 1998.

TABLE 4.13B

No. of Living Children of Ever-married Women Workers

Age Group	Mean No. of Children of Currently Married Women		% of Women with no Children	
	Bangladesh Data (Mitra *et al.*, 1994)	Garments Factory Worker (Afsar 1998)	Bangladesh Data (Mitra *et al.*, 1994)	Garments Factory Worker (Afsar 1998)
15-19	0.6	1.0	44.5	90.2
20-24	1.6	1.3	10.5	60.0
25-29	2.6	1.7	3.5	35.9
30-34	3.5	1.8	2.7	25.0
35-39	4.3	2.7	1.7	25.0
40-44	5.2	2.5	0.7	0.0
All Ages	2.8	1.7	9.9	57.8

Source: Mitra *et al.*, 1994; Chaudhury and Majumdar 1996 and Afsar 1998.

their fertility more effectively, than their predecessors as well as Bangladeshi women in general. In her recent study, the author found that more than 90 per cent of the married garments factory workers use contraceptives, compared to nearly three-fifths of their urban sisters of eligible age (Mitra *et al.* 1994: 47). The main reason for which they use contraceptives is the fear of job termination and pay-cut on account of pregnancy. By and large, garments factory workers neither enjoy paid maternity leave, nor are there facilities to look after their children. Nearly three-quarters of married garments factory workers depend on their kin for child care services and a quarter manage by themselves. Given the fact that they face intense pressure in meeting their own basic needs and that of their family, and given the pressure of the work load in a competitive market environment, it is natural that they try to defer pregnancy until higher income levels are achieved. Delayed marriage and effective control of fertility by the garments factory workers would help in reaching the goal of replacement level fertility by the year 2005, set by the government (GOB 1994:6). Following one projection, it is hoped that if the trend of fertility reduction among garments factory workers and other women of reproductive age continues with the same vigour, the population of Bangladesh is likely to stabilise at 211 million by 2056.

Economic Characteristics: Earnings and the Ability to Save and Remit

Explaining Wage Differentials

The earnings of the sample female workers of garments and other manufacturing units are three-quarters and ninety per cent respectively of their male counterparts (Table 4.11). The gender based divergence in average wages of the female garments factory workers is comparable with the income ratio of the male and female heads of households in urban areas (BBS 1995). However, Chaudhury and Majumdar (1993) found a much wider gap between male and female earnings (the ratio being 0.66) in the garments factories. They also found gender based disparity across job categories. In the present study, the highest gender disparity is found at the supervisory level and this is consistent with Rahman's (1993: 103) findings of workers from the export processing zones. The smaller gap in the earnings ratio found in the present study compared to Chaudhury and Majumdar's (1993) study and the highest gender differential at the supervisory level can be explained as follows:

- Whilst other studies derived the data by means of a random sample, the sample for the present study was drawn from a quota of different categories of workers by matching age of the male and female workers. Hence, the gender differential caused by demographic characteristics and subsequent socio-economic entitlements is minimised in the present study.
- Due to the nature of the sample, the gender gap in earnings is smaller at the unskilled and skilled production workers level than for supervisor/quality control officer or other technical/ managerial category. At the managerial level, the total number of workers were often selected as in sample due to availability of a small number of women in this category. This may have biased the results so that the female-male earnings ratio in this category is lower for both garments (0.73) and non-garments (0.83) than either skilled (0.87 and 1.02) or unskilled (0.82 and 1.02) production workers of the respective garments and other manufacturing industries (Table 4.11).

The above discussion suggests the importance of age in determining income. However, it also reveals that a sample female worker on average earns 10 to 25 per cent lower wages compared to her male counterpart even after controlling for age. Hence, there are other socio-economic factors, which can explain this significant gap. Both number of years of schooling and the extent to which experience is gathered from other factories are some of the important variables influencing earnings of the worker. On an average, a male garments factory worker had 3 years of schooling and about 2 years of experience as opposed to 2.6 and 1.6 years respectively of his female counterparts. Similarly, a male worker on average has 0.2 and 1.6 years of additional schooling and experience compared to a female worker of other manufacturing industries. It should be noted that given the extremely limited opportunities for training, workers often learn the skills from their fellow workers informally in the garments industry. Once, for example, workers learn machine operations, they apply directly for the job of an operator or skilled production worker in another factory. In her recent study on the garments factory workers the author found that nearly seven out of every ten respondents acquired informal training in this way and the bulk of them (85 and 75 per cent respectively of female and male respondents) are currently working as operators (Afsar 1998). Subsequently, the turnover rate is very high in those factories as revealed through interviews with the employers of the garments factories, and results of some existing studies (Majumdar and Chaudhury 1993). Even at the managerial level, where men and women had almost similar levels of education, experience matters a good deal. This is because the gender gap with regard to experience is very wide, one year for garments, and 13.8 years for other manufacturing industries, whilst the opportunity for informal training is not as easy as in the case of skilled operators.

Results of a multi-variate regression analysis run by Chaudhury and Paul (1996: 51-52) on determinants of income of the garments factory workers show that education beyond primary level, skills and experience are the most important factors affecting gender difference in earnings. They also found that even after controlling for all relevant variables, the income difference between male and female workers remains at a quarter. A significant positive impact of the length of stay in Dhaka city on income was also found in the regression analysis.

However, given the smallness of the sample and purposive nature of the data drawn for the present study, it is difficult to isolate the importance of migration in influencing income from other socio-economic variables. However, Table 4.11 shows clearly that gender based wage differentials are the highest in the case of recent migrants and least for non-migrants. Clearly, it points to the positive impact of longer duration of stay on income. This can be strengthened from the author's recently conducted survey data (Afsar 1998). As two-thirds of the female, compared to nearly three-fifths of the male workers were recent migrants, one could find at least some partial justification of the higher male compared to female wages. It also shows that compared to nearly three-fifths of the recent migrant workers (irrespective of gender), who had informal training, the figures for the male and female long-term migrants increases to 92 and 82 per cent respectively, explaining further the gender differential in the income earned by respondents (Afsar 1998).

Coping Mechanisms

One of the key purposes of this paper is to examine the coping mechanisms adopted by female migrant workers in the urban labour market and society. The pertinent findings related to coping mechanisms are highlighted next with data on income, expenditure, savings and remittances, to study whether migration is adopted as a strategy for income maximisation by men and women alike.

The workers' coping mechanisms include an effort to gain experience, making the most of opportunities, information and networking to improve their scope for upward mobility. Thus for example, a sample women worker from the garments factories, who migrated between 1991 and '96, earns on average nearly two-thirds of her male counterparts (Table 4.11). The gender ratio in wage increases to 0.73 and 0.86 respectively, for the long term migrants of those factories. A long term female and male garments factory worker thus earns 2.4 and 2.2 times higher wages than their recent migrant counterparts. Although the gap between male and female income still exists, the dramatic increase in women's wages from Tk. 772 to Tk. 1838 between 1980-1990 and 1991-'96 suggests that women garments factory workers are coping well within the urban labour market[3]. They have, thus, been able to acquire skills, information and to establish strong network connections to strengthen their stake in the labour market.

Many of these female workers had not worked before in the formal labour market so that migration provided an opportunity to them to secure an urban job and to earn a wage for the first time. Although nearly 40 per cent of the total male and female garments

---

[3] The corresponding figures for their male colleagues from the same industry were Tk. 1168 and Tk. 2522 wage. As none of the sample female workers from other manufacturing industries migrated between 1991 and 1996, it was not possible to compare wage between long-term and recent migrants in the case.

factory workers respectively earn less than the prescribed minimum wage[4], yet from a position of almost no cash income, 12 per cent of female garments factory workers earn more than Tk. 2000 per month (Table 4.14). Indeed, the magnitude of the proportion of female workers in the garment sector compared to other manufacturing industries, who earn the same amount as their male counterpart is much higher (one-third and a half respectively). However, it should be recalled that a female garments factory worker is younger and comes from a poorer background (in terms of their level of education and average landholding). Had they not migrated, these women would have remained either un or under employed or would have been involved in expenditure saving or home-based income earning activities, with a few working as wage labourers in the rural economy.

In the rural areas, 83 per cent of the employed women aged 15 years and over, compared to 15 per cent of men, are engaged as unpaid family helpers. Excepting only four per cent, who work as employees, the remaining 13 per cent are self-employed (7 per cent) and day labourers (5.6 per cent) (BBS, 1996: 48). Thus rural women have limited options for paid employment, and the wage/salary they receive is far below the urban average. The latest labour force survey data shows that 62 per cent of rural women, as opposed to 44 per cent of urban women in salaried service, get less than Taka 250 per week. Those who get more than Taka 500 per week constitute 26 and 15 per cent of urban and rural women respectively. Similarly the average wage rate for a female day labourer in the urban areas is Taka 36 per day, which is higher by Taka 11 compared to a rural women's daily wage (BBS 1995). Existing micro-studies indicate that female workers in the rural and informal sectors earn between a third and half of male wages. The situation in the urban formal sector thus appears to be much better, with the ratio of female to male wages ranging between 72 per cent and 97 percent, depending on the skill level (World Bank 1996).

Conversely, had a women worker in the formal manufacturing industry been employed as a domestic servant, she would have earned, an average, only Tk. 690 (ADB 1996) per month, which is half of

[4] Minimum wage was Tk. 900 per month for the year 1993 (Mondol 1993).

TABLE 4.14

Percentage Distribution of Respondents by Wage Group in 1996 and 1993

Respondent*	Up to Tk. 500		501-900		901-1300		1301-1500		1501+		All (No.)	
	Male	Female	Male	Female	Male	Female	Male	Female	Male	Female	Male	Female
Garments	6.6	26.0	28.9	11.7	18.4	23.4	3.9	13.0	42.1	26.0	76	77
Other Industries	–	–	–	6.7	16.7	13.4	–	10.0	83.3	70.0	30	30
Respondent**	3.6	15.7	8.6	27.1	24.3	28.5	10.7	4.8	52.9	23.9	140	376

Note: *Respondents refer to the sample workers of the present study; ** Chaudhury and Majumdar, 1993.

Source: Sample survey of migrant workers of Dhaka's formal manufacturing sector, 1, 1996 and Chaudhury and Majumdar, 1993.

the present average wage (Tk. 1389) of an RMG worker. Obviously migration and absorption into garments factories opened up better earning prospects for younger women drawn from landless and marginal farmer's households with low levels of education.

Non-Migrant women workers resident in the urban areas whether employed in garments or other manufacturing industries, earn more than a migrant woman and a non-migrant male worker (Table 4.11). The average monthly wage of a female worker working in garments factories is two-thirds of their non-migrant counterparts, but increases to 85 per cent and declines to 35 per cent in the case of long-term and recent migrant co-workers. The ratio between the average wage of female workers of other manufacturing industries and non-migrant counterparts is 0.46 and it almost remains the same for long-term and migrant women workers.[5] On the other hand, a non-migrant male worker from a garments factory earns 71 per cent of the income earned by a long-term migrant. It suggests that men have greater opportunity to bargain and acquire skills through a longer stay in Dhaka city, compared to their female colleagues. Women workers also face greater burdens due to poor living conditions, compared to male garments factory workers and also remain exposed to the hazards of commuting to and from their work place even at night. These female workers in the RMG work, on average, as long as their male counterparts (11 hours per day including overtime) with no relief from overtime work at night.

Savings and Remittances

Migrants save more than non-migrants and a good number of them (nearly two-fifths) are able to send remittances to their families of origin. The proportion of female workers who save is higher than for male workers, and the savings of a female worker as a proportion of her urban income, is also higher than that of her male colleagues. Two out of every five female workers from garments and other manufacturing industries, respectively save 8 and 14 per cent of

[5] However there are very few non-migrants (less than 5%) among the garments factory worker and most of them (nearly three-quarters) are settled migrants who migrated before 1980. On the other hand, workers of other manufacturing industries comprised of almost the same proportion of migrants and non-migrants.

their incomes (Table 4.15). On the other hand, one-third of their male counterparts from garments and other manufacturing industries reported respectively saving 6 and 10 per cent of their urban income. Similarly, a non-migrant worker saves only one per cent of his/her urban income, as opposed to 8 and 6 per cent, in the case of long-term male and female migrants of garments factories. Although a recent migrant worker saves nearly half that of a long-term migrant worker, yet they save four times as much as a non-migrant worker. This reflects the varying compulsions of those who still retain links with their village and those who have become fully urbanised. In the case of other manufacturing industries, women outnumber men in their propensity to save and a migrant worker saves proportionately more of his/her urban income than a non-migrant worker.

The propensity to save appears to increase with the increase in the age of the worker. Thus workers belonging to the 30 and 39 years age group save nearly one-fifth of their urban income, as opposed to around 3 per cent saved by their youngest counterparts (between 10 and 19 years) in garments factories. This holds equally for both male and female workers. However, only a few respondents belong to the 30-39 years age group, since majority of the workers in garments factories are younger compared to other manufacturing industries. Notwithstanding this one can still observe a positive correlation between age and ability to save in the case of garments factory workers (Table 4.16). It should be noted that the monetary wage of a garments factory worker also appears to increase with their age, which is not the case for the workers of other manufacturing industries in the sample. Consequently, no such clear and systematic pattern could be observed in this case. Hence, while the study suggests the influence of income in enhancing the saving capacity, one has to go beyond this and rigorously examine the impact of other factors in determining saving capacity of the workers.

An analysis of remittances shows that the average size of the remittances as a proportion of the monthly urban income is higher for garments factory workers than those of other manufacturing industries. On an average, a migrant male and a female garments factory worker respectively remit home nearly two-fifths and one-third of their urban income per month (Table 4.16). The corresponding figures for

TABLE 4.15

Average Savings of Respondents by Migration Status and Age

Respondents*	Average Savings of the Total Income (Tk.)		Savings as a Proportion of Income (%)		Total (No.)	
	Male	Female	Male	Female	Male	Female
Garments						
Non-migrant	66.7	20.0	1.4	0.4	3	5
Long- Term Migrant	261.4	144.1	8.6	6.2	35	37
Recent Migrant	43.4	46.9	2.7	4.1	38	35
All	144.7	145.1	6.4	8.0	76	77
10-19	27.3	32.6	2.2	2.9	33	33
20-29	145.7	136.7	5.2	6.7	35	38
30-39	625.0	816.7	14.6	20.7	8	6
Others						
Non-migrant	584.6	493.8	6.0	5.6	13	16
Long- Term Migrant	383.3	550.0	7.9	15.8	12	14
Recent Migrant	–	–	–	–	5	–
All	406.7	520.0	9.9	14.2	30	30
20-29	321.4	800.0	7.1	16.6	14	12
30-39	616.7	280.0	14.9	8.8	12	10
40+	75.0	533.3	3.2	17.8	4	6

Note: *Income here refers to average monthly wage and overtime.

Source: Sample survey of migrant workers of Dhaka's formal manufacturing sector, 1996.

TABLE 4.16

Average Remittances of Respondents by Migration Status and Age

	Average Remittances (Tk.)		Remitters (%)		Remittances as % of Income*		Total (No.)	
	Male	Female	Male	Female	Male	Female	Male	Female
Garments								
Long- Term Migrant	1033.3	600.0	51.4	33.4	34.1	25.8	35	37
Recent Migrant	625.0	457.1	36.8	20.0	39.3	39.6	38	35
All	874.2	535.0	43.8	26.4	38.5	29.6	73	72
10-19	462.5	525.0	12.9	12.5	38.6	45.4	31	32
20-29	880.0	507.1	73.5	40.0	31.4	24.7	34	35
30-39	1250.0	750.0	50.0	40.0	29.3	21.1	8	5
Others								
Long- Term Migrant	1450.0	300.0	83.3	35.7	29.9	8.6	12	14
Recent Migrant	1200.0	–	40.0	–	–	–	5	–
All	1411.1	466.7	70.6	35.7	34.6	12.7	17	14
20-29	1450.0	250.0	54.5	28.6	32.1	5.4	11	7
30-39	1466.7	600.0	150.0	83.3	46.5	23.8	6	6
40+	1166.7	350.0	–	–	–	–	–	–

Note: *Income here refers to average monthly wage and overtime.

Source: Sample survey of migrant workers of Dhaka's formal manufacturing sector, 1996.

their counterparts in other manufacturing industries respectively were 35 and 13 per cent. The proportion of remitters out of the total workers from other manufacturing industries is, however, higher (45 per cent) than those of garments factories (34 per cent). In both cases, a high proportion of men compared to women workers remit home. Nearly a quarter and a third of the female workers respectively from garments and other manufacturing factories, as opposed to 44 and 70 per cent of their male colleagues sent remittances regularly to their families at origin. A study of female labour migration in Bangkok Metropolis in 1988 found more women (56 per cent) than men (38 per cent) were sending remittances back to their village (Phongpaichit 1993: 189). In Thailand, like some other Southeast Asian countries, eldest daughters often bear the responsibility of bringing up the other siblings. Since the mid '70s women constituted a sizeable proportion of rural-urban migrants, because they were more likely to be un and under employed in rural areas and can be released from the rural households without greatly affecting the household agricultural productive capacity (Phongpaichit 1993: 182). On the demand side, the growth of tourism and export oriented labour intensive industries has attracted many young women from the rural areas to the city.

In Bangladesh, men are often considered to be the principal bread winners and they thus tend to dominate the overall rural-urban migration flows. Men continue to migrate and send remittances for the survival and betterment of their families in the villages. Three-quarters of the men as opposed to half of women from garments factories are still single. Hence, more men than female workers are likely to send remittances to their families at origin. Respectively, three-fifths and nearly two-fifths of currently unmarried men and women workers from garments factories remit to their home. Further, younger migrants from garments factories (aged between 10-19 years) are found to remit a much higher proportions (45 per cent) of their urban income compared to their older counterparts (25 per cent). Thus unlike savings, which appears to be influenced by income, the size of the remittances on the other hand, also depends on the intensity of the social ties and responsibilities respondents have at their place of destination and origin. For example, nearly a quarter of the female respondents from RMG factories had either single parents or siblings at the origin, whom they need to support.

The rates of current expenditure in relation to income tend to be higher for female garment workers compared to their male counterparts. Thus, women workers spend 52 per cent of their income on their accommodation in the city, compared to their male colleagues, who spent about a third of their monthly income on this item. Whether living with a relative or husband, women generally surrender almost the entire income or a lion's share for their basic subsistence. Furthermore, women spend about 13 per cent of their income for their medical treatment and that of other family members. Moreover, expenditure on clothing, sandals and cosmetics, transport and tiffin also consumes about a tenth of their total expenditure. Hence, women often have to borrow from their co-workers, relatives and friends to make ends meet. Not getting their salary and overtime payment together and on a fixed date or week aggravates their problem of indebtedness. Women workers in garments factories tend to feel such financial pressures more than their male colleagues, who have greater options to augment their income through part-time jobs and also by acquiring higher skills, because of their greater scope for mobility and lower burden of household chores. Therefore, male workers on average receiving higher income and incurring lower expenditures as well as with less family obligations in the city, can afford to save more and to thereby have a better capacity to remit money home, compared to their female colleagues.

Based on a review of five empirical studies, Rempel and Lobdell (1978: 333) concluded that the size of remittances varied directly with the strength of social and economic ties with the rural areas and inversely with how well migrants are established in the urban areas. Elsewhere, the author found a statistically significant correlation between the size of remittances, age and marital status of temporary migrants (Afsar 1995: 256). The majority of remitters (more than 90 per cent) sent money for both family maintenance and education of siblings (Table 4.17), so that the purposes for sending remittances tend to be similar for both male and female workers, though there is some variation in the motivation of female workers in other manufacturing industries.

TABLE 4.17

Percentage Distribution of the Sample Workers by Purpose of Sending Remittances to Families at Origin

Respondent's Category	Family Main-tenance	Education of Siblings	Treatment & Medication	Religious Ceremonies	Family Maintenance & Education	Others	All Remitters (No.)
Garments Factory							
All migrant							
Male	37.5	10.0	–	10.0	35.0	2.5	40
Female	40.0	40.0	5.0	5.0	25.0	–	20
Long-term Migrant							
Male	36.4	9.1	–	4.5	40.9	–	22
Female	30.8	23.1	7.7	7.7	30.8	–	13
Recent Migrant							
Male	38.9	11.1	–	16.7	27.8	5.6	18
Female	57.1	14.3	–	–	14.3	14.3	7
Other Industries*							
Migrant Male	16.7	8.3	–	–	75.0	–	12
Migrant Female	42.9	14.3	–	28.6	14.3	–	7

Note: *As only five male respondents were classified as recent migrants, it was decided to present data from other manufacturing units as one category. Data presented here denote multiple responses.

Source: Sample survey of migrant workers of Dhaka's formal manufacturing sector, 1996.

A large number of studies from Bangladesh, India, Indonesia and Africa, demonstrated that expenditures on current consumption absorbed between 80 and 90 per cent of poorer migrants' remittances (Afsar 1995: 260; Connell *et al.* 1976: 98; Prakash 1978: 110; Hugo 1978: 273). Elsewhere the author argued that in a country such as Bangladesh, where half of rural households fall below the poverty line, priorities on consumption expenditure can be viewed as consonant with the 'basic needs' approach to development without which the survival of the families of the migrants living in their place of origin would have remained precarious (1995: 260). Thus, remittances sent by sample respondents which could move beyond family maintenance and finance the education of siblings is surely a step forward to achieving sustainable development through investment in human resources. It suggests that labour migration is adopted not only as a strategy for income maximisation, but also to strengthen the human resources capabilities of the sending families.

4.4 COPING MECHANISMS OF MIGRANT WORKERS IN THE URBAN LABOUR MARKET AND SOCIETY

Women's Attempt to Change their Working Conditions

Evidence from the information collected in the course of survey work indicates that women workers are perceived by their employers to be docile, hard working and ready to work long hours and have less contacts, exposure and bargaining power compared to their male counterparts. Findings of the present study also point to lower wage and horizontal mobility of women workers, compared to male workers, particularly in the RMG industries. Hence it is important to examine whether women workers make any effort to improve their working conditions.

Demand for Paid Leaves, Higher Wages and Change in Night Duty

Half of the sampled women workers of garment factories have on occasion demanded paid leave and nearly three-fifths bargained for higher wages (Table 4.18). The proportion of men, who made similar demands, are slightly higher than women (63 and 62 per cent

TABLE 4.18

Proportion and Profile of Workers who Demanded Better Working Conditions

Respondents' Category	Paid Leaves				Average Education (years)		Length of Service (years)		Proportions whose Demand was Sanctioned (%)	
	Male		Female		Male	Female	Male	Female	Male	Female
	Total	%	Total	%						
% demanded paid leaves										
Garments	76	63.2	77	50.6	3.0	2.9	2.9	4.4	72.9	79.5
Other manufacturing	30	76.7	30	90.0	3.7	3.7	6.9	8.5	86.9	96.3
% demanded higher wages										
Garments	76	61.8	77	55.8	2.9	2.5	2.7	3.4	36.2	30.2
Other industries	30	3.3	30	6.7	2.0	4.0	12.0	12.0	100.0	50.0
% demanded change in night duty										
Garments	76	27.6	77	29.9	2.8	2.6	1.9	3.7	42.9	43.5
Other industries	30	13.3	30	10.0	2.7	3.0	3.0	11.3	50.0	100.0

Source: Sample survey of migrant workers of Dhaka's formal manufacturing sector, 1996.

respectively). The sample women on the other hand, outnumber their male counterparts marginally in their demand to be relieved of night work. However, the magnitude of both male and female workers of garments factories, who demanded less night work was much lower (30 per cent and 27 per cent), than those who demanded paid leave and higher wages.

Women workers from other manufacturing units mainly asked for paid leave and here they outnumbered their male counterparts. It should be noted, that unlike garments factories, which remain open even on weekly and public holidays, other manufacturing industries do not have such strong aberrations from normal working hours. Yet more women bargained for paid leave because of their dual responsibility of earning a livelihood and taking care of children. Workers in those factories do not have to bargain for higher wages as they generally have well-designed terms of contract and most of them are recruited on a regular rather than a casual basis. Conversely, a large number of workers in garments factories are hired on a casual basis, mostly without stipulated terms of contract.

Consequently, very few (3 per cent male and 6 per cent female) workers of other manufacturing industries demanded higher wages and a tenth of the sample workers from these industries, irrespective of gender, bargained to reduce the extent of their night work. Although very few of the sample workers bargained for overtime, here too the share of women workers from garments factories is much higher (13 per cent) compared to their male colleagues (8 per cent) or sisters at other manufacturing units (3 per cent). This is explained by the fact that garments workers were in the lowest wage category, and remained exposed to a higher level of night work.

Although the differential between the proportion of male and female garments factory workers, who bargained for higher wages, paid leave and changes in night shift remains narrow, it still calls for an explanation. Education is often considered as a means to raise the level of awareness/consciousness. Although a sample male worker has a higher level of education than a woman, the latter, on an average, have longer lengths of service in the same factory than the former (Table 4.18). This longer length of service of female workers might have conscientised women workers to a similar level of awareness demonstrated by more educated male workers to demand better terms and conditions. More than 90 per cent of the sample workers, irrespective of gender and types of factories, through the help of supervisors, applied for better terms and conditions. The workers did not involve unions or other external sources such as employers' agents in making their demands. As garments factories are operated by private entrepreneurs purely for profit, more aggressive forms of assertion of worker's rights is not tolerated by the owners in the RMG sector. Given the heavy competition for wage employment, the RMG workers, irrespective of gender, tend to generally abide by the existing rules and regulations of the factory and try to avoid confrontation.

Results of Bargaining by Respondents

As regards outcomes from efforts at bargaining by employees, notwithstanding the fact that women workers are paid lower wages than men, women have, if anything, proved more effective than males in realising their demands. For example, paid leave was sanctioned to 80 per cent of women and 73 per cent of male workers of the garments factories (Table 4.18). The corresponding figures for other manufacturing units are 96 and 87 per cent respectively. Similarly, one-fifth of the women workers who demanded overtime realised their demand whilst none of their male counterparts managed to do so. Conversely, more women had their request for higher wages (70 per cent) turned down than their male colleagues (64 per cent). Apart from the question of profit, need for cash income and meeting the demand schedule of the buyers, it is difficult to understand why employers so frequently reject the demands of their employees since most of their demands tend to be modest in their claim on the firms resources. Furthermore, not all that is conceded by employers are implemented in practice.

For example, nearly one-third of the respondents experienced a salary cut for taking leave of absence mainly due to sickness. The onus in this regard falls more heavily on women (one-third) compared to their male counterparts (one-fifth). Women workers are more susceptible to sickness and fatigue arising out of their double burdens of domestic chores, child care and office work, and also as a result of systematic deprivation of their nutritional needs to which they remain exposed from childhood. In her more recent survey, the author found that among those who took leave, seven out of every ten women, compared to 53 per cent of their male colleagues, took sick leave. More than four out of very five took 5.1 days of sick leave, on an average in the month preceding the survey, due to their own sickness. Nearly a fifth of women, as opposed to 7 per cent of their male counterparts also took sick leave because of other family members, including children (Afsar 1998). Results of the same survey also showed that 42 and 26 per cent of the female and male respondents from the sample garments factories were sick in the month preceding the survey. As a result women remain more vulnerable to wage cuts. This greater incidence of sickness amongst workers of garments factories, particularly women, suggests that on humanitarian grounds as well as due to financial benefit to employers, investments need to be made in providing preventative health care for the RMG workers. Furthermore, some form of contributory health insurance is needed, as well the creation of conditions of work and living for women workers which could not make them so vulnerable to illness.

Nari Udyog Kendra's (NUK, an NGO) health insurance scheme, which ensures periodic medical check up for women workers with the help of some employers, and immunisation and other reproductive and general health related services provided by another NGO, known as Unity Through Population Services (UTPS) in 93 garments factories of Dhaka city, represent a constructive welcome move in providing health care for women, but efforts needs to be replicated on a large scale. Research on the type of diseases suffered by women and their children should also be undertaken in order to design a health programme for garment workers.

The issue of employer responses to work demands suggest the need for discussion on the issue of labour relations in the RMG sector, the role of trade unions, and legal procedures for factory inspection and collective bargaining. The issues are discussed by Khan in his paper in this volume. It may leaves not be mentioned here that most demands by workers in the RMG sector tend to be handled on an *adhoc* basis and no formal bargaining of procedures appear to be in place in RMG units.

Living Arrangements of Migrant Women in the Urban Society

Living with family members and relatives at the current place of destination (Table 4.19) remains the most common arrangement among migrant female workers from garments factories. Three-quarters of the female workers live either in their own nuclear units or as a member of the extended family. The remaining one-quarter of those workers either live in sub-let arrangements (16 per cent) or in shared housing with other co-workers, (mess) (9 per cent). Those who live in sub-let arrangements either live with siblings and cousins (41.7 per cent) or co-workers (41.7 per cent). A few also live with single parents. Only 7 female garment workers were found to live in shared housing with other co-workers. These women are mainly divorced or separated, a few are currently unmarried, and except one, all migrated between 1991 and 1996. None of the female workers from other manufacturing units were found to live in a mess or boarding house and only 3 out of a total of 30 respondents lived in sub-let arrangements. Thus whilst nearly a quarter of garments factory workers, live with co-workers, be it relatives or friends, this type of living arrangement is almost non-existent among female workers of other manufacturing units.

Living arrangement of these women can also be related to some of the socio-demographic characteristics of workers. As opposed to a large number of female workers from garments factories, who are young and currently unmarried, their counterparts from other manufacturing industries are predominantly married (two-thirds) and live in family units either nuclear (60 per cent) or joint-extended (40 per cent). Moreover, garments factory workers tend to be first generation settlers in Dhaka city, whereas women workers from other manufacturing industries are either non-migrants or long-term migrants. Hence, they (the latter) are already absorbed in an existing family set up and do not have to find various ways and means to survive and sustain themselves in the urban society.

Unlike the family based living arrangements of female garment factory workers, living in a mess or boarding house is much more common among male workers of garments factories. One in three male workers of garments factories live in a mess or boarding house mostly with co-workers, and the bulk of them, nearly three-quarters,

TABLE 4.19

Percentage Distribution of Respondents by Types of Living Arrangement in the Place of Destination and Migration Status

Respondents*	Family Unit		Mess/Boarding House		Sublet		Others*		All	
	Male	Female	Male	Female	Male	Female	Male	Female	Male	Female
Garments										
Non-Migrant	66.7	80.0	33.3	–	–	–	–	20.0	3	5
Long- Term Migrant	65.7	75.7	17.1	2.7	8.6	16.2	8.6	5.4	35	37
Recent Migrant	36.8	65.7	44.7	17.1	7.7	17.1	–	–	38	35
All	52.6	70.0	31.6	9.1	7.9	15.6	9.2	–	76	77
Others										
Non-Migrant	61.5	75.0	7.7	–	15.4	–	15.4	25.0	13	16
Long- Term Migrant	16.7	78.6	25.0	–	8.3	21.4	50.0	–	12	14
Recent Migrant	40.0	–	60.0	–	–	–	–	–	5	–
All	–	–	–	–	–	–	–	–	–	–
All (Garments & Others)	87	123	5	4	14	12	7	10	34	15

Note: *Others include employer's land and squatting government/public land.

Source: Sample survey of migrant workers of Dhaka's formal manufacturing sector, 1996.

are also recent migrants. Living in messing units or boarding house is an age old practice for men, which was in vogue in this sub-continent with the introduction of English education and the subsequent emergence of city based employment.

Living arrangement of the workers at the place of destination shows the importance of family support for migrant workers. Female workers, in particular, depend largely on family members to cope with an urban environment. To overcome the existing negative attitude towards independent female workers as well as the lack of low-cost housing or hostel facilities in Dhaka city, women workers live with one or two family members in sub-let arrangement or with single parents or with their brothers or sisters, or with families of their relations. Family based living arrangements give these women necessary protection from theft and other untoward incidents and provides some support services e.g., child-care. This perspective can be substantiated from the fact that nearly a tenth of female garments factory workers, and one-fifth of their male counterparts, experienced theft in their place of residence while out for work. Incidence of theft is even higher in the case of male workers of other manufacturing units. It should be noted that half of the men, as opposed to a quarter of women garments workers had none to look after their houses when they went out to work (Table 4.20). Moreover, one out of every seven female workers in garments factories, compared to a fraction (3 per cent) of their male counterparts, drew on the support of their neighbours to look after their habitations. In the absence of responsible family members and relatives who can look after the house during working hours, a good number of male workers who live in messes remain susceptible to theft much more than female workers.

In meeting the day to day sustenance needs, the bulk of the female garments factory workers face intense hardship. A large number of helpers and operators live in low rental accommodation, where they have to share latrines, bathrooms and cooking gas burners or heaters with 15-30 families. In the city proper, viz. Karailer Math in Mohakhali and Kalapani area in Mirpur, they live in crowded quarters with an area of approximately 3 metre^2 for each person in a semi-durable type of structure at the cost of Taka 600 per month,

TABLE 4.20

Distribution of Respondents by Migration Status and Sources who Look after the House/mess when Out to Work

Year of Migration	Family Members/ Relatives (%)		Neighbour/Friend (%)		Maids/Servants (%)		None (%)		All (No.)	
	Male	Female	Male	Female	Male	Female	Male	Female	Male	Female
Garments										
Non-migrant	66.7	80.0	–	–	33.3	–	–	20.0	3	5
Long Term Migrant	57.1	59.5	2.9	16.2	14.3	8.1	25.7	16.2	35	37
Recent Migrant	36.8	51.4	10.5	14.3	15.8	8.6	36.8	25.7	38	35
All	47.4	57.1	6.6	14.3	15.8	7.8	30.3	20.8	76	77
Others										
Non-migrant	61.5	56.3	7.7	12.5	–	12.5	30.8	18.8	13	16
Long- Term Migrant	16.7	42.9	–	–	16.7	42.9	66.7	14.3	12	14
Recent Migrant	40.0	–	–	–	20.0	–	40.0	–	5	–
All	40.0	50.0	3.3	6.7	10.0	26.7	46.7	16.7	30	30
All (Garments and Others)	48	59	6	13	15	14	3	21	106	107

Source: Sample survey of migrant workers of Dhaka's formal manufacturing sector, 1996.

which constitutes nearly a half of the total salary of the operators and almost the entire wage of the helpers. Here respondents share two or three latrines and 5/6 gas burners or heaters with 15-30 families for cooking. Consequently, these women wake up earlier than their male colleagues and yet, are more vulnerable to pay cuts as they are often 10-15 minutes late to reach the factory due to their later start from their place of abode. The women generally lack proper bathrooms within a covered space or running water facilities for bathing. It is learnt from the respondents, their family members and neighbours at their community of residence, that there is an acute crisis of running water supplied by the Dhaka Water and Sewerage Authority (WASA) in those areas of the city proper. The workers have to pay for collecting water from a few tubewells that are found in the area, and also travel a long distance for this purpose, adding to the women's existing workload.

Female garments factory workers thus do not live in adequate lodging facilities. Being first generation workers in a metropolis, which is unplanned and infrastructurally least equipped to meet the needs of the poorer people, female garments factory workers pay a higher price to surmount the heavy odds in the settlement process, compared to their male counterparts. Nonetheless, they have managed to cope and to achieve the status of an independent earner. This is a significant achievement for illiterate or semi-literate and unskilled rural women from landless households exposed to both urban living and factory work for the first time in their lives. Only a few cases of return migration of female workers were cited in the community based FGDs, further highlighting the ability of these young female workers to cope with urban life.

Support from family members in terms of child care is also an important factor, which facilitate female workers to work outside home (garments factory), in the absence of any institutional support. Among female workers from garment factories with children under 5, almost 9 out of 10 depend on family support, as opposed to nearly three-fifths of their counterparts in other manufacturing units. A large number of the latter group (nearly two-fifths) depend on domestic help to look after their children. Male workers on the contrary, depend overwhelmingly on family members for child care. Lack of child care facilities in many of the emerging mega cities poses a big problem for women's outside work and occupational mobility. Although families still provide the necessary support for child care, how long this can continue needs to be examined, especially in a situation where a large majority (52 per cent) of the female garments workers are currently unmarried.

Mechanisms to Combat Odd Working Hours

Young migrant women, walking long distances, often after dusk, need protection against violence, physical or sexual assault on their way from home to office or vice versa. Such protection is usually provided by their co-workers and family members, in the absence of a cheap and safe public transportation system or office transport facility. Nine out of every 10 female garments factory workers live in the same ward as the factory or nearby, and walk to their workplace. The remaining 10 per cent of the female workers travel either by tempo or rickshaw. However, whether they walk or ride on a rickshaw, they are always accompanied by co-workers and or family members (Table 4.21). They seldom go to office alone, particularly at night. Their strong group identity on the road works as a protective shield in the otherwise unprotected lonely dark roads and lanes. Only a fraction of female garments workers (3 per cent) reported that they were teased while walking from office at night. However, the survey technique is not useful to capture sensitive areas such as sexual abuse/harassment, since women often have inhabitions, about sharing their personal experiences. Both men and women unanimously considered *mastaans* or musclemen as the principal potential threat. The bulk of the workers, three-quarters of men and three-fifths of women garments factory workers consider *mastaans* from the same locality as dangerous, while the remaining male and female workers perceived *mastaans* from other communities as potential threats. Hence, the issue of *mastaans* and violence should be addressed urgently.

Community based FGDs applied by the author in the other study mentioned here, revealed many instances of threat from *mastaans* and other forms of sexual abuses/ harassment faced by female garments factory workers. *Eve teasing* on the road and cases of

TABLE 4.21

Source of Respondents by Source who Accompany when go Out to Office at Night by Year of Migration

Respondents*	Go with Male/ Female Worker (%)		Male Neighbours (%)		Rickshaw (%)		Office Transport (%)		Others (%)*		All (No)	
	Male	Female	Male	Female	Male	Female	Male	Female	Male	Female	Male	Female
Garments												
Non-migrant	33.3	40.0	–	–	33.3	20.0	–	–	33.3	40.0	3	5
Long Term Migrant	42.9	70.3	–	–	11.4	16.2	–	–	45.7	13.5	35	37
Recent Migrant	65.8	82.9	5.3	–	2.6	5.7	–	–	26.3	11.4	38	35
All	53.9	74.0	2.6	–	7.9	11.7	–	–	35.5	14.3	76	77
Other Industries												
Non-migrant	23.1	25.0	7.7	18.8	30.8	–	15.4	37.5	23.1	18.8	13	16
Long Term Migrant	16.7	35.7	16.7	7.1	16.7	21.4	41.7	28.6	8.3	7.1	12	14
Recent Migrant	–	–	–	–	40.0	–	–	–	60.0	–	5	–
All	16.7	30.0	10.0	13.3	26.7	10.0	23.3	33.3	23.3	13.3	30	30
All (Garments & Others)	87	123	5	4	14	12	7	10	34	15	106	107

Note: *Others include family members for female workers at large and no companion for male workers.

Source: Sample survey of migrant workers of Dhaka's formal manufacturing sector, 1996.

kidnapping of the female garments factory workers are also reported. In Kalapani area, a young girl was kidnapped by the *mastaans* while coming home alone at around 10 o'clock at night. Next morning, they left her in the same place after raping her. She was badly injured and was under treatment for some time. After her recovery, she felt too embarrassed to work in the same garments factory and to live in the same area. Hence, she left the factory and the area. They also cited another rape case in Madhya Badda, the eastern fringe of Dhaka city. Within the factory, some women complained ironically that their male co-workers treats them as garments, which is to be used for some time and then discarded. Taking advantage of women's economic hardship, male co-workers, technical and even some managerial staff make false promises of marriage or even promotion. Finally, once they establish a sexual relationship, male partners often do not sustain the relationship. There are also cases, where women workers establish close relationships with technical and or managerial staff and use this to elevate themselves above other workers. Some of there liaisons even led to separation from their husbands. Being young and exposed to a less protective environment to work and live, both male and female workers remain susceptible to sexually transmitted diseases (STD). From her latest survey, the author found that one in every five garments factory worker, irrespective of gender, knew about a STD affected co-worker (Afsar 1998). Therefore, it is urgent to give a training to these workers on the dangers of STD and AIDS and ways they spread, as well as advise them on protective measures.

4.5 SUMMARY AND POLICY IMPLICATIONS

Summary

This study was primarily undertaken to explore the ways and means by which migrant women enter and cope with the demands of the urban labour market and urban society and how these differ from the coping strategies of male and non-migrant workers. Using a quota sampling technique, 213 workers were drawn from 5 garments and 3 other manufacturing industries viz., pharmaceuticals, electronics and food processing in Dhaka city from a list of 530 workers. The number of male and female workers was 107 and 106 respectively. A larger sample from garments (153), compared to 60 workers from other manufacturing was drawn, as the RMG industries have generated considerable female employment since the 1980s. The workers were interviewed both at their workplace and at home. The sample garments factories were established between 1984 and 1994, and excepting the pharmaceutical industry (CIBA Geigy Ltd.), the remaining two (food processing and electronics) were established in the '60s. The size of the sample garments factories varied between 250 and 2500 workers. The other sample manufacturing units cover nearly 100 employees. However, the food processing industry employed 530 workers. The share of women workers was almost double that of men in the sample garments factories, and except for pharmaceuticals, there was almost equal representation of male and female workers in the other manufacturing units

- For the purpose of the present study, migrants are defined by both geographic and temporal criteria. A person who is not born in Dhaka and migrated here between 1980 and 1996 is defined as a migrant. Further, those who migrated between 1991 and 1996 are defined as recent migrants, whereas those who migrated between 1980 and 1990 are deemed long-term migrants. It is assumed that 15 years is sufficient time to adjust to the urban environment. Hence, those who came before 1980 were treated as non-migrants. In this process, about 37 per cent of the sample were classified as recent migrants and 46 per cent as long-term migrants, yielding a total of 83 per cent migrants and 17 per cent non-migrants.
- Growth of RMG industries have led to women independently migrating, a phenomenon reflected in the gradual decline in the sex ratio of Dhaka city dwellers.

Female workers of garments factories came pre-dominantly in search of a job as did their male counterparts in both garments and other manufacturing units. Nearly three-quarters of women and men came for work related reasons (Table 4.3). Although two-fifths of women migrants from other manufacturing industries came for economic reasons, a quarter of them were associational migrants, who accompanied their husbands to Dhaka. A global review of reasons for women's migration by the UN Secretariat (1993) along with some recent studies reveal that worldwide more women migrate for family than economic reasons, for instance, to accompany other family members or a spouse and to get married. While the findings of the present study departs significantly from the above pattern, it is consistent with the findings from Bangkok Metropolis (Phongpaichi 1993).

Although women workers in general are landless, female garments factory workers are more disadvantaged in this regard. On an average they have 1.3 acres of land as opposed to 2.0 acres for their male counterparts in the same factory and 2.3 acres for female counterparts from other manufacturing units. Female workers from garments and non-migrants had 2.5 and 3.3 years of schooling respectively prior to migration. The corresponding figures for their male counterparts was 3.0 and 3.9 years respectively. Obviously, push factors alone cannot explain women's independent migration. Rather, a combined effect of demand pull and push facilitated by social networks can be put forward to explain this phenomenon.

Women's entry into formal manufacturing industries, particularly garments factories, still remains largely dependent on informal sources of information and social networks. Such an informal system of recruitment ensures loyalty and docility. On the other hand, securing employment through known sources might be considered safer for daughters by their parents. In many cases, the respondents who migrated for the present job, also had information about the nature of the work and wages. The propensity to have such information is higher among female recent migrant workers (half) from garments factories, compared to their long-term migrant colleagues (one-third) (Table 4.5). Increased access to information by female workers suggests wider and greater networking among recent migrant female workers from garments factories, compared to their long-term migrant sisters. Particularly, the role of social networks in supplying job related information to migrant workers of the garments factories can be considered to be an important factor in the labour migration process.

One major change in rural-urban migration over the past decade has been the increasing proportion of young women with low levels of educational attainment originating from rural areas. Employed migrants of both sexes tended to be young, but women were considerably younger than men. At the time of migration, a woman worker was on average at least two years younger than her male counterpart. Majority of women workers (52 per cent) from garments factories are currently unmarried, compared to nearly three-quarters of their male counterparts from the same and a quarter of female counterparts from other manufacturing industries (Table 4.6). Nearly one-tenth of the women workers from garments or other factories were reported to be divorced/separated and widowed. Both ever and currently married women in the garments factories have significantly fewer number of living children than Bangladeshi women in general. More than 90 per cent of them use contraceptives, compared to nearly three-fifths of their urban counterparts. Hence, the employment opportunities generated by the RMG sector for the young migrant rural women appears to contribute to fertility reduction.

The sample female workers of garments and other manufacturing industries earn three-quarters and ninety per cent respectively of the earnings of their male counterparts (Table 4.11). The gender gap is highest in the case of supervisor/technical/managerial category which is evident in the lower female-male earning ratio for both garments (0.73) and non-garments (0.83), than either skilled (0.87 and 1.02) or unskilled (0.82 and 1.01) production workers of the respective garments and other manufacturing industries. There is a significant increase in women's wages from Tk. 772 to Tk. 1838, for those who migrated to Dhaka between 1980-90 and 1991-1996, which suggests that women garments factory workers are coping well with the urban labour market situation. Obviously, migration and absorption into garments factories opened up better earning avenues for younger women from landless and marginal farmer's households with low levels of education, compared to rural wage labourers or those migrants who work as housemaids. It is important to note that whilst long-term male migrants earn more than their non-migrant counterparts, the reverse holds true for their female colleagues. As the latter started on an unequal footing compared to male workers and also have limited scope for upgrading their skills and education, they need more time than their male counterparts, to supercede their non-migrant counterparts in terms of income.

Migrant workers from garments factories save more than their non-migrant counterparts, irrespective of gender. Relatively older workers in garments factories (aged between 30 and 39) save (41 per cent) more and earn more than their younger counterparts. An analysis on remittances shows that the average size of the remittances as proportion of the monthly urban income is higher for garments factory workers, than those of other manufacturing industries.

Three-quarters of men as opposed to half of the women from garments factories are still single. Hence, more men than women are likely to send remittances to their families at origin. Those who remit constitute respectively three-fifths and nearly two-fifths of currently unmarried men and women workers from the garments factories. Further, younger migrants from garments factories (aged between 10-19 years) are found to remit a much higher proportions (42 per cent) of their urban income than their older counterparts (25 per cent). Moreover, female workers from garments industries spent much more on housing and medical treatment on themselves and their family members, than their male colleagues in the city, which circumscribes their ability to remit. Thus, unlike savings, which appears to be influenced largely by income, the size of the remittances, on the other hand, also depends on the intensity of the social ties and responsibilities migrants bear at their place of destination and origin. Remittances sent by sample respondents for both family maintenance and education suggests that labour migration is not only adopted as a strategy for income maximisation, but also to strengthen the human resources of the sending families.

Female migrant workers depend largely on family members to cope with the urban situation. To overcome the existing negative attitude towards independent female migrants and lack of housing or hostel facilities, they live with one or two family members in sub-let arrangements or with single parents or with their brothers or sisters, aunt's or uncle's family. In sharp contrast to female garments workers, living in a mess or boarding house is much more common among male workers of garments factories. Family based living arrangements gives women the necessary protection from theft and other untoward incidents and provides necessary services, e.g., child care.

Family members and co-workers of female garments factory workers generally act as a protective shield against violence, physical or sexual assault on their way from home to work or vice versa. In the absence of a cheap and safe public transportation system, almost 9 out of 10 female factory workers live in the same ward as the factory or nearby, and walk to their workplace. The remaining 10 per cent of the female workers travel either by *tempo* or rickshaw. However, whether they walk or ride on a rickshaw, they are always accompanied by co-workers and/or family members. This is particularly true at night. Through direct survey the incidence of sexual harassment of the garments factory workers on the roads is reported to be very low. FGD on the other hand revealed that eve teasing is very common and kidnapping and raping of lone female garments factory workers by *mastaans* are not rare. It has also been revealed that women are more susceptible to abandonment by their co-workers and husbands, and sexual abuses by other male technical staff such as mechanics, electricians, etc. Moreover, the risk of spread of STD and AIDS among garments factory workers cannot be ignored.

It is encouraging to learn that not only did a large number of women bargain for better working conditions but they remained no less pro-active in this respect than their male counterparts, and the outcome does not differ much by gender. Yet, women remain exposed to greater hazard from salary cuts due to higher propensity to take sick leave. Women garments factory workers live under adverse circumstances for themselves and their family as they largely have to share toilets, bath rooms, taps for drinking water and gas burners or heaters with other families. Such pressure of day to day living not only impinges on their time use, but makes them more vulnerable in-terms of salary cuts and frequent sickness. Support from family members with regard to child care is also an important factor which enables female workers to work outside home (garments factory), in the absence of any institutional support. Lack of child care facilities in many of the emerging mega cities poses a big problem for women's outside work and occupational mobility. Although families still provide necessary support for child care, whether this can be sustained needs to be examined.

Policy Implications

The above discussion on migrant women workers' coping mechanisms in the urban labour market and society suggests some important areas for policy intervention. One such important area is housing and efficient delivery of basic amenities. Public sector housing so far has provided only one per cent of urban housing needs. Hence, the informal private sector provides the bulk of housing while the formal private sector is confined to upper middle and high income housing. There is only one hostel for working women run by the Department of Women's Affairs but that remains for middle class working women in Dhaka city. On a very limited scale, *Nari Uddyog Kendra* (NUK) started hostel schemes for low income female garments factory workers. NUK has two rented structures accommodating a total of 200 women with facilities of food, education, skill development and recreation. However, as it charges Tk. 700 (Tk. 300 for food and Tk. 400 for room rent), it is not often affordable by helpers or unskilled production workers of garments factories who on an average earn Tk. 500 per month, though it remains a good bargain for RMG women operatives. During field work it was observed that helpers are the most transient category, and are often denied accommodation by their relatives, on account of inadequate monetary contributions. Hence, they have to move from one relative to other in search of a house or look for a steady co-worker or single working cousin with whom they can live in sub-let arrangements. Thus, whilst there is a general need for low income housing in the urban areas, low cost hostel facilities for working women, particularly unskilled garments factory workers needs urgent attention for policy intervention.

Often planners and policy makers are hesitant to implement low-cost housing schemes fearing that this might 'pull' more migrants from the rural to urban areas. Hence, many governments in developing countries (e.g., Bangladesh) tried to discourage migration by not addressing any resettlement policy in the urban areas and have instead aimed to divert investment into rural development. Such policies have not prevented rural-urban migration. For example, in India, out-migration is found to be higher from those districts that show better agricultural performance. Similarly in Equador, efforts to improve living conditions through integrated rural development, though otherwise successful, failed to significantly reduce rural-urban migration. Values generated by modernisation and high aspirations could not be counterbalanced by the socio-economic changes brought about by rural development (Bilsborrow 1993). In countries such as Bangladesh and Thailand, where rapid growth takes place in the capital city, migration occurs so as to avail of economic opportunities generated by those cities. Women's independent migration, in particular, occurred as a direct response to the demand generated by the export oriented manufacturing industries in the metropolis. Hence, along with efforts to reduce migration, the government must undertake migration responsive policies. Migration responsive policies in this case cover a broad range of concerns and include access to housing, basic amenities, health care and consciousness raising about diseases such as STD and AIDS/HIV, education and training, transport and child care services. Any policy that facilitates the provision of adequate housing and other services to female migrants will accelerate the wheel of economic growth by facilitating female mobility in response to economic incentives. Some of the recommendations made by the proceedings of the United Nations expert meeting on the *Feminization of Internal Migration* (1993) can also be emphasised for the present study. These include:

- Governments, the private sector and non-governmental organisations should provide adequate support services to first time migrants in urban areas, including job placement services and accommodation for migrant women.
- There should be more low-cost but technologically appropriate public housing projects and housing credit schemes for women. Government should also ensure that existing legislation and administrative practices shall grant equal ownership and tenancy rights to women as to men.

The findings of the present study also draw attention of the policy makers on the need for cheap and safe public transportation. It showed heavy concentration of women in those wards where garments factories are located. The private sector, more preferably NGOs, can start city shuttle services for female workers of garments and other manufacturing industries at peak hours in the morning and evening to enable women to perform their normal and overtime work. Employers can also use their pick-up vans to pick and drop off women workers during odd hours and can charge for the petrol cost.

Elsewhere, the author has argued that the government should invest more to improve roads and transportation facilities between rural and urban areas, which will encourage more temporary rather than permanent migration. This proposition was derived from one pertinent finding of her thesis which shows that temporary migrants came from those villages which are better connected with Dhaka city (Afsar 1995).

The present study confirms that women are underrepresented in technically skilled and in senior grades in industry, a universally common pattern. It also shows that the wage gap between men and women workers at this level is the highest compared to skilled and unskilled production workers' level. This finding is consistent with Rahman's (1993: 103) results[6]. These findings call for a more gender-equitable spread of students at secondary and tertiary levels of education and revision of curriculum and teaching practices to achieve more scientific orientation and technological relevance. Demand based vocational training, particularly for migrant women should be organised by both government and non-government organisations. Women workers should also have opportunities for 'on the job training'. As the RMG industries are run largely by private entrepreneurs, it is difficult to impose 'on-the job' training through government directives. They may agree on paper but not in principle, or implement it half-heartedly. Moreover too many impositions may lead to closure of some of the factories and hence many women will be deprived of job opportunities. Therefore, some incentive schemes along with orientation and education of employers, as well as advocacy programmes can be more effective. Incentives to employers can be provided in the form of tax rebate, sales promotion, discount of up to 10 per cent on the duty and value added paid by them. Donors can come forward with funds for training of women workers. Those factories that will organise such training on a regular basis

[6] Some possible explanation for contradictions are offered in Chapter 3, Section 3.2.

and efficiently, can be made eligible for the fund after thorough scrutiny and assessment by independent research bodies.

The study also reveals that women are not lagging behind men in making demands for better working conditions such as paid leave, higher wages and changes in night duty. However, they remain more penalised through salary cuts for availing of more sick leaves than men. A women worker takes more sick leave because she is more vulnerable to sickness than her male colleagues. A women worker has to bear the double burden of domestic chores almost without any support and in a situation where sources of basic amenities are shared with 15-30 families, whilst also doing a full-time job in a factory. The lack of child care facilities for the urban working women exposes them to constant conflict and tension. Similarly, there is a need for better and more efficient delivery of water and sanitation facilities as well as protection of tenants rights. Dhaka Water and Sewerage Authority (WASA) can distribute those facilities adopting progressive rating based on use rather than land ownership, and a fixed rate criteria. City Corporation along with NGOs, and landowners as well as tenants should look after the maintenance and care of water and sewer lines. Moreover, there should be some measures to protect the rights of the tenants so that the landlord cannot frequently increase the house rent at their own will. Any policy that improves health and lowers fertility is likely to foster women's spatial mobility, economic opportunities and productivity.

A health insurance scheme initiated by the *Nari Uddyog Kendro* was adopted by employers of some garments factories who organise regular health check ups of their workers. Similarly, immunisation, regular health care including reproductive health and treatment provided by another NGO, known as *Unity Through Population Services* (UTPS) in 93 garments factories in Dhaka should be supported by the employers and the government. Whilst these initiatives should be replicated on a larger scale both in the factories and communities, there should also be a set of basic safety standards to be followed by these factories. Here too, similar types of incentives outlined for training can be adopted as cost effective policy measures. Considering the threat of spread of sexually transmitted diseases and AIDS among the garments factory workers, there should be crash training programmes to raise their consciousness about dangers of these diseases and ways to get protection.

Finally, recognising that the formulation of policy requires an adequate data base, it is urged that both garments and other manufacturing factories have a list of gender disaggregated data by age, education, length of service and migration status.

References

Afsar, Rita (1991): "Struggle for Better Future", Paper Presented at the International Conference on the Urbanisation and Urban Poor, Dhaka: Bangladesh Institute of Development Studies, July 27-29.

Afsar, Rita (1995): "Causes, Consequences and Challenges of Rural-Urban Migration in Bangladesh" Ph.D. Thesis, Submitted to the University of Adelaide, Australia.

Afsar, Rita (1996): "Onus of Poverty on Women in the Poorer Settlements of Dhaka City", A Paper Presented at the National Committee on Women and Poverty, Organised by the Women for Women, Dhaka, October, 27-29.

Afsar, Rita (1996): "Application of Demographic Analysis in Assessing Gender Based Urban Poverty in Bangladesh", A Paper Presented at the 8th National Conference of the Australian Population Association, Adelaide, Australia, 2-7th December, 1996.

Afsar, Rita (1998): "Too Early or Too Inadequate: A Situation and Impact Analysis of UTPS Programmes on the Garments Factory Workers, Their Families and the Garments Factory Workers, Their Families and the Garments Factory Management", A Report Prepared for Disability and AIDS Control Unit, ACTIONAID, Bangladesh, Dhaka, Mimeo.

Anker, Richard and Catherine Hein (1986): "Sex Inequalities in Third World Employment: Statistical Evidence", In *Sex Inequalities in Urban Employment in the Third World*, Richard Anker and Catherine Hein, Eds. Essex, United Kingdom: Macmillan Press.

BBS (1995): Bangladesh Bureau of Statistics, Statistics Division, Ministry of Planning, Government of the Peoples Republic of Bangladesh.

Bilsborrow, Richard E. (1993): "Issues in the Measurement of Female Migration in Developing Countries", Chapter VI, Internal Migration of Women in Developing Countries, Proceedings of the United Nations Expert Meeting on the Feminization of Internal Migration, Aguascalientes, Mexico, 22- 25 October, 1991.

Caldwell, John C. (1969): African Rural-Urban Migration: Movement to Ghana's Towns, Canberra, Australia: The Australian National University Press.

Chant, Sylvia, ed. (1992): *Gender and Migration in Developing Countries*, London: Printer.

Chaudhury, S. and Majumdar, P. P. (1991): " The Conditions of Garments Workers in Bangladesh: An Appraisal", Dhaka: Bangladesh Institute of Development of Studies, Mimeo.

Chowdhury, S. and Majumdar, P. P. (1993): "Garments Workers in Bangladesh: Economic, Social and Health Condition", *Research Monograph: 18*, Dhaka: Bangladesh Institute of Development Studies (BIDS).

Connell, John, and Others (1976): *Migration From Rural Areas: The Evidence From Village Studies,* New Delhi: Oxford University Press.

Findley, Sally E., and Linda Williams (1991): "Women Who Go and Women Who Stay: Reflections of Family Migration Processes in a Changing World", Population and Labour Policies Programme, Working Paper No. 176, Geneva: International Labour Office.

Gore, M. S. (1971): Immigrants and Neighbourhoods: Two Aspects of Life in a Metropolitan City, Bombay: Tata Institute of Social Sciences.

Hossain *et al.* (1996): "1987-1994: Dynamics of Rural Poverty in Bangladesh", Dhaka: Bangladesh Institute of Development Studies, Mimeo.

Hugo, Graeme J. (1993): " Migrant Women in Developing Countries" Chapter III, *Internal Migration of Women in Developing Countries*, Proceedings of the United Nations Expert Meeting on the Feminization of Internal Migration, *Aguascalientes*, Mexico, 22- 25 October.

Hugo, Graeme J. (1978): Population Mobility in West Java, Yogyakarta, Indonesia, Gadjah Mada University Press.

Hugo, Graeme J. (1981): " Village-Community Ties, Village Norms, and Ethnic and Social Networks: A Review of Evidence from the Third World", *in Migration Decision Making Multidisciplinary Approaches to Microlevel Studies in Developed and Developing Countries*, Gordon F. De Jong and Robert W. Gardner, (Eds.) New York: Pergamon Press.

Khan, S. I. (1996): "Gender Issues and the Ready-Made-Garment Industry of Bangladesh: The Trade Union Context", A Paper Prepared Under Centre for Policy Dialogue (CPD) and United Nations Research Institute for Social Development (UNRISD) Sponsored Project on Changing Patterns of Women's Employment in Bangladesh, Dhaka, Mimeo.

Lansing, J. B. and Mueller, E. (1967): *The Geographical Mobility of Labour,* Ann Arbor: Survey Research Centre, University of Michigan.

Lopez, Maria de la Paz, Haydea Izazola and Jose Gomez de Leon (1993) *Characteristics of Female Migrants According to the 1990 Census of Mexico, Internal Migration of Women in Developing Countries*, Proceedings of the United Nations Expert Meeting on the Feminisation of Internal Migration, Aguascalientes, Mexico, 22- 25 October.

Majumdar, P.P., Mahmud, S. and Afsar, Rita (1995): *The Squatters of Dhaka City, Dynamism in the Life of Agargaon Squatters*, University Press Limited, Dhaka, Bangladesh.

Mitra *et al.*(1994): *Bangladesh Demographic and Health Survey*, National Institute of Population Research and Training, 1993-94, Calverton, Maryland.

Phongpaichit, Pasuk (1993): "The Labour Market Aspects of Female Migration in Thailand", Internal Migration of Women in Developing Countries, Proceedings of the United Nations Expert Meeting on the Feminization of Internal Migration, Aguascalientes, Mexico, 22- 25 October.

Rahman, S.H. (1992): Macroeconomics Performance, Stabilisation and Adjustment: The Experience of Bangladesh in the 1980s, Indus, New Delhi.

Rempel, H. and Lobdell, R. A. (1978): "The Role of Urban to Rural Remittances in Rural Development", *The Journal of the Development Studies*, 14(3): 324-341.

Ritchey, P. Neal (1976): *Explanations of Migration*, Annual Review of Sociology, 2: 363-404.

Skeldon, Ronald (1990): *Population Mobility in Developing Countries*, London and New York: Belhaven Press.

UNINSTRAW (1994): "The Migration of Women", Methodology Issues in the Measurement and Analysis of Internal and International Migration, UNIRTRAW, San Domingo, Dominican Republic.

United Nations Secretariat (1993): "Types of Female Migration", *Internal Migration of Women in Developing Countries*, Proceedings of the United Nations Expert Meeting on the Feminization of Internal Migration, Aguascalientes, Mexico, 22- 25 October, 1991.

Annex 1

SAMPLING FRAME: PROBLEMS OF ENLISTING FACTORIES AND CONTACTING WORKERS

It was decided to select factories from those thana where there is concentration of RMG factories. Existing studies reported such concentration in Mirpur, Motijheel, Tejgaon and Gulshan (Chaudhury & Majumdar 1991). The Bangladesh Trade and Commercial Guide which documents all formal sector establishments, was used as a sampling frame. However one major problem was encountered while contacting those factories. The directory was published in 1991. Between 1991 and 1996, the telephone numbers in many areas such as Motijheel, Eskaton, Moghbazar and Gulshan were changed or digitised and it was not possible to capture factories in those thanas with the help of this guide book. This problem was partially addressed with the help of the directory prepared by the Bangladesh Garments Manufacturers and Employees' Association (BGMEA) in 1995. In this case too, the *thanas* which were digitised after 1995 could not be covered. Hence the sample factories were selected from the following *thanas*:

- Tejgaon
- Mirpur
- Mohammadpur
- Gulshan
- Tongi

Apart from telephone, getting permission to enter into garments factories and interview the workers required endless telephonic conversations, persuasions and strong advocacy for the need of research. Whilst there is a generally research phobia or apathy among common public in this country, the employers of those factories are not immuned from such feelings. A host of other factors are also responsible for making those factories highly restrictive or inaccessible. These are:

- Generally RMG industries operate to meet some specific demands of the external market, exclusively at private initiative. Here the entire production is linked to a chain of activities performed simultaneously such as assembling, cutting, stitching, finishing, ironing and packaging. Hence temporarily withdrawing one worker from any of these activities hampers the entire production process. Subsequently the sample workers were interviewed mainly during lunch time, after office hours and in their homes. It was not so easy to contact a worker at his/her home address mainly because, the addresses they gave were often incomplete and in some cases wrong. Helpers or unskilled production workers of garments factories were the most mobile category as many of them lived with their relatives and often thrown out on account of insufficient monetary contribution. As many workers from garments factories worked overtime, they were not found at home until 10 o'clock at night. Upon return, they were often too tired to respond to the questionnaire. Thus in order to interview the helpers of garments factories they were approached during lunch time and provided with lunch. In this way, the time they would have spent in going home or other food centres, was saved and utilised for the purpose of interviewing. However, excepting helpers, all other categories of workers were interviewed at home either at night or those days when they did not work overtime, given the funding constraints.

- Excepting the sample pharmaceutical factory, it was not difficult to get access to the workers of other manufacturing industries selected for this study. In the case of pharmaceutical industry, although the permission was procured from the head office, the factory manager of the manufacturing unit in Tongi was reluctant to give permission to interview workers mainly because he thought that labourers would be politicised through their active participation in the research process and this would jeopardise the factory's interest in the long run. With great persuasion, permission was obtained to interview workers mainly inside the factory and occasionally in current place of residence of the worker.
- Finally the data collection for the study was started immediately after the general strikes when work pressure was greater than the normal time. All these factors hampered the progress of data collection considerably and it took four months to collect data from 213 workers.

Chapter 5

GENDER ISSUES AND THE READY-MADE GARMENT INDUSTRY OF BANGLADESH: THE TRADE UNION CONTEXT*

Shamsul I. Khan

5.1 INTRODUCTION

Various studies have pointed out that there has been a considerable expansion in female employment in Bangladesh during the last decade (Paul-Majumdar and Chaudhuri-Zohir 1993; Bhuiyan 1991; Wahra and Rahman 1995). Female employment, due to both "push" and "pull" factors, has expanded in an unprecedented manner in the formal export-based sectors, particularly in ready-made-garments (RMG) manufacturing. In fact, at present, there are about 2,400 garment factories operating in Bangladesh, though, till July 1996, 2,357 garment factories were registered with the Bangladesh Garments Manufacturers and Exporters Association (BGMEA) (Nahar 1996). The growth, indeed, has been phenomenal since the ready-made garment industry began modestly as late as the 1970s.

However, the rapid growth in the female labour dominated export-based manufacturing industries is now also raising new issues

* The Author would like to thank Nasreen Khundker, Department of Economics, University of Dhaka, and Shahra Razavi and Yusuf Bangura, both from the United Nations Research Institute for Social Development, Geneva, for their incisive comments on the first draft. The author would also like to express his gratitude to Carol Miller, United Nations Research Institute for Social Development, for providing the author with relevant literature at short notices.

and concerns about the evolving industrial relations in the RMG sector and their possible future consequences for wages and labour productivity in general and changing working conditions for the women labour force in particular. One particular reason for this concern is the possible 'organisational impact' of the phasing out of the Multi-Fibre Arrangement (MFA) on the overall workplace environment of the factories by the year 2005. One of the crucial factors behind the boom in ready-made garment manufacturing in Bangladesh was the search by several East Asian countries — mainly in the late seventies — for ways around the MFA. Through the MFA — first introduced in 1974 under the General Agreement on Tariffs and Trade (GATT) — mainly US, Canada and some West European countries sought to protect their own garment industries from cheap imports of garments from the developing countries.

Bangladesh, however, was able to escape these import quotas because it was not perceived as a particular threat to the industries of those countries. As a result, many East Asian firms, unable to export to countries like the US because their countries' quotas had already been exhausted, simply relocated to Bangladesh, either in the form of direct investments (FDI), or as joint ventures, or even as 'Buying Houses'. However, instead of going for the establishment of backward linkages or developing indigenous raw material sectors, most of these firms preferred to import almost all raw materials from their own countries for making their ready-made garments in Bangladesh. In other words, they used only the amply available cheap labour force of the country. These garments were then exported to USA, Canada, and some West European countries as Bangladeshi goods, thereby avoiding import restrictions placed on goods from East Asian countries.

Taking advantage of "informal" labour recruitment and workplace policies — which included, recruiting workers without proper 'appointment letters' and providing the supervisory staff full authority to hire and fire 'semi-skilled' casual workers (from other factories or the unemployed) whenever necessary — the owners of these enterprises generally maintained their "strong grip" over the overall management and labour relations and tended to oppose any kind of unionisation.

Around the mid-eighties, when a new generation of Bangladeshi entrepreneurs, a majority of whom started operating primarily as local suppliers to these 'Buying Houses', joined the RMG manufacturing sector, they also followed the path of the RMG pioneers. Barring a few relatively new garments manufacturers like, say, the Beximco Knitwear & Fabrics Ltd., all went for cheaply available imported raw materials. All of them also employed mainly 'unskilled' teenage girls, drawn primarily from the rural areas. There were three main reasons for this deliberate feminisation of the work force: (i) it was perceived by the garments factory owners that, as Guy Standing has already pointed out with reference to export-led industrialisation in other Asian Newly Industrialised Countries (NICs), these poor women had been socially and economically oppressed for so long that they were certain to have low "aspiration wages" when they took up their jobs and also low "efficiency wages" once they were in employment (Standing 1989); (ii) since these women were already in a precarious situation due to their socio-economic vulnerability, they were more likely than their male counterparts to work "extra hours" if necessary, and in case of any decline in their performances in terms of productivity, they were much more easier to "get rid-off"; (iii) they were also perceived by most garments owners as "docile", "to a large extent, trustworthy", "manageable", "less confrontational" and therefore "less susceptible" to any "anti-management propaganda by outsiders"

It would be interesting to note in this connection that, from the very outset, most of the above mentioned RMG factory owners tried their best to keep the factory units as "informalised" as possible because that would provide them with greater flexibility in terms of labour management, unit production and working hours without significant social obligations to their workforce. Any kind of unionisation, including 'in-house' unions, was also perceived as "undesirable" by most garments factory owners because, as they argued, "at the formative phase of their manufacturing businesses" they could not afford to be distracted by "unreasonable" workers' demands and "unnecessary disruptions" by the trade union leaders who, at one point or other, "might try to pursue their own selfish agenda in the name of worker's participation". It is alleged by some trade union leaders that even in very few factories where a kind of 'in-house' unionisation was allowed, say, for example, Desh Garments, the union leaders were "hand-picked " by the management who sooner or later became "the agents of the owners" in the name of "management-labour solidarity".

It is actually in the backdrop of the above mentioned scenario that one has to analyse the future of the labour-management relations in the RMG industries in Bangladesh in the new millennium and its consequences for labour productivity and gender equity. More so, because there is a risk that after the dismantling of the MFA and the consequent opening of the garments market to free trade, most Bangladeshi garments manufacturers might try desperately to be competitive in terms of price in the existing world market, both for retaining old orders and for winning new orders, and would, thus, need to exercise all available options for cutting cost. The possible consequences of these competitive pressures could be (a) to lock the RMG sector, into a vicious cycle of low-wage, low-efficiency, and low-technology production; (b) shrinking of the existing modest 'on-the-job training' and other facilities for the predominantly female workers; (c) further deterioration of factory conditions.

However, the cost-cutting option could, in the long run, turn out to be a 'Trojan horse' for the manufacturers, since in an industrial sector where labour costs are already among the lowest and where the working environment is in dire need of improvement, any such endeavour is bound to make the Bangladeshi manufacturers vulnerable to new types of non-tariff barriers in the name of humanitarian concerns, as happened earlier on the issue of 'child labour' (Nahar 1996). Therefore, for their enlightened self-interest, the RMG manufacturers from Bangladesh, must find some ways of minimising production costs, without heavily clamping down on wages and other benefits. Their success in this respect would ultimately depend on whether or not they manage in striking a balance between wage structures, the working environment and labour-management relations on the one hand, and labour productivity on the other. It is in this context that one has to consider the role of the trade unions in the RMG manufacturing sector in Bangladesh. Although the post Cold War debate on the consequences of globalisation for trade and industrial policy reforms in developing countries seems to be far from settled, there is a growing consensus that those issues cannot be addressed in isolation from the broader debate on labour standards, trade unions and gender equity (Çagatay 1996; Standing 1989, 1990; Olukoshi 1996; Khundker 1997).

Relevance of the Study

That the state of industrial relations in the ready-made garments industries of Bangladesh outside the Export Processing Zones — on which very limited information is available — is quite dismal is evident from various news reports published in leading vernacular and English dailies of the country regarding the increasing trend of physical assaults, *Gherao*, demonstrations, rallies, work stoppages and lay-offs (*The Bhorer Kagoj,* 05.03.1994; 18.05.94; 19.02.1995; 27.02.95; 03.04.95; 07.08.95; *The Dainik Sangbad* 20.02.1994; 27.05.1995; 06.01.1996; *The Banglabazar Patrika* 24.07.1995; 27.01.1996; *The Dainik Janakantha* 11.02.1995; 13.02.1995; *The Dainik Ittefaq* 03.06.1995; 09.09.95; 02.01.1996; *The Daily Star* 19.08.1995). As the *prima facie* evidence of the investigation by the author suggests, the effect of the above mentioned "unhealthy" management-labour relations on workers, particularly female workers in terms of loss of wages, and on the management as well as on the overall RMG sector in terms of loss of productivity, is appalling. If no new *modus operandi* is immediately evolved for institutionally resolving the above-mentioned disputes, these could do incalculable damage to management-labour relationships and the morale of both. Since it has not been possible, so far, to quantify the loss directly attributed to the existing poor industrial relations in the RMG sector, the specific impact of this deteriorating relationship still remains largely unrecorded.

Despite the obvious problematic state of management-labour relations in the RMG enterprises in Bangladesh, no systematic effort has so far been made at understanding the basic dynamics of industrial relations in the private sector in general and the problems of unionisation in the female-dominated RMG sector in particular. There might be various reasons for an apparent lack of academic interest in management-labour relations in the private sector. However, the single most important reason seems to be that, so far, the role of the trade unions in the private sector has remained quite peripheral in the overall political calculus of industrial management in Bangladesh. On the other hand, the trade unions in the public sector, with their pervasive "patron-clientelist" political nexus, have kept on playing a dominant role in the political decision-making process. Besides, the admixture of booty capitalism and patron-clientelism has created particular types of 'ruling elite' in Bangladesh, known as neo-patrimonial, in which the power holders' arbitrary will has often intermeshed with legal-rational organisations. This has, in effect, encouraged rent-seeking behaviour on the part of members of the ruling elite through granting special privileges to politically influential actors such as the trade union leaders in big public sector organisations who, in return, have served as support bases of this same ruling elite both at the local and national levels (Khan *et al*, 1996). Even today, there is a general trend among the large trade unions in the public sector to remain affiliated, as long as it is possible, with different political parties so that they can use their political leverages, whenever necessary in their course of action.

In addressing the issue of trade unions, one has to take note of two important points. First, the apparent politicisation of trade unions in large public sector organisations has more to do with the structural ensemble of the Bangladeshi political parties — which have consistently failed to make the "rent-seeking" industry of Bangladesh subject to a diseconomy of scale — than with the functioning of the trade unions in the public sector. Therefore, the responsibility of transforming such affiliated trade unions so that they can contribute to build harmonious industrial relations lies primarily with the political leadership in Bangladesh. We should, however, keep in mind that not all the trade unions in the public sector are politically sponsored, and the percentage of formally unionised workers in the modern manufacturing sector today remains between 5 to 7 per cent. The second, structurally relevant point to be noted is therefore that the coverage of the trade unions in the work force is very limited.

In the prevailing circumstances, it is not surprising that almost all the pioneering work on industrial relations in Bangladesh focus specifically on issues related to the public sector (Sobhan and

Ahmad 1980; Ahmad 1980; Quddus 1982; Murtaza 1982; Islam 1983; Mondal 1992). In his paper on industrial relations in Bangladesh, Islam (1983) concludes that most problems at the labour front originate from the government, which is both the law-maker and the largest industrial employer in the country. In contrast to the role of the government in the public sector, its role in influencing management-labour relations in the RMG sector appears negligible. This has ensured that labour relations in the RMG sector is largely determined by market forces. Thus in our view, the elastic supply of female labour, the threat of unemployment, and the negative attitude of management towards any kind of unionisation, are mainly responsible for the non-emergence of healthy management-labour relations in this vital sector. This argument provides the premise of this paper.

Objectives of the Study

The following explain the objectives of the present study:

a. To critically evaluate the unionisation process in the RMG sector outside the Export Processing Zones in Bangladesh.

b. To illustrate the role of the federations of trade unions in organising trade unions in various RMG industrial units.

c. To analyse the general responses of the owners towards the processes of unionisation in their respective industrial units.

d. To study the general trend and explain causes of disputes among activists of trade unions and/or federations of trade unions on the one hand and owners of different RMG enterprises on the other.

e. To examine the effectiveness of various federations of trade unions and their basic industrial units in voicing female labours' demands on issues related to wage negotiations, specification of contracts, job assignment and promotions, skill development and training, as well as welfare agendas like housing, security, etcetera.

f. To underline the opinions of both the trade unions and the management regarding 'piece work rate' wages in RMG enterprises.

g. To evaluate the policies of the government in facilitating the unionisation process in RMG enterprises.

h. To find out how industrial disputes regarding unionisation are generally handled by labour courts and how suitable the existing legal framework is in terms of meeting female labours' needs as regards to maternity leave, wages, night work and other forms of "protective" legislation.

i. To analyse the relationship between the federations of trade unions and their basic units and the structured trade unions of the country, which are often labour front organisations of various political parties, in order to understand to what extent these federations and/or their basic units have succeeded in influencing the attitudes of the structured trade unions towards the concerns of female labour in the RMG sector.

j. To review the policy agenda of two major political parties of Bangladesh in order to find out to what extent these political parties have taken cognisance of the changes in the employment pattern of women in Bangladesh and whether this has had any impact on the policy proposals of political parties.

Methodology of the Study

During the pre-testing, it was found that almost all existing and active trade unions were involved in one way or other with some of the garments workers' federations. No unionisation process was found that could sustain itself for a considerable period without the help of any of the existing federations. The reasons were: (i) high turnover of basic unit workers and/or sympathisers — who are mostly female — from one factory to another for economic betterment; (ii) inactivity of the basic unit workers and/or supporters after a certain period of time because of the fear of harassment by the management or due to inducement on behalf of the management for refraining from becoming supporters and/or members of any such union; (iii) expulsion or dismissal of the basic unit union leaders by the management on flimsy grounds such as "misconduct" under section 18 of the Employment of Labour (Standing Orders) Act, 1965, although such an action amounts to bypassing the legal protection extended to union leaders by the Industrial Relations Ordinance, 1969 (Section 15); and, (iv) the so-called "voluntary restraint" shown by the unit union leaders after being "bought-off" by the management or being threatened with physical violence by the hired ruffians of the owners.

Nevertheless, we endeavoured to interview the office bearers of all of the 72 RMG unit unions registered in the Dhaka Division by the office of the Registrar of Trade Unions of the Directorate of Labour, Government of Bangladesh. Despite our repeated attempts, however, we failed to interview any unit union leader directly in or around the factory premise. We found that most of the RMG factories remained open from 8 AM to 10 PM, and since the workers had very little time for leisure, few factory workers were found free during that period. Besides, almost all factories kept their gates locked during that period and their management would not allow us to talk to the workers, let alone union leaders, without the prior permission from the owner. We, therefore, decided to follow a 'multi-stage' sampling, beginning with the federations.

However, since most of the federations did not have proper sampling frames, i.e., office records of workers and/or units — though they were obliged to maintain, under the Industrial Relations Ordinance of 1969 (Section 7-B), a register of members showing particulars of subscriptions paid by each member, an accounts book showing receipts and expenditure, and a minute book for recording the proceedings of meetings of the trade unions, we had to opt for 'non-random' sampling. In this case it was 'purposive' sampling which meant that we had to take as many samples of the unit level unions from the federations as could be made available to us by them. Besides, the study was based on five types of samples: the first comprised the people who have been involved with the initiation of the unionisation process in the RMG sector, namely, the office-bearers of both the garments federations and their unit unions; the second comprised the people who were involved with the management in RMG enterprises, namely, the owners; the third comprised the officials of the Labour Directorate who were responsible for both monitoring and implementing various labour institutions and employment related acts, as well as resolving those industrial disputes which could not be settled through collective bargaining procedures; the fourth comprised the people from the compulsory dispute resolution machinery of the state who were primarily responsible for both arbitration and adjudication through formal judicial procedures; and the fifth comprised the "interested outsiders" in the positions of leadership in different working-class organisations. These organisations were found to be merely front organisations of various political parties. After carefully weighing all the merits and demerits of different kinds of interview techniques, we finally settled for 'non-formal' interviews at each of the stages with different check-lists of queries.

Plan of the Study

The study consists of five sections. This introductory section describes the background, rationale and methodology of the study. It discusses the deteriorating state of industrial relations now prevailing in the RMG sector, and emphasises the positive role that unionisation can play in improving industrial relations in this vital sector where the labour force remains predominantly female, by opening various new avenues for workers' participation, ensuring a better working environment with its effect on labour productivity. The history of the unionisation process, the basic *ensemble* of the federations, as well as the role of the garments federations and their basic units in promoting the causes of the predominantly female labour force, are summarised in Section II. Section III analyses general views as well as responses of the owners of various RMG enterprises to the initiatives of either the federations or of some workers in their respective factories for unionisation. Section IV evaluates government policies towards labour in general, and regarding the formation of federations of workers union and/or unit unions in particular. It also makes critical assessments of procedural activities as well as monitoring policies of both the offices of the Registrar of Trade Unions and Federations of Trade Unions, and the Chief Inspector of Factories and Establishments of the Directorate of Labour. In this connection, it also describes the legal framework of handling disputes with particular reference to the unionisation process and issues related to the dismissal or other punitive measures taken against the office bearers of unit unions. The somewhat ambivalent relationship existing between the federations of the garments workers' unions and the structured trade unions — meaning labour front organisations of various political parties — have been illustrated in Section V. Finally, Section VI wraps up the study by bringing together the main conclusions derived from the previous sections.

5.2 DAVID VERSUS GOLIATH: WORKERS' MOBILISATION AND THE UNIONISATION PROCESS

Review of the Federations of the Garments Workers' Union

The Registered Garments Federations in Bangladesh

As far as the office records of the Directorate of Labour are concerned, there should be at present 4 registered federations of garments workers unions operating in Bangladesh (see Annex 1). However, despite the existence of four federations on paper, our investigation suggests the existence of only two federations in reality: namely, Bangladesh Garments Shramik Federation and the Jatiya Garments Shramik Federation. The Bangladesh Jatiyatabadi Garments Shramik Federation is only partially active and is characterised by occasional labour related activities while the Bangladesh Janashwadhin Garments Shramik Federation seems to be defunct. It should be mentioned in this connection that after repeated attempts we failed to locate even the office of the Bangladesh Janashwadhin Garments Shramik Federation in the address given in Form C [see rule 4(2) of the Industrial Relations Rules, 1977] that was submitted to the office of the Registrar of Trade Unions while applying for registration. We even failed to find the whereabouts of its office bearers. We were rather surprised to find out that despite its virtual non-existence for a considerable period, its registration was not cancelled. For us it is a glaring example of the negligence habitually displayed by officials at the Registrar of Trade Unions in monitoring the activities of the registered federations of trade unions, although they are legally obliged to do so under Section 21 of the Industrial Relations Ordinance, 1969. Such negligence certainly provides a *prima facie* case in support of those owners and workers who regularly complain about the prevalence of widespread corruption both in the offices of the Registrar of Trade Unions and the Chief Inspector of Factories and

Establishments. At any rate, all of the three active registered federations claimed to have sufficient numbers of unions at the unit levels. Most of the unit unions, they claimed, were established with their direct support. They extend, they stressed, all kinds of legal support to the workers of their unit unions in case of dismissal or any other wage or work related disputes. They also claimed to have negotiated with the owners of some factories on behalf of their unit unions. The Bangladesh Garments Shramik Federation and Jatiya Garments Shramik Federation further emphasised that they also provide paralegal and other job-related training to members and supporters at the unit union level.

The Non-Registered Garments Federations in Bangladesh

Beside the above mentioned registered federations, we found from different sources, including newspaper reports, the names of 10 more non-registered federations who are purportedly involved with garments workers (see Annex 2). However, again, according to our findings, among these 10 federations only the Bangladesh Independent Garments Workers Union (BIGWU) is active almost on full-time basis with various female labour-related activities, e.g., providing medicare facilities to female garments workers, running night-shift, and weekend schools, conducting paralegal and socio-political awareness-building programmes, extending legal support to individual workers and its affiliated unit unions etc. As for the nine other federations, we failed, despite all our efforts, to trace either the office bearers or their offices or to find even one clue regarding the existence of the four federations. They are: Bangladesh Biplobi Garments Shramik Federation, Sammilito Garments Shramik Karmachari League, Bangladesh Garments Shramik League, and Garments Shramik Karmachari Union. However, one Mr. Tauhidur Rahman, whose name was given both as the General Secretary of Bangladesh Biplobi Garments Shramik Federation and Garments Shramik Karmachari Union, was reported to have organised, in his individual capacity, a few demonstrations of garments workers in the Mirpur area when there were lay-offs or labour-management conflicts in some factories of the locality. Although we did locate him once, we failed, despite repeated attempts, to get any appointment for an interview till the writing of this report in mid-October 1996.

Of the remaining five, the Garments Shramik Oikkya is a comparatively new organisation, established by the former left-leaning female student leader Mosharefa Mishu. To the best knowledge of the author, this organisation is yet to start any activity worth mentioning. The Bangladesh Garments Shramik Karmachari Federation is the second best organisation among the non-registered federations in terms of organisational activity. Besides providing legal and institutional help to its unit unions, it also conducts, from time to time, as it claims, various socio-political and paralegal awareness-building programmes for garments workers. The remaining three federations are mostly engaged in *mousumi* (seasonal) activities like organising rallies and demonstration in front of factories or the National Press Club, arranging processions to the National Press Club, sending workers' delegations to the management on behalf of the garments workers in respective factories and so on in time of labour-management disputes. The reason why the National Press Club in Dhaka gets pre-eminence in terms of their organisational activities is the simple fact that, rightly or wrongly, most federation leaders believe that it is the simplest and most convenient place for attracting media coverage.

Pattern of Interviewing the Office Bearers

We interviewed the Presidents and General Secretaries of all the three 'active' registered federations whereas from the unregistered federations, we succeeded in interviewing the office bearers — Presidents or Vice Presidents and/or General Secretaries — of only four federations till the writing of this report. The reason for this is that the office bearers of some 'seasonally active' (*mousumi*) federations were very busy with their work and 'other activities'. This seemed to consist of participation in the election campaigns of different candidates contesting for national elections for the 7th Parliament at the time of our survey. Some others, although apparently not busy, pretended to be always pre-occupied, thereby indirectly refusing co-operation despite our repeated attempts to engage them.

Consequently, even after stretching the stipulated time frame for interviewing as much as we could till the very last date (20 October, 1996) we were able to interview the office bearers of only seven federations altogether. They represented the following:

1. Bangladesh Garments Shramik Federation.
2. Bangladesh Jatiyatabadi Garments Shramik Federation.
3. Jatiya Garments Shramik Federation.
4. Jatiya Garments Shramik Jote.
5. Jatiya Garments Shramik Karmachari Federation.
6. Bangladesh Garments Workers Federation.
7. Bangladesh Independent Garments Workers Union (BIGWU).

Tapping the Gender Issues within the Federations/Unions

Beside the office bearers of the federations, who were mostly male, we also sat independently on several occasions, with the Unit union leaders, who were mostly female, as well as other female members and supporters of the above-mentioned federations in or outside their office premises. During our 'group discussions' with the female members and supporters we wanted to know from them particularly to what extent their "own issues" and "sentiments" such as for example, ensuring separate toilets and changing room facilities at the work place, fighting against sexual harassment, ensuring personal security and safety both in and outside the workplace, overcoming various hazards of long working hours, ensuring maternity leave, health and child care facilities and so on, were echoed in the activities and demand charters of the federations.

We also wanted to verify whether any "gender subordination" existed in the hierarchy of the federations in terms of decision-making. While most of the workers spoke positively about the inclusion of "all feasible women's issues" in the activities and demand charters of the unions, their responses on issues related to "gender subordination within the unions" were varied. Some were quite ambivalent in their expression of opinions. Some accepted the prevalence of male domination within union leaderships as merely a *fait-accompli* given the existing socio-political conditions in Bangladesh which, to their mind, were not conducive to women leadership, particularly when it came to industrial dispute resolution. For them, the industrial disputes in Bangladesh are always "confrontational" and therefore, male leaders would be better equipped to "withstand the management onslaught" in times of crisis. Some argued that given the opportunity and, at times," a little outside support", women workers would be equally able to lead their unions or federations. In support of their argument they pointed out that both the President and the General Secretary of the Bangladesh Independent Garments Workers Union (BIGWU) — a federation established with an active support from the Asian-American Free Labour Institute, a Washington, D.C. based American NGO — were women. For the majority of them, however, the issue of leadership within unions or federations did not really matter because the women workers constituted more than ninety per cent of their total membership.

The Garments Federations: Formation and Network

During our interviews with both the federation leaders and female members, the first thing we wanted to know from them was how their federations were established and whether there was any political or NGO involvement during the inception of any of the federations. These consultations helped us to explore the extent to which the predominantly female garments workers in the RMG sector were in a position to provide their own leaders, be they at the federation or at the unit union level. This required an understanding of whether these women felt constrained by their lack of experience as new entrants into formal employment, societal vulnerability, and the threat of unemployment, so that it would have been relatively difficult for them to form federations or unit unions without having some interested "outsiders" as their patrons. Legal, political and other support from either various political quarters or from a particular NGO seems to have played a vital role in the formation of most federations. Even the two out of seven federations which grew out of workers' movement were initially backed by supporters of one left-leaning political party and a left- leaning trade union.

Socio-Political Background of the Founding Leaders

In order to have a sharper view of the extent of the role played by the interested male "outsiders" in the formation of those federations — whose membership was comprised almost exclusively of female garments workers — we wanted to know next about the socio-political background of the founding leaders. We were not surprised to find that very few garments workers, particularly female workers, were able to establish their federations themselves. Among our seven respondent federations, only in one case the leadership came originally from the garments workers themselves, and these, incidentally, were female. However, we must mention here that a foreign NGO played a significant role, both in terms of finance and organisational support, in promoting the above-mentioned female leadership. In six other cases, the leadership came either directly from former and active male political activists of various centrist or left-leaning political parties, or from former student leaders or activists (again, mostly male) affiliated with student front organisations of different political parties.

It is interesting to note here that none of these political activists and former student leaders had anything to do with the RMG sector or the garments workers until they decided to launch, or get involved in garments federations. Some of them were interested out of political conviction, in a new kind of trade unionism in this particular export-based private sector and have joined the union movement with the revolutionary zeal of organising the oppressed "neo-female proletariat" who had become politically "de-classed" in the process. However, some others have joined the struggle, as we understood, simply with some long-term "career ambitions" in mind and with the hope of being able to use these federations, if and when necessary, as 'spring-boards' for reaping the ensuing politico-economic benefits "in these hey-days of NGOs in the developing world".

The rest, according to our observations, have ventured into this new avenue of labour politics primarily to gain political esteem in their own political parties or in the student or labour front organisations of those parties where, otherwise, their status as activists and leaders would have remained rather marginal. The secondary reason for their venturing into RMG labour politics is, of course, again economic.

With the possibility of the emergence of a larger private sector in the horizon, the above-mentioned leaders, by becoming a part of labour-management relationship in that sector, also want to have a say in the state of affairs of the country, where politics has already become a kind of business with two methods of exchange: money and connections. In fact, during interviews, most of the federation leaders blamed each other for misusing their labour organisations for their own personal interests. Some even called the other federations' leaders *agent provocateurs* of owners.

Sources of Finance of the Federations

Our next area of interest was the sources of finance of the garments federations. We hypothesised that a vulnerable financial base might have been one of the reasons why federation leaders, as it is often alleged by some of the federation leaders themselves, readily fell back on graft. During interviews, we were repeatedly told by most federation leaders that the overall financial situation of the federations were not very healthy. In the same breath, we were also told that they had been extending various legal and other material support to their unit unions.

During our interviews, when we asked the seven respondent federations how they met the costs incurred for supporting unit unions, Jatiya Garments Shramik Jote mentioned annual subscriptions by worker-members as its only source of financial earnings. On the other hand, Jatiya Garments Shramik Federation and Bangladesh Jatiyatabadi Garments Shramik Federation identified workers' subscriptions along with financial contributions from 'friends' and 'well wishers' as its sources of finance. Jatiya Garments Shramik Karmachari Federation stated membership fee as its only source of finance, while Bangladesh Garments Shramik Federation and Bangladesh Garments Workers Federation claimed that their money came from friends and well-wishers. Only the Bangladesh Independent Garments Workers Union (BIGWU) admitted that it receives financial assistance regularly from the Asian-American Free Labour Institute (AAFLI), a Washington, D.C. based American NGO. Its leaders expect the AAFLI to continue to support it financially until, as they put it, it completes developing its institutional infrastructure and becomes financially solvent.

Two points seem to be worth noting here. Firstly, though most federations have mentioned the worker's contributions and annual subscriptions as their main sources of finance, the amount, as is clear from their modes of subscription in the ensuing pages, is so meagre that it hardly accounts for their stated volumes of activities and amount of incurred expenditures. This suggests that they must be receiving large sums of money from elsewhere which they remain unwilling to disclose. Secondly, though half of our respondent federations were established through direct initiative and support of various political organisations and their affiliated trade unions, none of them have given any indication of receiving any amount of financial help from those parent political organisations. When we directly asked them from where they were getting all the money they needed to meet their regular expenses, in most cases, they were as vague as possible in their responses. When pressed, almost all of them observed that from time to time, they receive a certain amount of financial assistance from, "friends" and "well-wishers". They, however, categorically refused to reveal the names and whereabouts of those "friends" and "well-wishers".

In order to have a clearer picture about the sources of finance of our respondent federations, we decided to ask them more questions regarding the mode of subscription by the members of those federations. We found out at this stage that the mode of subscription varies from federation to federation. Bangladesh Independent Garments Workers Union (BIGWU), for example, takes Taka 10 (ten) per person as admission fee from all workers. Jatiya Garments Shramik Jote, on the other hand, claims that it charges a monthly subscription fee for general members. However, despite our repeated queries, both the President and the General Secretary of this *Jote* refused to reveal the exact amount of the subscription. They kept on insisting that it was a "pittance". Bangladesh Jatiyatabadi Shramik Federation usually takes monthly subscriptions at a rate of Tk. 2 (two), but in times of any financial crisis of the workers, the federation accepts any "token amount" as subscription.

Unlike these federations, Jatiya Garments Shramik Federation and Bangladesh Garments Workers Federation do not have any hard and fast rule regarding subscription from its workers. They normally charge membership fees and a "small amount of subscription" while granting new membership to a garment worker. Although, there is a provision for subsequently asking for annual subscriptions, it is not made binding on its members. The Jatiya Garments Shramik Karmachari Federation does have a provision for an annual membership fee at the rate of Taka 10 (ten). However, its President made it clear to us that, due to the poverty of the workers, the federation hardly collects any subscription from its members. As for the Bangladesh Garments Shramik Federation, it does not have any provision whatsoever for collecting subscriptions from workers. As its General Secretary pointed out, considering the grave financial condition of most garments workers, one could hardly expect them to pay membership fees and/or subscriptions.

Obviously, most of the federations are too reluctant to demand membership fees from garment workers. Most leaders of federations are of the opinion that garment workers might consider the provisions for membership fees as well as subscriptions as an added burden which, in turn, might discourage them from seeking membership in a federation. Almost all the leaders of our respondent federations were unanimous in their "off the record" opinions that their provisions for the so-called membership fees and subscriptions in their respective federations were merely a token which they were obliged to keep at least on paper for submitting their yearly returns under the requirements of the Industrial Relations Rules, 1977 [Section 5 (a & b)]. During the audit, as we were told by those leaders, what they present as membership fees or subscriptions to the officials of the Department of Labour are actually "donations" or "help" which they receive from time to time from their "friends" and "well wishers". The federations, normally, do not keep any official document on the donations.

Problems of Formation and Sustainability: Examples of our Respondent Federations

Available evidence suggests that starting with nine clothing factories in 1977, the number of Bangladesh's garment enterprises had reached the impressive figure of 2400 by the year 1995. However, until recently there has not been any significant trade unionism in this particular export-oriented sector. This is rather surprising since almost 19 years ago the Industrial Relations Rules of 1977 clearly provided a *modus operandi* as well as a legal guideline regarding the formation of both the federations of trade unions and their unit level representation. The reasons for this rather slow growth of unionism in the RMG industries could be numerous: lack of job security of the garments workers due to the non-issuance of valid appointment letters by the owners, the heavy work load of the workers, widespread illiteracy, lack of consciousness particularly among the female workers regarding their legal rights, lack of a professional attitude as well as professional background of the garment owners, and so on. Furthermore, as indicated by the federation leaders, numerous bureaucratic impediments make the formation of unions a formidable task. In this context, the federation leaders pointed out the problems they faced while trying to get their federations registered. For example, Bangladesh Garments Shramik Federation was formed fifteen years ago; even so, it was registered as a federation only in 1984. The second oldest federation, both among the registered and non-registered categories, seems to be the Jatiya Garments Shramik Jote which, as its leaders claim, was formed sometime in the mid-eighties. However, since it is not registered as yet with the Directorate of Labour, we have no way of verifying the claim. When we asked them why this *Jote* could not get itself registered as a federation with the Directorate of Labour despite its formation such a long time ago, they directly put the blame on the "corrupt" officials of the Directorate of Labour. On the other hand, the Labour officials claimed that the *Jote* did not even try to get itself registered since it did not have sufficient unit unions as required under the Industrial Relations Ordinance, 1969 [Section 3 (d)] for obtaining registration as a federation.

Among the two other federations which have been in place for little more than five years, the registered one, Bangladesh Jatiyatabadi Garments Shramik Federation, has only been in official existence for less than five years, while the non-registered Jatiya Garments Shramik Karmachari Federation, has been functioning, as its leaders claimed, for more than six years. Here too, when we asked the leaders why it was not as yet registered, its leaders cited some unspecified "procedural difficulties" but then hastily added that it was "on the way of getting registration soon". Of the remaining two, the registered one, *Jatiya* Garments Shramik Federation, obtained its registration only in early 1996 though, according to its leaders, it had been functioning for quite some time. Bangladesh Independent Garments Workers Union, on the other hand, at first tried to form a 'National Federation' combining all the federations; but its attempt failed, its leaders claimed, due to the objections of the leaders of other federations. Currently, it is in the process of forming various unit unions before it emerges as a federation.

Current Unit Unions under Each Respondent Federation

According to the records of the office of the Chief Inspector of Factories and Establishments, Directorate of Labour, there are more than 2000 RMG factories in Dhaka city, while the current number of the existing unit level trade unions in Dhaka is, according to the figures provided by the office of the Registrar of Trade Unions, only 72. Assuming that there is only one trade union in each factory, this means that only around 3.6 per cent of RMG factories in Dhaka city have registered unit unions. However, the statistics given by the federations regarding their respective unit level trade union members indicate an unit union membership of around 130 which does not tally with the official figures. More specifically, the federations who were covered in our study claim that they have around 92 unit unions in Dhaka whereas the records of the office of the Registrar of Trade Unions put the figures at around 22.

One can, of course, raise questions regarding the validity of the statistics provided by the office of the Registrar of Trade Unions. There may be more than one union in some factories, since having a thirty per cent representation of workers in a factory is enough to form a unit union. There may also be some genuine unions in some factories which have not been officially recorded yet by the office of the Registrar of Trade Unions. Even allowing for the numbers presented by the federations covering their members, the number is still quite low, given the fact that there are already quite a few garments workers' federations operating in and around Dhaka city.

TABLE 5.1

Current Unit Unions under Each Federation

Names of Respondent Federations	No. of Unit Unions as Federations Claim	No. of Unit Unions as per Labour Office Records
Bangladesh Garments Shramik Federation	27	11
BD Jatiyatabadi Garments Shramik Federation	11 (Altogether 17 in BD)	05
Jatiya Garments Shramik Federation	28	06
Jatiya Garments Shramik Jote	13	No Office Record Available
Jatiya Garments Shramik Karmachari Federation	07 (Altogether 10 in BD)	No Office Record Available
Bangladesh Independent Garments Workers' Union	03	No Office Record Available
Bangladesh Garments Workers Federation	03	No Office Record Available

This indicates that though most of these federations maintain some contacts with garments workers in many factories, and though they might have some members and supporters in some of those factories, only a few federations have been able to muster enough support to form unit unions in the factories so that the bulk of the factories remain non-unionised. Since the federations do need to show the enrolment of some unit level unions in order to be registered with the Directorate of Labour as federations, some of the few non-registered federations might also be citing the same unit union as their own member or more than one federation may have unit members in the same factory.

Federations-Unit Unions Interactions: A General Picture

Our next area of interest during the survey was to find out how and actually upto what extent our respondent federations were interacting with the garments workers in general and with their basic units in particular. Table 5.2 contains the information regarding the modes of contact of the federations with their unit unions.

As will be evident from the above table, most of the federation leaders communicate with the workers and unit union leaders, most

TABLE 5.2

Modes of Contact with General Workers and/or Unit Union Leaders

Modes of Contacts	No. of Respondent Federations
i. Making door to door contacts; plus ii. Meeting workers and unit union leaders at different venues near their factories during their free time; plus	02
iii. Workers and unit union leaders come to meet federation leaders at some stipulated places on Fridays i. Making door to door contacts; plus ii. Meeting workers and unit union leaders near factory premises during their free time; plus iii. Workers and unit union leaders come to federation offices during their free time	02
i. Making door to door contacts; plus ii. Meeting workers and unit union leaders near factory premises during their free time; plus. iii. Workers and unit union leaders come to federation offices during their free time or whenever they require any help	01
i. Meeting the workers and unit union leaders near factory premises during their free time; plus ii. Workers and unit union leaders make their own contacts whenever necessary.	02

of whom are female, either by meeting them near their factory premises during their lunch breaks or by visiting them at their houses during their free time. However, at times, it becomes quite difficult to meet workers and unit leaders when they work from 8 A.M. to 10 P.M. In that case, the workers and units leaders can come to the federation offices only during the Fridays or other holidays. In fact, such long working hours often keep many female workers away from any union-related activities and seriously constrains the workers' participation in these activities. Only in some factories where they are not required to work for more then one shift, do those female workers come to the federation offices regularly (normally in the afternoon). However, most of the female unit union leaders we met during our interviews were "temporarily" out of work; they were either sacked or were, forced by the management to give up their jobs because of their involvement with union-related activities.

The next thing we wanted to know from the federations was what type of help they have so far rendered to their unit unions. Their responses are summarised in Table 5.3.

TABLE 5.3

Kinds of Help Federations Rendered to Unit Unions

Types of Help	No. of Respondent Federations
i. Legal help; plus ii. Financial help; plus iii. Providing institutional support in organising labour movements; plus iv. Educating the general workers and unit union leaders regarding relevant labour laws in Bangladesh; plus v. Negotiating with owners on behalf of the workers and unit unions.	03
i. Legal help; plus ii. Providing institutional support in organising labour movements; plus iii. Negotiating with the owners on behalf of the workers and unit unions.	02
i. Legal help; plus ii. Providing institutional support in organising labour movements.	02

It is obvious from the responses of the federation leaders that all our respondent federations have provided legal help to the unit union members. All of them have also provided institutional support to the unit union members in organising labour movements. These were, as we were told later by our respondent unit union members, the two most important factors which have influenced the unit union members as well as other garments workers — particularly female workers — to look to the federations for support in times of crisis: be it unlawful dismissals, labour-management disputes, or even lay-offs. In all probability, it is this possibility of availing of organised institutional support which has influenced the general garments workers, as will be explained in Table 5.4, to seek the patronage or even support of federations while forming unit level unions. As we were told by the federation leaders, 43 per cent of our respondent federations have also provided financial assistance to the unit-union leaders in times of crisis. Seventy one per cent of our respondent federations have also negotiated or have tried to negotiate with the owners on behalf of their unit union leaders and members.

TABLE 5.4

How are the Unit Unions Generally Formed?

Modes of Forming Unions	No. of Respondent Unions
Through federations' initiatives only	02
Through joint initiatives of both the federation and unit level.	05

However, not all female unit union members are happy with the idea of delegating their right to negotiate to the federation leaders. In fact, this issue has still remained the most controversial and at times even hotly debated feature of federation-unit union relations. On the one hand, most female garments workers feel technically too weak to negotiate, both individually and through their indigenously created unit unions, with the owners, because most owners are often quite autocratic and patrimonial in handling industrial disputes. Female garments workers thus welcome the intervention of federation leaders on their behalf in solving disputes with the management both in bipartite negotiations and extended conciliation, as well as in compulsory adjudications. On the other hand, many female garments workers and unit union leaders confessed to the author that they are quite apprehensive about many male middle class "professional" leaders of federations, who might be pursuing their own agendas rather than pursuing the interests of the female garments workers and their unit unions. Many garments owners have also labelled some federation leaders simply as "trade unionist brokers" who "milk" both sides, the RMG workers and/or their unit unions and the owners, in the name of solving industrial disputes. According to them, in times of industrial conflicts, some of these federation leaders take money from the owners to "buy-off" the prospective male "trouble-makers" among the garments workers (interestingly, most of the owners have confessed to the author that it is much easier to bribe a male leader than a female one). At the same time, the federations also try to squeeze out money from mostly female workers by promising them protection from harassment either by the members of the law enforcing agencies or by the hired musclemen of the owner.

Though some of our respondent federations have claimed that they try to educate the female garments workers and their unit union leaders regarding their legal rights and obligations through various workshops, group discussions and other means, during our survey, we observed only the Bangladesh Independent Garments Workers Union (BIGWU) to be conducting weekly classes on various legal, social, and other issues related to female workers. The leaders of BIGWU, however, confessed that they have often encountered difficulties in getting enough female garments workers to participate in their training courses.

Formation of the Unit Unions

As the data in Table 5.4 suggests, unit unions in the RMG sector in Bangladesh are formed in two ways. Firstly, the federations try to form unions in as many factory units as they can, mainly in order to increase their power bases in the RMG sector, so that, as umbrella bodies of various unit unions, they can emerge as "legitimate bargaining agents" in this specific area of the private sector. In this process, the federation leaders themselves organise the workers in various units, secretly obtain the signatures of the interested thirty per cent "would be members" of unit unions in the 'Form D' [See rule 5 (1) of the Industrial Relations Rules, 1977] and do all the necessary leg-work, including as they claim, "bribing" the officials at the office of the Registrar of Trade Unions. Secondly, when workers of any factory face problems such as delay in payments of wages and overtime benefits, scrapping of holidays, and deterioration in the factory work environment, they come to the federations for assistance. Then, in most cases, the federations provide various forms of assistance, such as organising demonstrations and moving the matter before the relevant labour courts and so on. Following such solicited interventions by the federations on a particular unit they slowly explore the possibility of forming unit unions in the concerned unit, and then try to persuade RMG workers to do so by explaining how easy it would be for them to bargain in industrial disputes if they had their own unions in place in the unit. When the workers become interested, they explain to them the required procedures for obtaining registration as a union, and if necessary, provide the workers with legal, institutional and other support to realise this objective.

Theoretically speaking, of course, the workers of any factory can form their unit unions independently of the effort of a federation if they can only muster support of thirty per cent of workers of that factory and get their signatures in the 'Form D' before submitting it to the office of the Registrar of Trade Unions. The Registrar, on being satisfied that the signatories have complied with all the requirements of the Industrial Relations Ordinance of 1969 for being registered as a trade union, is supposed to register the trade union in a prescribed register and issue a registration certificate in the prescribed form within a period of sixty days from the date of receipt of the application. However, as can be seen from our survey, such procedures are rarely followed in Bangladesh, firstly because very few of the garments workers, most of whom are females and rural migrants, are aware of the procedures regarding the formation of trade unions. Secondly, even if they know the procedure, they are worried about possible harassment from the management. Nevertheless, the author can attest that some workers did try in certain factories to form 'independent' trade unions. But after some time, they were forced to seek the assistance of different federations for various reasons including the bureaucratic hassles involved in unionisation. It is, therefore, no wonder that five of our seven respondent federations were formed through the joint initiative of both the general unit level workers and the federations. In the second part of this section we will elaborate on different issues related to unit level unions.

Review of the Unit Level Unions

The Respondent Unit Unions of Our Survey

As has already been mentioned in Section I, we tried to interview as many female unit union leaders as could be brought together with us by the federations. Since all but one of our respondent federations have claimed to have more than seven unit unions in Dhaka, we at first decided to interview at least seven unit unions from each federation. However, till the writing of this report in the middle of October 1996, we were able to interview the office bearers of only 28 unit unions. The reason for this is that even after duly fixing the date of appointment with the federations for interviewing their unit union leaders, some federations repeatedly cancelled their appointments with us at the last moment. Many unit union leaders did not turn up simply for interviews at the stipulated place and time despite having made prior appointments with us through their affiliated federations. In fact, we have now come to the conclusion that there is a strong possibility that many federations might have claimed to have a rather larger representation at the unit level than they actually do. Table 5.5 contains the number of unit unions of our respondent federations whom we were able to interview.

TABLE 5.5

Unit Unions of Our Respondent Federations

Name of Respondent Federations	No. of their Unit Unions
Bangladesh Garments Shramik Federation	05
Bangladesh Jatiyatabadi Garments Shramik Federation	05
Jatiya Garments Shramik Federation	03
Jatiya Garments Shramik Jote	03
Jatiya Garments Shramik Karmachari Federation	07
Bangladesh Independent Garments Workers Union	04
Bangladesh Garments Workers Federation	01

Formation of the Unit Unions and their Current Status

We hypothesised that one of the most important reasons why female garments workers could not form their 'independent' unit unions was their reluctance to be involved in any kind of organised industrial dispute with the management unless they were forced to do so. We were proven to be correct on this account. The reason is very simple. Coming from different rural backgrounds marked by pervasive poverty, widespread illiteracy, and various kinds of social exploitation, most of the female garments workers were quite happy at the beginning merely to get jobs in various urban and suburban localities which, for the first time, provided them with the "hope" of leading "decent lives". That is why, at the beginning, it did not bother them much that their wages were quite low, and their working environment not very congenial, nor were they troubled at not having valid 'appointment letters'. Being unaware of modern industrial concepts such as "job security", they simply tolerated the prevailing unhealthy working conditions, hoping to get better wages later by doing "overtime" and, in the process, acquiring "on-the-job-training". But when their hopes were dashed by the "unprofessional" attitudes of some garments owners, these workers started thinking of developing some collective capacity to deal with the management where workers could take joint action to protect their rights through such actions as *gherao*, demonstrations, and/or work stoppages. It was at this stage that the workers started contacting the federations, several of whom were already in touch with some of the workers, to seek support for their future course of action, including clandestinely forming unit unions. Tables 5.6, 5.7 and 5.8 represent the formation process, current status of the registered unit unions, and causes of inactivation of the unit unions.

Table 5.6 makes it clear that two-third (18) of our respondent unit unions were formed with the direct initiative and support of the federations. Even those unit unions (09) which tried to form their unions 'independently' at the initial stage, had to seek the help and support of a federation at one stage or other. Only one union succeeded in obtaining its registration through its own initiative. But even this unit could not sustain the union for long because the owners simply fired the office bearers on charges of "misconduct", taking advantage of the vaguely defined terminology in Section 3 of Article 17 of the Employment of Labour (Standing Orders) Act of 1965, though the Industrial Relations Ordinance of 1969 (Section 15) protected their jobs as trade union leaders. Subsequently, the office bearers of the concerned union, with the help of a federation, Jatiya Garments Shramik Karmachari Federation, filed a case at the 1st Labour Court. The case is still awaiting the judgement of the Labour Court.

TABLE 5.6
Modes of Formation of the 28 Respondent Unit Unions

Modes of Formation	Number of Unions
Through the initiatives of the Federations	19
Initiated by the general workers and later helped by the Federations	09

TABLE 5.7
Present Conditions of the Respondent Registered Unions

Present Conditions of Unit Unions	Number of Registered Unit Unions
Still active	02
Still registered but not active	08
Claim to be registered but have no committee	01
Cases pending in labour courts	02

TABLE 5.8
Causes of Inactivation of the Unit Unions

Causes of Inactivation	No. of Respondent Unions
Migration of the office bearers for better job prospects	02
Owners forced the office bearers to leave the factory through various intimidation tactics	01
Office bearers "voluntarily" became inactive due to the fear of harassment by the owner	04
Transfer of factory ownership and/or the venue of the factory	01
Office bearers were bribed by the owner for becoming inactive	01

During interviews it was revealed to us by the federation and unit union leaders that among the 28 respondent unit unions only 13 unions (12 from the 19 federation-initiated unions and 1 from the 9 independently formed unions) were able to complete the full registration process and had succeeded in obtaining registration. However, it should be mentioned that though the federation and unit union leaders claimed that 13 unit unions succeeded in obtaining registration, office records of the Registrar of Trade Unions showed the number of registered unit unions among our 28 respondent unions to be only 8, and not 13. At any rate, in the two factories where the unit unions were still found to be active despite continuous harassment on the part of the management, the unit union leaders have been successful in obtaining recognition from their owners as legitimate 'Collective Bargaining Agents'. Furthermore these unit unions have also successfully negotiated with the owners on behalf of the workers on issues related to timely payment of wages and improvement of the working environment in their respective factories.

Among the 14 unit unions, whose efforts at registration were claimed to be fruitless by the federation and unit union leaders to have been infructuous, in 5 cases the registration procedure was stopped due to "harassment" by the owner. In the remaining 9 cases, the applications for registration were rejected by the office of the Registrar of Trade Unions on what the federation and unit union leaders termed "flimsy grounds".

The reasons for inactivation and non-existence of 9 unit unions, as indicated in Table 5.7, were attributed both to the voluntary migration (for better job prospects) and forced migration (due to the fear of harassment) of the office bearers of various unit unions. In fact, our *a priori* assumption is that if a survey is made to determine the main reasons for inactivation of the unions in all of the registered units, the above mentioned reasons would top the list.

TABLE 5.9

Events that Led to the Formation of Unit Level Unions

Causes of Formation	No. of Respondent Unit Unions
i. Delaying the payment of monthly wages; plus	12
ii. Non-payment of bonus and overtime benefits; plus	
iii. Deterioration of working environment; plus	
iv. No provision for holidays, maternity and sick leave; plus	
v. Physical and verbal harassment by the owner.	
i. Delaying the payment of monthly wages; plus	08
ii. Non-payment of bonus and overtime facilities; plus	
iii. Deterioration of working environment; plus	
iv. No provision for holidays.	
i. Delaying the payment of monthly wages; plus	
ii. Deterioration of working environment.	08

The Formation, Activities, and Achievements of the Unit Unions

It is clear from the above table that most garments workers became interested in forming unions mainly to realise their legally sanctioned fundamental rights, including timely payment of wages, proper remuneration for overtime work, maternity and other leave, *et cetera*. Since, in the absence of proper collective bargaining bodies the workers remained at the mercy of the owners for realising their goals, they found no other way but to form unions with or without the help of the federations. The unionisation process of the RMG workers, therefore, remains radically different from that of unions in the public sector whose underlying dynamics is largely political.

TABLE 5.10

How Effective have the Unit Unions been in Upholding Workers' Rights?

Industrial Dispute Related Activities	No. of Respondent Unions
Placed the demand charter	07
Could not place any demand charter	06

Among the 13 registered unit unions only 7 were able to place any demand charter before their management. The other 6 unit unions not only failed to place any demand charter but also became inactive within a short span of time. In the above mentioned 7 units, the demand charters were placed before the management on many occasions. The main demands were:

i. Timely payment of wages and overtime remuneration;
ii. Payment of two Eid bonuses and other legitimate incentive payments;
iii. Provisions for maternity leave with half payment for a period of three to six weeks depending on the health condition of the female workers;
iv. Provisions for child-care facilities for the female workers;
v. Provision for sick and casual leave with and/or without half payment depending on the nature of urgency of the request;
vi. Improving hygienic conditions and working environment in the factories;

vii. Ensuring adequate toilets and dining facilities for the workers;
viii. Provisions for providing security for female workers while returning home at night;
ix. Issuance of 'Appointment Letters' and ensuring "job security";
x. Payment of wages according to the tripartite charter if on minimum wage scale;
xi. Re-appointment of workers who were fired during industrial disputes with the management in particular factory units.

In 2 factories, after the submission of the demand charter, the owners not only rejected the charter outright but also fired the workers whom they thought were behind the formulation of the charters. In 5 factories, the owners, after long struggle and a few *gherao* and work stoppages, met some demands of the charters. Those demands were: timely payment of wages and overtime remuneration, payment of two Eid bonuses, improvement of hygienic conditions, providing adequate toilet and dining facilities, and re-appointment of fired workers. Besides, in one factory, the owner even agreed to provide child-care facilities and to issue 'Appointment Letters'. However, in most cases, after a certain period of time, owners reneged on the agreement. Nevertheless, in 3 factories the workers were successful, through agitation as well as litigation, in forcing the owners once more to meet some of their demands. No owner, however, agreed to provide maternity leave to female workers with half payments. They agreed, at best, to grant unpaid leave to female workers in "advanced stages" and to ensure that their jobs would be restored should they decide to come back to the factory again.

Federations' and Unit Unions' Opinions Regarding Linking Wages to Labour Productively

According to the leaders of our respondent federations and unit unions, wages in the private sector are supposed to be fixed through the collective bargaining process. However, due to the inadequacy or almost non-existence of the collective bargaining procedure in the RMG industries, wages must be fixed by the Minimum Wages

Board (MWB) established in 1957 and reconstituted in 1961. Most of our respondent federations and unit unions did not object to the idea of linking the wage structure to the labour productivity ratio. But they emphasised that one of the preconditions for that would be to ensure first of all that the garments workers are paid, what they termed, a "fair wage" which should on no account be less than the minimum wage. In other words, while the lower limit of the "fair wage" must be the minimum wage, the upper limit could be determined by the level of efficiency of the workers on the one hand, and a fair return on capital on the other. It is only within this framework that they are willing to accept wages on a piece rate work basis.

5.3 BATTLING THE HYDRA

The Owners' Response to Unionisation in RMG Sector

It goes without saying that the structure of ownership and management determines both the structure of trade unions and the mechanisms for resolving industrial disputes. In the emerging formal private sector of Bangladesh, particularly in the field of RMG industries, the owners who generally tend to be patrimonial as a class, still try to resolve industrial conflicts through autocratic and unilateral decisions. One reason for this could be a historically sustained in-built authoritarianism in all spheres of our entrepreneurship. The earlier dominance of the semifeudal and large land-owners has influenced the attitudes of most of the industrialists of Bangladesh in their dealings with subordinates and workers. Just as the agricultural workers were treated as virtual serfs on the landed estates of *Jamindars* a few decades ago, so workers in the RMG enterprises, barring a few exceptions, are still dealt with by a mixture of authoritarian and paternalistic managerial practices. Against such a backdrop, it is no wonder that most RMG owners do not look at the possibility of unionisation in the RMG industries with a positive attitude.

Of course, to be fair to the owners, most of their apprehensions emanate also from what they have seen during industrial conflicts in the public sector, particularly of the workers' organisational strength and the militancy of some of their "professional trade unionist" leaders, linked with the broader political agendas for seeking power. It would, probably, not be inappropriate to mention here that the workers and their unions in the public sector industries of Bangladesh have quite often displayed all the characteristics of early industrial development, including multiplicity of unions, serious inter-union rivalries, and allegiance of workers to different unions (Khan 1986). But then, the reason for these multiplicity as well as inter-union rivalries may partly lie, as Nasreen Khundker correctly points out, also in the management structure of the public sector industries which is often centralised and is normally in the hands of the civil servants. The civil servants are generally perceived as "unsympathetic to the labour cause" by the union leaders. And this, along with a somewhat restricted collective bargaining mechanism where wages and other benefits are determined by National Pay Commissions (for government and public sector employees) and National Wages and Productivity Commissions (for industrial workers in the public sector) — influence the trade union leaders to rely heavily on political parties in pursuing their objectives (Khundker 1997).

There is also another factor which one needs to take into consideration while discussing the state of affairs of the unions in both the public and private sectors: their weak financial position. In Bangladesh, generally the workers remain inclined to pay their union dues only at those times when their particular demands are being raised. Some union leaders therefore try to ferment disputes simply for the purpose of replenishing their union funds. However, this problem can easily be addressed by evolving an institutional mechanism in which union dues may be deducted from a worker's wages on specific authorisation from him or her. The revenues thus collected from the workers should then be made available only to the union freely elected as a bargaining agent of the workers in a factory.

At any rate, in order to 'cross-check' the information provided by the federation and unit union leaders regarding the issues related to unionisation as well as to obtain an impression of their possible response in this sensitive matter, we tried to interview the owners of all of our 28 respondent factory units. However, till the writing of this report in mid-October 1996, we have been able to interview only 11 garments factory owners. Ten owners flatly refused to give any appointment for interviews. Nor were they interested in either contradicting or confirming the information provided by the federation and unit union leaders regarding industrial disputes in their respective factories despite our sending the information to them in writing. Two owners pretended to be busy all the time and kept on shifting the dates for interviews, and finally, in early October 1996, indirectly refused to give the interviews. Five owners were out of the country most of the time during our survey and could not be contacted till the writing of this report.

Emergence of Industrial Conflict: Unions Vs. the Owners

Unionisation Process and the Owners

What affects labour-management relations in the RMG industries is the lack of mutual trust, both among union leaders and owners in handling industrial disputes through direct negotiations. That is why while union leaders always try to pursue their unionisation process as secretly as possible, the garments owners always try to keep themselves informed of the activities of the federations and garments workers in their respective factories. In fact, most of the male federation leaders as well as female unit union leaders, whom we interviewed, have claimed that in order to remain informed about the 'activities' of the federations and their activists, most garments owners always place people in 'crucial places' both in the factories and at the Directorate of Labour. Tables 5.11 and 5.12 explain at what stages and how the owners — as the federation and unit union leaders claimed — came to know about the unionisation processes of the 28 respondent federations and unit unions. It should be mentioned here that none of our respondent owners have contradicted the information provided in Tables 5.11 and 5.12 which was, in fact, provided to us by the federation leaders. In other words, the owners tacitly corroborated the information cited in Tables 5.11 and 5.12 regarding the unionisation process, though this was provided mostly by the garments federations.

It is obvious from Table 5.11 that in 7 factories the owners had planted informants amongst the workers so that they could know

TABLE 5.11

The Stage at Which the Owner Came to Know about the Unionisation

The Stage of Knowing about Unionisation	Number of Respondent Unit Unions
Before submitting the application to the office of the Registrar of Trade Unions	07
After submitting the application to the office of the Registrar of Trade Unions	15
After getting registration certificate from the office of the Registrar of Trade Unions	06

TABLE 5.12

How Does the Owners Come to Know about Procedures?

Channels through which Owners come to Know about Unionisation	No. of Respondent Unit Unions
Through the agents of the owners among the workers	07
Through unofficial channels of the office of the Registrar of Trade Unions	15
Informed by the union leaders themselves after obtaining Registration Certificates	06

beforehand which workers of their factories were trying to form unit unions, in order to force those workers out from the factories before they could even submit applications for registration to the office of the Registrar of Trade Unions. It was important for the owners that, if they had to go for this kind of "preemptive attack", they did so before the submission of the applications for registration because once the application for registration was submitted, it would have become not only difficult for the owners to stop the process of unionisation but any attempt to do so could also expose them to legal prosecution for 'misconduct' under Article 15 of the Industrial Relations Ordinance, 1969. As Table 5.12 further reveals, the owners had also their informants in the office of the Registrar of Trade Unions, who informed the relevant owners as soon as they learned about the submission of the applications for registration. In most cases, the owners then traced the office bearers in their units who were involved in the unionisation process and tried to frustrate the process in various ways.

We were informed by federations and/or unit level leaders that in seven cases, where the owners were not informed beforehand regarding the unionisation process, either the office bearers of the unit unions or the federations bribed officials at the Registrar of Trade Unions or the unit unions, or the federations had such 'political backing' that the officials of the Registrar of Trade Unions did not dare to disclose the information to owners. The general response of the owners, as described to us by the federation and unit union leaders, are discussed in Table 5.13. Of course, the majority of our respondent owners did not agree with the information provided in Table 5.13. Others, who did not contradict the authenticity of the information, however, claimed that they themselves never resorted to any such activity.

TABLE 5.13

Immediate Response of the Owners Toward Unionisation Process

Owners Reactions to Unionisation Process	Number of Respondent Unions
i. Verbal threats; plus (ii) Physical assaults; plus (iii) Threatening through hired musclemen; plus (iv) Filing police based on false criminal charges; plus (v) Dismissing the principal union leaders without compensation on charges of "gross insubordination".	06
i. Verbal threats; plus (ii) Physical assaults; plus (iii) Threatening through hired musclemen; plus (iv) Firing the main leaders with compensation on charges of "misconduct".	03
i. Verbal threats; plus (ii) Physical assaults; plus (iii) Bribing the Main Leaders.	02
i. Verbal threats; plus (ii) Physical assaults; plus (iii) Threatening through hired musclemen; plus (iv) Police harassment with false criminal charges; plus (v) Pressure on the main leaders, through various means, to give up their jobs.	04
i. Verbal threats; plus (ii) Physical assaults; plus (iii) Threatening through hired musclemen; plus (iv) Firing the main leaders with compensation on charges of "misconduct"; plus (v) Fulfilling some demands.	05
i. Laying-off.	03
i. Transferring ownership and/or selling factories.	02
i. Forming counter unions.	03

The findings above clearly show that owners used various methods to stop the unionisation process, and also to destroy, wherever they could, the unit unions. To achieve their goals, they first tried to employ all possible pressure tactics, including verbal threats, physical assault, and intimidation through hired musclemen. When the pressure tactics failed to bear any fruit, they tried to stop the process simply by bribing influential federation and/or unit union leaders. When even that ploy did not work, they started filing a variety of criminal charges against union leaders in order to harass them with the help of the police. Since most of the unit union leaders were female and also often poor, they could not withstand the above-mentioned pressure indefinitely. At the end, many unit leaders left the factories. In a number of such cases the unions, if constituted but not yet registered, ceased to exist. In other cases, the owners simply dismissed union leaders. It was often quite easy for owners to dismiss union leaders because many union leaders did not have valid 'Appointment Letters', and hence no proof that they were working in a particular factory. If the unions were registered, the owners sometimes tried to fire the union leaders but with a compensatory package of three months wage to discourage them from any strong response. However, in some cases, where the unions were very strong and the general workers were united, the owners either declared a lock-out of the factories or met, at least for the time being, some demands of the workers.

The Owners Attitudes Toward Trade Unions

Irrespective of their educational, socio-cultural and economic background, most of the garments owners seem to have a very negative attitude toward the existing garments federations and their affiliated unit unions. The root cause of this negative attitude seems to be in their perception of trade unionism which, again, emanates from what they have seen of the activities of the trade unions in the public sector. According to most of our respondent owners, the Bangladeshi entrepreneurs currently involved in the RMG sector invariably face some common labour-related problems. These include: (i) indiscipline among workers, (ii) lack of commitment of most workers towards raising their productivity, (iii) illegal and unreasonable demands often placed by "representatives" of garments workers, (iv) an unfavourable labour code which lays down privileges but does not spell out the duties of workers, (v) politicisation of trade unions, (vi) multiplicity of federations and unit level unions, and consequent rivalries between them, and (vii) too many work stoppages.

In the backdrop of such a scenario, according to some of our respondent garments owners, the situation is not yet mature to allow full-fledged unionism in a nascent industrial sector such as RMG. However, three of our respondent owners claimed that they would have no objection to the formation of unit unions if they were formed independently, and not through, what they termed, the instigation of outsiders or "professional trade unionists". But before these unions are formed, the workers must be adequately educated regarding existing labour laws, basic rights, and their obligations so that they cannot easily be manipulated by "professional unionists" with vested interests. These owners suggested that NGOs might like to chalk out certain awareness-building programmes for female garments workers which could educate them about their legal rights. They also suggested that there should be provisions for 'on-the-job-training' programmes for garments workers but that these should be linked to their duration of service in a factory.

Most of our respondent owners admitted that many garments factories do not have a conducive working environment and adequate facilities for their workers, largely due to the "corrupt" inspectors from the office of the Chief Inspector of Factories and Establishments. According to those owners, the inspectors are more busy in collecting 'tolls' from the garments owners than checking the real conditions of the factories. In this connection, one owner compared the role of the Inspectors of Factories and Establishments with the inspectors of the Bangladesh Road Transport Authority who are responsible for providing 'Fitness Certificates' for automobiles. He added that no inspector would issue a 'Fitness Certificate' even for a brand new car unless he received something in cash from the owner of the car. Likewise, no Inspector of Factories and Establishments would be satisfied with the prevailing condition and working environment of any factory — however excellent the condition of that factory might be — until and unless he is paid-off with a few thousand *taka* from the owner. Consequently, for some garments owners it really does not matter whether or not the working conditions in their factories remains commensurate with the provisions of the Factory Act if they can escap their legal obligations by paying a few thousand Taka monthly to the inspectors, to encourage them to turn a blind eye to such violations of the law.

Most of our respondent owners refuted the allegations of the federation and unit union leaders that they resorted to various acts of intimidation to sabotage the unionisation process in the RMG industries. Rather, they identified the lack of time of the garments workers and their high turn-over rates as two most important factors inhibiting the process of unionisation. As regards the prevailing state of labour-management relationship in the garments industries, most of the owners admitted that they maintained contacts with the general workers primarily through the Floor Supervisors and/or Production Managers. Only two owners claimed that they sat with the workers in general meetings at least once a month. Two other owners claimed that they always encouraged the general workers to come to them, with prior appointments, whenever necessary.

Regarding the linkage of wages with labour productivity, most garments owners were of the view that the RMG industries' capacity to pay the workers a minimum wage should be linked to their profit-ability, which, again, depended on the prices of their products relative to material input prices, and on labour productivity trends. However, the owners were divided on the issue of providing wages on a piece rate basis. Some favoured the idea but the others expressed appre-hensions that this could increase the costs of supervision. The reason for this is the fact that in the RMG industries the workers tend to work on an assembly line according to their job specialisation, thus, a piece rate work wage system would require much better co-ordination of this work in terms of speed and specialisation.

Federation leaders and garments workers were equally divided on the issue of piece rate work. For some garments workers, the main benefit of piece rate work was that it would make their work more quantifiable in terms of production performance and therefore it would be easier to link it with the wage structure as well as the pay for "overtime". It would also help to take into consideration the existence of different levels of expertise in the work force and the value of "overtime" work could then be measured in terms of the production rate instead of the prevalent time-based system. Others, however, argued that a piece rate system would work to the disadvantage of workers because in the name of differentiating between different levels of expertise in the work force, the owners would then simply try to "manipulate" wages around the principle of "equal wage for equal work" to use it to their own advantage and, if and when necessary, try to play-off one worker against the other.

5.4 WATCHING FROM THE SIDELINE

The So-called Resolution of Rights Disputes

The rights disputes relate to conflicts over matters of rights resulting from a contractual relationship, which may include grievances in respect of unfair treatment, denial of entitlement as well as unjustified punishments (Pakistan Labour Policy, 1969). Such disputes may either be of an individual or collective nature but more frequently tend to be individual cases. As far as the problematic of unionisation in the RMG industries is concerned, two state machinery are involved here: (1) Directorate of Labour, and (2) Labour Courts.

Directorate of Labour

In conformity with the requirements of ILO Conventions No. 87 and 98, in Bangladesh, workers and employers have been granted the right to establish and join associations of their choice without permission from any authority. Furthermore, they have the right to draw up their own constitutions, to elect their representatives in full freedom, to organise their programmes, to establish and join federations, confederations and international organisations of workers and employers. There are no restrictions or requirements to form and organise an association. It is only when an association is to be registered as a trade union that certain formalities have to be addressed. Among these requirements the most important one, under the Industrial Relations Ordinance of 1969, is that it must have a minimum membership of thirty per cent of the total number of workers employed in the establishment or group of establishments in which it is formed. Besides, the Industrial Relations Ordinance, 1969 also stipulates that non-worker trade unionists cannot become members or office-bearers of any trade union unless it is a federation of trade unions.

In the RMG industries after submitting the application on behalf of a garments federation or an union, if the Registrar of Trade Unions is convinced that the aforesaid federation or union has complied with all the requirements of the Industrial Relations Ordinance, 1969, including the minimum membership of thirty per cent, he/she will issue the Registration Certificate. Before issuing the Registration Certificate, normally, the inspectors of the office of the Registrar of Trade Unions try to verify all factual evidence germane to the application by visiting the garments factories. There are allegations that it is at this stage that the owners try to sabotage the whole process of unionisation. The Registrar of Trade Unions did not rule out the possibility that some garments owners might try to bribe the inspectors so that they do not write "positive reports" regarding the federations' and/or unions' fulfilling all their requirements for obtaining Registration Certificates; however, he claimed that his office always tries to cross-check those reports through other factual evidence before deciding whether or not to issue any such Certificate.

The controversy, however, does not end there. The Industrial Relations Ordinance, 1969 also stipulates that the registration of any trade union can be cancelled by the Registrar of Trade Unions after obtaining permission from the Labour Court if, among other things, the membership of that trade union does not cover at least thirty per cent of the workers of the establishment or group of establishments for which the union was formed. Our survey elicited allegations from the workers that the owners always sought to keep the inspectors in "good humour" to encourage them to report that the union membership has fallen short of the required thirty per cent. When the author raised this issue with the Registrar of Trade Unions he did admit the possibility that his office may not be in a position to monitor the activities of the trade unions all the time, but, he added, that if there is a dispute regarding the current legal status of a federation or an unit union, his office attempts to resolve the dispute in accordance with the law and to the satisfaction of the parties concerned. If, however, the efforts of his office proved infructuous in resolving union-management disputes, the Directorate of Labour issues a certificate to that effect, and then, the concerned parties are free to seek remedies through other legal and judicial procedures.

The Labour Courts

In the event of failure of efforts for resolution of union-management disputes regarding the formation of unions or dismissal of union workers, the Labour Courts are responsible for providing legal redress to the concerned parties. The verdict of a Labour Court in a rights dispute is termed as a "decision". All decisions of the Labour Courts are final and cannot be called into question in any manner by, or before, any other court or authority. But the main problem with the compulsory adjudication of the Labour Courts, as some of the garments federation and unit union leaders have pointed out, is that most such adjudications often take a long time. In at least three cases, where we were able to trace the final stages of the courts' proceeding in the 1st and the 3rd Labour Courts of Dhaka, the proceedings took 7 to 9 years before they came to a "decision". The reasons for this long delay can be attributed to the enormous number of cases that the three Labour Courts of Dhaka are required to deal with. During the period from August to September in 1996, there were more than three thousand cases pending in the 1st and the 3rd Labour Courts. Moreover, the penalty for non-compliance of the Courts' orders seems to be very minimal: a maximum of three months simple imprisonment or a fine of maximum Taka one thousand. Therefore, many garments owners do not take the verdicts of the Labour Courts seriously.

5.5 NO EASY PARTNERS

The Structured Trade Unions and the Garments Federations and Unions of Bangladesh

Since the early 1980s, the government of Bangladesh has adopted a series of structural adjustment programmes. One major effect of the adoption of structural adjustments in our macro-economic policies is a somewhat lopsided emphasis on the private sector with the hope that through its profit maximisation policies, private enterprises will be able to raise the level of efficiency in industrial management. The major political parties of the land are now putting more emphasis on the private rather than on the public sector. Even the Awami League, the pioneers of the nationalisation programme in the early 1970s, has now acknowledged the importance of the private sector, though its party manifesto is still quite vague on issues related to trade unions and labour laws. Equally vague is the party manifesto of the Bangladesh Nationalist Party on issues related to trade unions, thought it claims itself as a champion of an 'open market' policy. Consequently, most of our structured trade unions — which are practically labour front organisations of various political parties, and are active mainly in the public sector — remain useful assets in the calculus of our domestic power politics.

Since most of these potential front organisations are yet to take cognisance of the phenomenal growth of the RMG industries with their predominantly female labour force, they have not yet been able to formulate a coherent industrial relations policy for this particular sector. It is no wonder then that though political connections play an important role in the 'life cycle' of most of the garments federation leaders, they still do not enjoy high esteem in the political hierarchy of structured trade unions. The reason for this comparatively 'low esteem' of the garments federation leaders could be that most of the leaders of major structured trade unions still take pride in "controlling" the largest enterprises of the public sector. Furthermore, it became obvious to us during our survey that most of the politically 'connected' garments federations leaders actually come from the lowest strata of the structured trade unions. In other words, the advent of the garments industries provided most of the marginalised leaders of the structured trade unions with a new opportunity to rise into political prominence. Though the structured trade union leaders do not take the garments federation leaders seriously, they do not mind bestowing them with their political blessings because they think that this could pay-off in the long run. In a sense it is a marriage of convenience for both parties; for the federation leaders, the support of the structured trade unions is important because it will provide them with the political clout which will enable them to prevail upon the garments owners, whereas for the structured trade unions this relationship marks a turning point in broadening their sphere of influence in hitherto uncharted territory.

5.6 CONCLUSION

The intrinsic points that emerge from the foregoing discussion are: (i) in Bangladesh, industrial conflicts in the private sector, particularly in the RMG industries, have so far been resolved through autocratic and unilateral decisions of garments owners; (ii) there has not been any healthy growth of trade unionism in the RMG industries, which has led to the creation of a pervasive patron-clientelist nexus of interested male "outsiders" and mostly female garments workers; (iii) the existing male-dominated garments federations have not been successful in addressing the main concerns of the female workers such as for example, the calculated exploitation of the societal "vulnerability" of female labourers due to lack of security both in and outside the workplace and from sexual harassment. However, the female unit union leaders and workers have generally failed so far to overcome "the fear of separatism" from their male counterparts and consequently, have failed to launch their own women's unions; (iv) despite the fact that the labour laws of the land are generally not observed by most employers in the garments industries, and in some cases the laws themselves have become outdated and hence inadequate, the Bangladeshi state apparatus, increasingly driven by export-oriented economic policies, has limited its role to that of a bystander in the area of industrial relations in the RMG sector.

As is obvious from the points indicated above, most Bangladeshi garments owners have failed, to a large extent, to see any causal connection between labour standards and productivity outcomes. Therefore, for many of them, to be competitive has so far meant to be "cost effective", mainly by lowering labour standards and taking comparative advantage of the "low-wage employment" due to the abundance of Bangladeshi female teenage labour. As a logical consequence of their above mentioned "economic rationality", many of RMG owners have also became virulently anti trade union because, according to them, trade unions as "market distorting entities" would not only "raise production costs" and "create industrial disorder" they would also "eventually off-set Bangladesh's comparative advantage" by dismantling the "low-wage" regime associated with a female dominated labour force.

However, the contention of this paper is that the position taken by most of the Bangladeshi garments owners on the issue of unionisation in the RMG industries is both simplistic and unjust. Contrary to their arguments, there are ample examples of causal connection between labour standards and productivity outcomes where improved standards enhanced productivity and encouraged the adoption of new technologies (Çagatay 1996). There is also clear correlation between unionisation, productivity and gender equity. In an example from the industrialising economics, Guy Standing has found that in Malaysia the unions have contributed both to productivity enhancement and a narrowing of the gender gap in wages (Standing 1990). Unionisation and on-the-job-training can also be helpful in arresting high labour turnovers in the RMG sector. There is evidence from Malaysia that unionised firms established a working environment that encouraged trained workers to stay on and to seek further training needed to enhance their productivity (Standing 1990).

In the backdrop of this comparative scenario, it is argued here, the time has now come for the garments owners in Bangladesh to look at the issue of unionism from a different perspective. There is enough evidence from our study to show that industrial relations in the RMG sector which is today the most important private sector in the country is taking the form of a "legitimate oligarchy" liable for ensuring such a hierarchical pattern of industrial relations which is likely to aggravate "class conflict" between management and unions. Under the circumstances both the owners and the unions should now for the sake of their own enlightened self-interest, explore new avenues for providing the predominantly female work force in the RMG sector with some opportunities for participation in the management of the enterprises where they work.

The Industrial Relations Ordinance of 1969 provides various avenues for workers' participation in management. At the level of the enterprise, works councils, joint consultation committees, and other systems of workers' participation in decision-making within undertakings provide the basis for a more active involvement of workers in the running of the enterprise with a view to making them stakeholders in the enterprises where they work. Such an initiative will not only lend itself to more harmonious industrial relations within the enterprise but could serve to make such enterprises more efficient. At the national level, the principle of tripartitism in making policies affecting labour has been accepted in most developed countries (Khan 1986). But, so far, such participation schemes have largely failed to produce the desired outcome in the private sector of Bangladesh. In the garments sector, for example, as has been analysed in greater detail in sections II and III of this paper, the owners are emphatically against such types of workers' participation because, rightly or wrongly, most garments owner fear that at some stage it would inevitably lead to an unhealthy collusion between political parties and trade unions. This, in turn, owners fear would be prejudicial to improvements in productivity and the creation of a congenial working environment in the private industrial sector.

In the given circumstance the most useful way for facilitating female workers' participation in industrial management in the RMG industries could be to resort to some form of enabling legislation on the part of the government, which could serve to at least secure the rights of the workers as a preclude to giving them a stake in management. Such measures could include the effective enforcement of freedom of association in the RMG industries through various binding and non-binding contracts involving the Department of Labour, the federations of trade unions and the garments owners, enactment of anti-discrimination laws as well as protective legislation relating to such issues as night work and maternity leave, enforcement of equal pay for equal work. Incentives could be provided to the RMG owners through provision for such tax rebate to the RMG industry in order to implement on-the-job-training, providing health care insurance and other measures to improve the conditions of work in the RMG sector. The government should also invest in such interventions in partnership with the owners. However, whether or not legislation and other measures would mark a dynamic change in the circumstances of the female garments workers is contingent upon the extent of their gradual socio-political empowerment through collective action, where they come to recognise their own enormous contribution to the sustainability of Bangladesh's most dynamic export industry.

References

Ahmad, M.1980: "Labour Management Relations in Bangladesh: A Study in Participation". *National Reports*, Vol. 1, International Centre for Public Enterprises in Developing Countries, Ljubljana, Yugoslavia.

Bhuiyan, M. 1991: "The Textile and Clothing Industry in Bangladesh", *EIU Textile Outlook International*, March.

Çagatay, Nilufer 1996: "Gender and International Labour Standards in the World Economy", *Review of Radical Political Economics*, September.

Islam, M.M. 1983: "Industrial Relations in Bangladesh", *Indian Journal of Industrial Relations*, Vol. 19, No. 2, October.

Khan, Abbas Ali. 1986: *Handling of Industrial Disputes in the Public Sector Industries in Bangladesh*, Unpublished doctoral dissertation submitted to the Department of Management Studies, University of Glasgow, February.

Khan, Shamsul I. *et al.*, 1996: Political Culture, Political Parties, and the Democratic Transition in Bangladesh, Academic Publishers, Dhaka.

Khundker. Nasreen 1997: "Globalisation and the Transformation of Industrial Relations in Bangladesh", Dhaka. (mimeo).

Murtuza, G. 1982: "Causes of Weak Trade Union Movement in Bangladesh", *The Personnel*, Vol. 2, December.

Mondal, Abdul Hye 1992: *Trade Unionism, Wages and Labour Productivity in the Manufacturing Sector of Bangladesh*, Research Report No. 1332, Bangladesh Institute of Development Studies, Dhaka.

Nahar, Tasneem. 1996: *Bangladesh's Garment Industry: Time for Reform*, An Oxfam UK and Ireland Report, Dhaka, August.

Olukoshi, Adebayo 1996: "Economic Crisis, Structural Adjustment and the Coping Strategies of Manufacturers in Kano, Nigeria" Discussion Paper 77, United Nations Research Institute for Social Development, Geneva.

Paul-Majumdar, Pratima and Salma Zohir Chaudhuri 1993: *Employment and Occupational Mobility among Women in Manufacturing*

Industries of Dhaka City: Bangladesh, Findings From A Survey of Employees, Asian Regional Team for Employment Promotion (ARTEP), International Labour Organisation (ILO), February.

Quddus, M.A. *et al.* 1982: *Labour Management Relations in Bangladesh*, Bureau of Economic Research, University of Dhaka (unpublished).

Sobhan, R. and M. Ahmad 1980: Public Enterprise in an Intermediate Regime: A Study in the Political Economy of Bangladesh, Bangladesh Institute of Development Studies, Dhaka.

Standing, Guy 1989: "Global Feminisation through Flexible Labour", *World Development*, Vol. 17, No. 7, 1989.

——, *Do Unions Impede or Accelerate Structural Adjustment? Industrial Versus Company Unions in an Industrialising Labour Market*, Working Paper No. 47, World Employment Programme Research, International Labour Organisation, Geneva.

Wahra, Gowher Nayeem and Ferdausur Rahman 1995: "A Right to Live: Girl Workers in the Bangladeshi Garment Industry", *Gender and Development*, Vol. 3, No. 2, June.

Annex 1

1. **Bangladesh Janashwadhin Garments Shramik Federation**
   (President: Delwar Hussain Khan
   General Secretary: Md. Abdul Baqui Dewan
   Registration No. # B-1801,
   Date of Registration: 09.10.1984)

2. **Bangladesh Garments Shramik Federation**
   (President: Khurshid Alam
   General Secretary: Md. Mubarak Hossain
   Registration No. # B-1804,
   Date of Registration: 19.10.1984)

3. **Bangladesh Jatiyatabadi Garments Shramik Dal**
   (now a Federation)
   (President: Md. Shahidul Islam
   General Secretary: Mrs. Selina Aktar
   Registration No. # 1049,
   Date of Registration: 03.12.1991)

4. **Jatiya Garments Shramik Federation**,
   (President: Aminul Haque Amin
   Registration No. # Not Available
   Date of Registration: 01.02.1996)

Annex 2

1. **Bangladesh Garments Shramik Karmachari Federation**
(President: Abul Hossain
General Secretary: Mohar Ali)

2. **Bangladesh Biplobi Garments Shramik Federation**
(President: Makbul Hossain
General Secretary: Tauhidur Rahman)

3. **Jatiya Garments Shramik Jote**
(President: Babul Sikder
General Secretary: Jainul Abedin)

4. **Sammilito Garments Shramik Karmachari League**
(President: Sirajul Islam Roni
General Secretary: Not Available)

5. **Bangladesh Garments Shramik League**
(President: Selim Reza
General Secretary: Not Available)

6. **Garments Shramik Front**
(President: Afroza Begum
General Secretary: Not Available)

7. **Bangladesh Garments Workers Federation**
(President: Mosharraf Hossain
General Secretary: Not Available)

8. **Garments Shramik Oikkya**
(President: Mosharefa Mishu
General Secretary: Not Available)

9 **Bangladesh Independent Garments Workers Union (BIGWU)**
(President: Hasna Hena
General Secretary: Nazma Begum)

10. **Garments Shramik Karmachari Union**
(President: Shahidullah Badal
General Secretary: Tauhidur Rahman)

Chapter 6

PROSPECTS FOR INTERNALISING GLOBAL OPPORTUNITIES IN THE APPAREL SECTOR IN BANGLADESH*

Debapriya Bhattacharya
Mustafizur Rahman

6.1 INTRODUCTION

Issues of Concern

Current adjustment policies in Bangladesh, coupled with ongoing industrial restructuring are expected to create employment opportunities in export-propelled activities. Data on the short-run impact of recent industrialisation efforts in Bangladesh indicate that women constitute the majority of the incremental labour absorption in the country's export-oriented manufacturing enterprises. Available information also suggests that conventional measures of gender bias (such as wage gaps, access to employment and lack of job security) are relatively less conspicuous in this organised segment of the manufacturing sector (Bhattacharya, 1994). These trends are present in units located in both export processing zones (EPZs) and the domestic tariff area (DTA). These are characteristics of the labour force of foreign-owned units in particular — which tend to have the most advanced technology and the highest productivity levels in the country (Bhattacharya, 1998). Notwithstanding such ostensibly

* The paper is also available as UNRISD occasional paper no. 10, Geneva, July, 1999.

The authors are grateful to Carol Miller, Shahra Razavi, Swasti Mitter and David Westendorff for comments on an earlier draft. Editorial comments provided by Jenifer Freedman are also acknowledged. The usual disclaimer applies.

positive features of part of the country's evolving labour market, concerns have been raised about the real nature and prospects for sustainability of these trends. It is widely held that "cheap and readily employable" labour underpins the competitive advantage of the country's export sector. To begin to understand the nature of women's industrial employment in Bangladesh, the pull and push factors that have contributed to the feminisation of trade-oriented manufacturing employment must be examined. Concretely, it is important to analyse whether it is the gender gap in the effective wage structure that underpins the growth of female labour in export-oriented industries. In other words, given the low opportunity cost of female labour in Bangladesh, is female labour attractive because women are paid less than men for similar jobs — even when productivity differentials are accounted for? This particular concern is heightened by the fact that entrepreneurs prefer to employ young, single, literate women in export-oriented units. Accordingly, non-wage factors (such as social docility and amenability to repetitive process functions) prompt entrepreneurs to opt for a distinctive set of female labour. Thus non-wage factors clearly influence employment patterns as well.

From a neoclassical perspective, one would expect that economic reforms leading to deregulation and liberalisation would cause prices in the various factor markets in different countries to converge over time. Accordingly, stimulated by an increasingly competitive labour market, a gender-neutral equilibrium price of labour would gradually evolve, particularly in the export-oriented industrial sector, since this sector is relatively more exposed to the dynamics of factor prices in the global market. However, the pattern of structural changes in employment in the export sector may inhibit the gradual evolution of gender-neutral wage levels expected from global integration. This rigidity may be accentuated by women's lack of occupational mobility. For example, the introduction of new technologies may affect women's employment through automation, de-skilling of workers and/or increased skill requirements in key jobs. Admittedly, the effects of such technological shifts have not been uniform either for women or for men. But persistent functional gender segregation in export-oriented units may prevent transformation of the structure of the female labour force, reinforcing a possible gender-based wage differential.

The sustainability of current trends in female labour absorption in the organised manufacturing sector is linked to the broader issue of competitiveness of Bangladesh's industry. The major source of creation and protection of industrial competitive advantage in the global economy lies in the adoption and diffusion of new technologies, which lead to growth in the productivity of factors of production. It is thus important to endow women workers with basic education and vocational training (including computer literacy). Female-oriented investment in human resource development may therefore be the most dependable deterrent to technological redundancies. Alternatively, with the changing nature of national competitive advantage, a mis-match may emerge between the skill and quality endowments of female labour and the skill and quality endowments demanded. Under these circumstances, if certain supply-side constraints are not addressed through public policy interventions (e.g., in the areas of skill development and healthcare), female employment in the export sector cannot be maintained and enlarged — in absolute or relative terms.

One also needs to take into account that the level of export-supported female employment is vulnerable to fluctuating global demand. This may be reinforced by the "footloose" nature of foreign investment (one of the major promoters of female employment), which may shift production locations in search of cost effective sources of labour, usually for their "old" technologies. While global demand may be an exogenous variable (predicated largely by the economic activity rate in the developed countries), the extent to which an exporting country can create a niche for itself depends on the availability of a quality workforce within a conducive policy framework.

It is thus important to look beyond the immediate benefits accruing to women workers in Bangladesh through increased access to wage employment as a result of trade expansion. A new set of issues with far-reaching implications for the industrial employment of women in the context of economic globalisation requires attention. While women's short-term material interests are served by such employment opportunities, fulfilment of longer term strategic gender interests may only be evaluated in terms of continued access to such opportunities in the future, coupled with enhanced gender equity in the labour market.

The Nature of the Study

Objective and Scope

The primary objective of the present paper is to assess the adjustment dynamics of the export-oriented manufacturing sector in Bangladesh in view of the opportunities and constraints created by changes in technology and the economy. This line of investigation has been pursued in the concrete context of the apparel industry in Bangladesh, which, with a predominantly female labour force, has experienced significant growth in the recent past.

An attempt has been made to identify structural changes in Bangladesh's manufacturing sector, and in apparel in particular, and their implications for the burgeoning female labour force. In this context, the paper examines the firm-level behaviour of ready-made garments and knitwear producers and its implications for the welfare of women workers. Apart from the domestic factors underpinning the prospects for female industrial employment growth, the analysis also considers the impact of global demand for textiles. Finally, the paper highlights the micro-macro linkages of public policies that affect the sustainability of female industrial employment in Bangladesh.

Data and Methodology

The present study builds on analysis of the available empirical information as well as new evidence on the ready-made garments (RMG) sector in Bangladesh. In particular, sectoral estimates generated by two independent research studies have been adapted to trace the inter-temporal changes in operational behaviour in the RMG sector.[1] Projections prepared at the Ministry of Commerce and the Ministry of Textiles, as well as data maintained by the Bangladesh Garments Exporters and Manufacturers Association and Export Promotion Bureau, have been extensively used in the study. Sources of secondary data also include various publications of the Bangladesh

[1] One of the two studies reported the extrapolated results of a stratified sample survey of 1,220 private manufacturing firms, including 72 RMG units. The survey, sponsored by USAID, was carried out by the World Bank in 1992-93. For details, see ISS (1993). The other study, based on a sample survey of 38 RMG units, was conducted in 1995 by one of the authors. For details, see Bhattacharya (1996a).

Bureau of Statistics and the General Agreement on Tariffs and Trade (GATT).

Primary data on the RMG sector were collected for the present study through micro-surveys and debriefing of key informants. A survey carried out in February 1997 elicited information on employment structure and wage rates for different types of jobs in the country's RMG industry. To generate the required data, a checklist was completed by the chief executives of 10 RMG units of average size (i.e., approximately 400 workers). Information provided by the chief executives was cross-checked through focus group discussions involving 126 randomly selected workers (mostly female) in the sample RMG units.

Structure

The paper is divided into six sections. Section II analyses the general features of female employment in Bangladesh's manufacturing sector. Section III takes a closer look at the growth trends in the country's apparel industry and their implications for female employment. Section IV considers adjustment behaviour of the RMG units and its consequences for female employment. Future prospects for female employment in Bangladesh's export-oriented apparel sector are assessed in section V, taking into account the evolving international trade regime and the projected global demand for textile products. The concluding section draws out some policy implications.

6.2 FEMALE PARTICIPATION IN INDUSTRIAL EMPLOYMENT IN BANGLADESH

Participation Rate

Compared to their male counterparts, women's participation in the formal economy has remained low in Bangladesh. This mirrors the general trend observed in the labour markets of developing countries. According to the most recent labour force survey (1995-96), women's share in Bangladesh's total labour force (i.e., the economically active population over 15 years of age) is around 38 per cent, or 19 million (see Table 6.1). The labour force participation rate (LFPR) of women

TABLE 6.1

Participation Indicators of Women's Employment (1995-96) (per cent)

Indicators	Age group (years)				
	15+	15-29	15-19	20-24	25-29
Women's Labour Force Participation Rate[1]	37.77	43.28	37.50	48.39	44.00
Rural	40.63	45.45	37.74	50.98	47.54
Urban	26.09	33.33	36.36	36.36	28.57
Women's Economic Activity Rate[2]	55.65	55.73	47.59	59.14	60.04
Rural	63.60	64.03	54.61	67.27	69.26
Urban	30.44	30.80	28.99	33.14	30.56
Share of female employees in total employment (10+ years)				38.10	
Share of female employees in total female labour force (i.e., not managerial or administrative)				97.73	
Women's share in non-agricultural labour force				23.38	
Women in non-agricultural activities: share in total employed female				22.60	
Women's share in total manufacturing labour force				36.59	
Female-male gap in manufacturing labour force (female per 100 male)				57.69	
Women in manufacturing: share in total employed female				7.04	
Women's share in total employed persons in service sector				20.81	
Women in services/commerce: share in total employed female				14.90	
Women's share in total employed persons in agriculture				46.67	
Women in agricultural sector: share in total employed female				77.40	
Women's share in total professional-technical personnel				34.72	
Women's share in total administrative-managerial personnel				4.92	

Notes: 1. Share of women in respective age cohort in total labour force;
2. Share of economically active women in respective age cohort.

Source: BBS, 1996b.

is lower in the urban areas (26.1 per cent) than in rural areas (40.6 per cent), where women are extensively involved in household-based and agricultural activities.

However, women's LFPR increases, particularly in urban areas, in the 15-19 and 20-24 years age categories: 36.4 per cent compared to the overall urban average of 26.1 per cent. Information on the female economic activity rate (EAR) reveals a similar trend: the

20-24 years age group in urban areas demonstrates the highest female EAR — 33.1 per cent — in comparison to the overall urban average of 30.4 per cent. This implies that the rate of female labour absorption is perceptibly higher among younger women in urban areas, where manufacturing units in Bangladesh are concentrated.

Less than a quarter (22.6 per cent) of the total number of employed females in Bangladesh are engaged in non-agricultural activities. While almost 15 per cent of the total number of employed females belong to the services/commerce sector, only a little over 7 per cent are involved in manufacturing activities. According to the 1995-96 Labour Force Survey (LFS), more than 1.5 million women were engaged in the manufacturing sector, including both formal and informal activities. The present study is more concerned with female employment in the organised manufacturing sector — to which almost all the export-oriented processing units in the country belong. Before we turn to this subject, it may also be noted from Table 6.1 that the proportions of women occupying professional-technical and administrative-managerial positions in Bangladesh are 34.7 per cent and less than 5 per cent, respectively, of total employment in these categories.

Table 6.1 provides a static picture of the state of female participation in Bangladesh's labour force in 1995-96. Have these indicators registered any improvement over time? Unfortunately, frequent changes in the definition of the categories used in the LFS do not readily allow comparisons. In spite of such discrepancies, however, LFS data do suggest that women's LFPR in the national economy in general, and in non-agricultural and manufacturing activities in particular, has improved in recent years.

Manufacturing Employment

According to the Census of Manufacturing Industries (CMI), approximately 200,000 women were employed in the manufacturing sector in Bangladesh in 1991-92 (the latest reference year for which information on sectoral aggregates is available from an official source). The CMI essentially covers formal sector registered enterprises with 10 or more employees. These are usually located in urban areas. However, in addition to being quite dated, the census estimate suffers from serious undercoverage. For example, in 1991-92, the RMG sector alone employed 700,000 female workers (as we will see later), whereas the comparable CMI (1991-92) figure is 150,000. In the absence of more reliable aggregate estimates, we may still analyse the CMI data assuming that it provides a representative set of cross-section information.

According to the figures presented in Table 6.2, women accounted for 15.3 per cent of the total number of manufacturing sector employees in Bangladesh in 1991-92.[2] More than 88 per cent of the women engaged in the sector were regular production workers ("operatives", in CMI terms) and another 9.6 per cent constituted hired casual workers. Less than 1 per cent of the women employees were involved in administrative and clerical activities, and about 0.3 per cent belonged to the entrepreneur category.

TABLE 6.2

Trends in Female Employment and Wage in the Manufacturing Sector

Indicator	1988-89	1989-90	1990-91	1991-92
Women's share in total mfg employment	14.1	14.20	15.72	15.30
Women's share in total operatives	16.41	16.55	17.76	18.06
Female-male wage ratio (all employees)	0.40	0.55	0.52	0.52
Female-male wage ratio (operatives)	0.46	0.51	0.47	0.57

Source: BBS, 1996a.

On average, a manufacturing enterprise in the organised sector in Bangladesh has seven women employees.[3] Female employment is highest in joint ventures (56 female employees per unit), followed by state-owned enterprises (more than 12 female employees per unit). The figure for the exclusively locally owned private sector units is a little above seven.[4] The overwhelming majority (98.7 per cent) of

[2] According to LFS data, in 1995-96 the share of women in total manufacturing employment was about 36.6 per cent (see table 1). This high estimate is attributable to inclusion of women involved in small and cottage level processing activities (e.g. handloom weaving).

[3] The average employment size of a manufacturing enterprise in the organised sector is 50 (1991-92).

[4] On average, a state-owned enterprise has a total or 1,335 employees, whereas the corresponding figures for joint ventures and domestic private units are 290 and 40 respectively.

the women employees are located in private sector enterprises (local and joint ventures taken together).

It may be observed from Table 6.2 that, between 1988-89 and 1991-92, women's share in total manufacturing employment increased from 14.1 per cent to 15.3 per cent, whereas operatives increased from 16.4 per cent to 18.1 per cent. The share of female workers in total manufacturing employment registered a fall between 1990-91 and 1991-92, but the extent to which this is a statistical artefact or a reflection of recent reform measures affecting the manufacturing sector remains to be seen.

Sectoral Distribution

The sectoral distribution of female manufacturing employment in Bangladesh remains highly skewed, as shown in Table 6.3 and Annex Table 6.1. The wearing apparel sector, categorised under Bangladesh Standard Industrial Code (BSIC) 323, alone employs about 85 per cent of the female industrial employees (which is about 12.9 per cent of total manufacturing employment). This is followed by textiles manufacturing including cotton, synthetic and jute textiles (BSIC 321 and 322), which account for about 6 per cent of female industrial employees or approximately 1 per cent of total manufacturing employment. The third most important provider of female employment is food processing (BSIC 311 and 312), which account for just over 3.2 per cent of female industrial employees or 0.5 per cent of all manufacturing employment. Wood work, cigarette manufacturing and pharmaceutical industries employ about 1.84 per cent, 1.47 per cent and 0.58 per cent of female industrial employees respectively. Annex Table 6.1 shows that this pattern of sectoral distribution for all types of female employees also holds true for female production workers.

The current state of industrial statistics, unfortunately, does not allow us to readily relate the market orientation of the enterprises with the gender composition of their labour force. Nonetheless, it is quite evident from the above figures that at least 91 per cent of female manufacturing employment is concentrated in enterprises that either produce for direct export (e.g., garments and jute), or that produce outputs "deemed exports", because they constitute export linkage industries.

TABLE 6.3

Share of Women in Employment and Wage Bill in the Manufacturing Sector

Ind Code	Sub-sectors	Total employees (no.)	Female as % total mfg employment	Total operatives employee (no.)	Female as % of total operatives	Total wage bill (000 Tk.)	Share of female in total wage bill (%)	Total operative wage bill (000 Tk.)	Share of female in total operative wage bill (%)
311	Food mfg.	44005	0.30	32609	0.34	774081	0.12	448017	0.16
312	Food mfg.	62099	0.19	42649	0.19	1777793	0.14	1071183	0.10
313	Beverage ind.	1715	0.01	873	0.01	55071	0.00	20026	0.01
314	Cigarettes	32829	0.22	30240	0.26	358954	0.04	296521	0.06
315	Animal feeds	63	0.00	42	0.00	886	0.00	416	0.00
321	Textiles mfg.	563969	0.80	500750	0.90	12634680	0.49	10001408	0.60
322	Textiles mfg.	19203	0.11	16390	0.13	348607	0.04	280379	0.05
323	Wearing apparel	215838	12.9	201074	15.18	2865818	6.78	2428562	9.45
324	Leather & its prod.	10802	0.00	8807	0.00	244659	0.00	156023	0.00
325	Footwear except Rubber	5290	0.01	4224	0.01	281313	0.00	157641	0.00
326	Ginning pressing	3997	0.00	3188	0.00	63968	0.00	38576	0.00
327	Embroidery of Textile goods	529	0.04	510	0.05	3240	0.01	3156	0.02
331	Wood & cork prod.	13252	0.28	11357	0.32	213588	0.10	156371	0.13
332	Furniture mfg.	2304	0.00	1930	0.00	41841	0.00	30897	0.00
341	Paper & its prod.	16743	0.02	11138	0.01	945490	0.26	516360	0.00
342	Printing & publishing	15447	0.01	10646	0.00	442984	0.01	263093	0.00
351	Drugs & pharma.	18103	0.09	7847	0.09	913031	0.19	316354	0.22
352	Industrial Chemicals	9766	0.03	5609	0.01	572957	0.16	266581	0.02
353	Other chemical Products	15306	0.03	11794	0.03	688702	0.05	363504	0.04

(Contd.)

(Continued)

Ind Code	Sub-sectors	Total employees (no.)	Female as % total mfg employment	Total operatives employee (no.)	Female as % of total operatives	Total wage bill (000 Tk.)	Share of female in total wage bill (%)	Total operative wage bill (000 Tk.)	Share of female in total operative wage bill (%)
354	Petroleum refining	889	0.00	620	0.00	150157	0.00	98366	0.00
355	Misc. petroleum Prod.	204	0.00	113	0.00	5019	0.00	2243	0.00
356	Rubber prod.	3663	0.00	3057	0.00	69042	0.00	54466	0.00
357	Plastic prod.	3214	0.00	2391	0.00	90918	0.00	59752	0.00
361	Pottery & Chinaware	3387	0.00	2598	0.01	57128	0.00	36040	0.00
362	Glass & its prod.	2051	0.02	1746	0.02	72664	0.01	43214	0.01
369	Non-metallic Mineral prod.	20567	0.03	18054	0.02	260746	0.02	153156	0.01
371	Iron & steel basic Indus.	14795	0.00	10689	0.00	590386	0.00	392604	0.00
372	Non-ferrous metal Ind.	459	0.00	324	0.00	15772	0.00	10410	0.00
381	Structural metal Prod.	13155	0.01	10949	0.01	219282	0.00	161279	0.00
382	Fabricated metal Prod.	6155	0.00	5342	0.00	121005	0.00	89123	0.00
383	Non-electrical Machinery	6594	0.01	4366	0.00	241794	0.01	128283	0.00
384	Electrical Machinery	13021	0.03	9733	0.03	359781	0.04	214736	0.04
385	Transport Equipment	12588	0.00	9530	0.00	434463	0.01	248502	0.00
386	Scientific precision Etc.	172	0.00	130	0.00	3328	0.00	2481	0.00
387	Photographic Optical goods	117	0.00	91	0.00	1764	0.00	1204	0.00
389	Mfg of sports Goods	198	0.00	170	0.00	3920	0.00	3238	0.00
391	Decorative Handicrafts	135	0.00	120	0.00	1279	0.00	1088	0.00
393	Other mfg. Industries	3312	0.09	2870	0.11	41913	0.03	32234	0.04
394	Other mfg. Industries	286	0.00	220	0.00	4139	0.00	2806	0.00
	Total	1156222	15.30	984790	17.76	25972163	8.52	18550293	10.96

Source: BBS, 1996a.

Wage Differentials

A little more than 8.5 per cent of the total wage bill in Bangladesh's manufacturing sector is attributable to all female employees, while the corresponding figure for women production workers is about 11 per cent (see Table 6.3). These shares compare unfavourably with their respective employment shares (15.3 per cent and 17.8 per cent). The divergence between shares of female employment and their wage bill is an explicit indication of the female-male wage differential prevailing in the sector. The compensation packages for female employees are systematically low across the sub-sectors. The average female-male wage ratio in Bangladesh's manufacturing sector in 1991-92 was 0.52 for all employees and 0.57 for production workers, suggesting a smaller gender differential in wage determination among production-related workers. The time series data presented in Table 6.2 indicate that while the female-male wage ratio for production workers improved somewhat between the late 1980s and early 1990s, the ratio in effect remained stagnant (or deteriorated) when all employees are accounted for.

It is also worth noting that female-male wage differentials are much lower in export-oriented industries. While we return to this issue later, it may be pointed out, based on data presented in annex Table 6.2, that in the wearing apparel industry (BSIC 323), female wages as a share of male wages constitute 70 per cent in the case of all employees and 90 per cent in the case of production workers — both these proportions are higher than their respective sectoral averages.

Growth Pattern

Prospects for growth in women's industrial employment are clearly conditioned by the pattern of manufacturing growth in Bangladesh. Bakht's 1993 study of the performance of the country's manufacturing sector in the 1980s found that the top 10 sub-sectors in terms of growth in value-added were the following (in descending order of their trend rate of growth): ready-made garments, silk and synthetic textiles, dyeing and bleaching textiles, compressed liquefied gas, soft drinks, fertiliser, hand and edge tools, china and ceramic wares, fish and seafood, and tanning and finishing. In the best-performing sub-sector (RMG) women constituted 70 per cent of all employees. In other sub-sectors female employment was negligible, with the exceptions of fish and seafood (10.4 per cent), silk and synthetic textiles (4.4 per cent), fertiliser (2.1 per cent) and china and ceramic wares (1.5 per cent). The top three in terms of female employment are export-oriented industries, while the other two have recently been demonstrating their export potential.

A more recent investigation (Bhattacharya, 1996a) found that two sub-sectors with significant weight in the manufacturing structure demonstrated robust growth in output between 1988/89 and 1995/96: RMG and pharmaceuticals. In pharmaceuticals (BSIC 351), 5.7 per cent of all employees and 12.5 per cent of production workers are women.

In sum, the economic activity rate of women in general, and the share of women in manufacturing employment in particular, are quite low in Bangladesh. However, there is evidence that both these indicators are experiencing an up-turn, particularly in the urban areas, and among relatively young women. The sectoral distribution of female manufacturing employment remains highly concentrated in RMG, although virtually all sub-sectors demonstrating growth in recent years are important from the point of view of the female-intensity of their labour force. There are substantial female-male wage differentials in the country's manufacturing sector, but these gaps are lower in the export-oriented industries. Wage differentials are also lower among production workers, and there are indications that the situation is improving. It is possible that such apparently positive trends in industrial employment of women in Bangladesh are a result of the increasing integration of the national economy into the global trade circuit. This, in turn, has been propped up by the deregulation and liberalisation measures that characterise current macroeconomic policies. The mechanisms that have led to such positive outcomes must be identified rather than assumed.

6.3 BANGLADESH'S APPAREL SECTOR: GROWTH CORRELATES

Genesis

Female workers in Bangladesh were traditionally linked to global markets through export of tea and raw jute.[5] It is only with the

[5] Women constitute almost 90 per cent of all workers in the tea plucking stage, while the percentage of women in processing and blending varies between 10-25 per cent.

emergence of the RMG sector in the late 1980s as Bangladesh's leading export industry that the country's female labour force was integrated into international markets in a more direct and intense way. The transition from traditional to non-traditional export-oriented activities is of considerable significance, because it brings out some critical dimensions of the evolving pattern of female employment in Bangladesh. First, export-oriented RMG, a manufacturing activity, differs from the previous agro-based exports. Second, RMG units are concentrated mostly in urban areas, whereas earlier female-intensive processing activities were located in rural areas. Third, the rapid growth of the apparel sector and its increasing share in the export basket testifies to the importance and potential of female employment in exports, as well as industrialisation, in Bangladesh. These three distinguishing features, *inter alia*, have important implications from a gender perspective, particularly in terms of employment opportunities, skill development and wage level.

Bangladesh's RMG industry has come a long way since 1977 when Reaz Garments made its first shipment of products to France. The Desh-Daewoo collaboration in 1978 catapulted Bangladesh's unknown RMG industry onto a trajectory of fast growth. Several factors contributed to this remarkable success. In 1980, the Bangladesh Bank (the central bank of the country) granted back-to-back letters of credit (L/C)[6] and bonded warehouse facilities[7] to RMG producers/ exporters, decreasing their working capital requirements and allowing duty-free access to inputs for the sector. Quotas imposed on some neighbouring countries compelled intermediate buyers to shift sourcing of RMG products to countries like Bangladesh where prevailing low wages ensured competitive prices. Moreover, in the US and Canadian markets quotas imposed on imports of apparel meant guaranteed

Women also account for a significant share (46.7 per cent) of the agricultural labour force.

6 Under the "back-to-back" letters of credit extended by commercial banks, the exporters of RMG are able to import inputs (i.e., fabrics and accessories) against the export orders placed in their favour by the RMG importers. Given this provision, Bangladeshi exporters do not need to invest their own resources to finance working capital.

7 Under the bonded warehouse facilities, the imported inputs can be cleared through the customs against export orders without paying any import duty. This ensures that the export-oriented RMG units can access imported inputs at zero-tariff.

access for developing countries like Bangladesh, while in the countries of the European Union preferential treatment under various schemes, such as the General System of Preferences (GSP), provided crucial price support and, consequently, a competitive edge for RMG exports from Bangladesh.

According to a recent study (Bhattacharya, 1996b), knit and woven RMG accounted for 7 per cent of units, 11 per cent of fixed assets, 21 per cent of annual investment, 30 per cent of the employment and wage bill, and 23.5 per cent of gross value added and returns on capital attributable to the private manufacturing sector in Bangladesh in 1992. More than 95 per cent of the output of the RMG units and about 90 per cent of that of the knitwear units catered to foreign markets.

Annex Table 6.3 shows that, in just over 15 years, the share of RMG in total exports increased from less than 2 per cent to about 66 per cent. Table 6.4 provides information on export growth rates registered by Bangladesh's RMG sector. Between 1987 and 1997, the compound growth rate of RMG exports was more than 25 per cent. The annual compound growth rate of exports between 1992 and 1997 was a robust 19.4 per cent, four times higher than the GDP growth rates registered in the country over the same period.

TABLE 6.4

Inter-temporal Compound Growth Rates of RMG Exports (1987-1997)

Exports	Last 10 years (FY 1987-FY 1997)	In the 1990s (FY 1990-FY 1997)	Last 5 years (FY 1992-FY 1997)
Woven RMG	21.6%	19.5%	14.7%
Knit RMG	–	75.5%	45.0%
Total RMG	25.4%	24.4%	19.4%

Source: Computed from Export Promotion Bureau (EPB) Data Base.

Employment Growth

The rapid growth of Bangladesh's RMG exports also meant a very high rate of employment expansion. In 1995-96, about 1.3 million workers were employed in approximately 2,350 RMG factories in the country. Table 6.5 presents information about the growth of

TABLE 6.5
Growth of Employment in the RMG Sector

Year	Workers	Supervisors	Managers	Total
1981-82	4200	315	28	4543
1982-83	6400	480	44	6924
1983-84	24000	1800	172	25972
1984-85	99350	7451	720	107521
1985-86	323200	24240	2348	349788
1986-87	346850	26014	2520	375384
1987-88	362250	27169	2632	392051
1988-89	391950	29396	2848	424194
1989-90	405700	30428	2948	439076
1990-91	514050	38554	3736	556340
1991-92	729100	54683	5300	789083
1992-93		–	–	804000
1993-94		–	–	827000
1994-95		–	–	1200000
1995-96		–	–	1294000

Source: BGMEA.

employment in the RMG sector between 1981/82 and 1995/96. In 1991-92 (the most recent year for which activity-specific data are available), about 92.4 per cent of all employees in the RMG sector were production workers. It is of critical significance that women constitute the majority of this workforce. According to the Bangladesh Garments Manufacturers and Exporters Association (BGMEA), in 1996 almost 1.2 million female workers (i.e., 90 per cent of total employment in the industry) were employed in the export-oriented RMG units.

As can be seen from Table 6.6, in 1994-95 about 46.7 per cent of the total workers employed in the textile sector of Bangladesh were women. It is interesting to note here that in almost all countries, irrespective of the level of economic development, women on average constitute almost three fourths of the total labour force in the textile sector. In contrast, in Bangladesh it is only in the export-oriented RMG industry and the silk sub-sector that women constitute the majority of the workforce: 9 out of 10 in the export-oriented RMG

TABLE 6.6

Gender Composition of Employment in the Textile Sector (1991-92 and 1994-95)

(million person-years)

Sub-sectors	1991-92			1994-95		
	Male	Female	Total	Male	Female	Total
RMG						
Local	0.720	0.080	0.800	0.752	0.084	0.836
Export-oriented	0.080	0.720	0.800	0.120	1.080	1.200
Dyeing/finishing	0.200	0.004	0.204	0.212	0.005	0.217
Weaving (powerloom)	0.191	0.006	0.197	0.100	0.003	0.103
Handloom	0.572	0.455	1.027	0.409	0.324	0.733
Silk	0.100	0.100	0.200	0.110	0.120	0.230
Knitting/hosiery	0.043	0.002	0.045	0.044	0.007	0.051
Spinning	0.115	0.006	0.121	0.120	0.013	0.133
Total	**2.021**	**1.373**	**3.394**	**1.867**	**1.636**	**3.503**

Source: Ministry of Commerce, Government of Bangladesh (1996).

sector and almost 1 in 2 in the silk industry. The other notable female-intensive sub-sector is the handloom sector, where women constitute a little less than half of the workforce. In the spinning and knitting sub-sectors, the female participation rates are not significant.

A substantial discrepancy in the female participation ratio is discernible between local and export-oriented RMG (see Tables 6.6 and 6.7). This is explained by the fact that, in Bangladesh the RMG units catering to the local markets are mainly small tailoring outfits with a majority of male workers, while the export-oriented RMG units are relatively large units with a predominance of female labour.

Table 6.7 also shows that between 1991-92 and 1994-95, the share of women in total employment has registered an increase from 5 per cent to 10 per cent in spinning and from 4 per cent to 14 per cent in knitting. Ministry of Commerce projections (presented in Section 5) envisage a substantial increase in the share of women in the workforce of these sub-sectors in the near future. But given the relatively low share of female workers in the non-export-oriented sub-sectors in Bangladesh's textile industry, these must be viewed with some scepticism.

TABLE 6.7

Share of Female Employment in Total Employment of the Textile Sector (1991-92 and 1994-95)

Sub-sectors	1991-92	1994-95
RMG		
Local market-oriented	1/10	1/10
Export-oriented	9/10	9/10
Dyeing & finishing	1/50	1/50
Weaving (powerloom)	3/100	3/100
Handloom	11/25	11/25
Silk	1/2	13/25
Knitting & hosiery	1/25	7/50
Spinning	1/20	1/10

Source: Ministry of Commerce, Government of Bangladesh, 1996.

Wages

Female participation in the RMG sector in Bangladesh is confined mainly to the low-paid segments of the production process. In general, the level of wages in the RMG sector is low, for both males and females. The daily wage rate of RMG workers compares unfavourably with that of similar categories of workers in both the public and private sectors.[8] Low wages go a long way in explaining the attractiveness of Bangladesh-made garments to foreign buyers.[9] Table 6.8 gives an indication of comparative wage levels in the RMG sector in some of the major textile producing countries. As can be seen from the table, Bangladesh's wage level is relatively low, even by South Asian standards. For instance, the average hourly wage in the RMG industry in Bangladesh is 50 per cent, 42 per cent and 33 per cent of those of Nepal, India and Sri Lanka respectively.

---

8 For example, according to the wage data provided by the BBS (1995) we find that the average monthly wages of skilled factory workers in textile and other sectors is 1.4 to 2.0 times that of similar workers in the RMG factories.

9 However, it is to be noted here that there is a limit to the extent to which low wages can be translated into low unit costs of production. Since the productivity of labour is also relatively low in Bangladesh, the cost of production per unit of output tends to be on the high side despite low wages. Bangladesh's apparel sector enjoys comparative advantage mainly because the sector is labour intensive and low productivity is somewhat offset by low wages.

TABLE 6.8

Average Hourly Wage Rates in the RMG Sector Across Countries

Country	Wage/hour (US$)
Germany	25.00
USA	16.00
South Korea	5.00
Mexico	2.40
Poland	1.40
Sri Lanka	0.45
China	0.35
India	0.35
Nepal	0.30
Bangladesh	0.15

Source: *The Financial Express*, Dhaka, 15 June 1995.

Abundant, readily available labour and its low opportunity cost lead to low wage levels, providing a comparative advantage to female labour in particular operations in the RMG production cycle. At the same time, inter-industry wage differentials indicate a depressed wage situation in the export-oriented RMG sector. This needs to be interpreted in the light of structural rigidities (e.g., enforcement of national minimum wages) that characterise the wage determination process in other formal manufacturing units, particularly in the public sector. In other words, wage rates in the RMG sector can be interpreted as market clearing wages established in a more or less flexible labour market.

Substantial differences in wage levels between male and female workers for comparable jobs are not discernible in the RMG sector. However, there is a caveat to this observation. In RMG production, female workers are predominantly concentrated in "low-skill/low-wage" operations and, thus, are low paid. As shown in Table 6.9, most women are either production workers or "helpers" (female workers constitute 40-60 per cent of the total workforce in the latter category).[10] Women employed as production managers, supervisors,

[10] According to the tripartite agreement signed in January 1994 (Statutory Regulatory Order No. 14 — Minimum Wages Ordinance) workers in the RMG sector are categorised into seven grades. Most of the female workers are concentrated in Grades

finishing and machine operators, and "in-charges" (drawing salaries varying from 2-10 times that of the average operator, depending on the type of operations) are extremely rare.

TABLE 6.9

Gender Intensity of Participation and Wage Rates in Export-oriented RMG

	Wage/pay per month Taka	Average female participation rate
Production workers		
Plain and overlock	1200-1600	80-95%
Flat lock	1500-1800	40-60%
Helper	500-700	40-60%
Supervisors	2000-3500	10-20%
Finishing in charge	4000-5000	0-5%
Production manager	12000-25000	Extremely rare

Sources: Based on (i) debriefing of chief executives of 10 RMG units and (ii) focus group discussions involving 126 RMG workers (mostly female). The Survey was carried out for the present study.

Export-oriented RMG entrepreneurs in Bangladesh argue that low wages in the RMG sector reflect the low productivity of workers in the sector.[11] Yet it is noteworthy that the overwhelming majority of the workforce in the RMG sector are non-unionised women, which has also enabled entrepreneurs to keep the wage levels depressed. Moreover, workers in RMG factories in the export processing zones (EPZs) are barred by law from organising trade unions of their own. Workers often try to complement their low wages by working overtime, which, in effect, is a mandatory practice in Bangladesh's RMG factories. As labour standards and labour rights are gaining prominence on the WTO's agenda (in addition to that of the ILO, which has long treated such issues), the working environment in Bangladesh's RMG sector is likely to undergo substantial

5 and 6 (junior sewing and knitting machine operators, and general sewing and knitting operators). Minimum wages fixed for these two types of operators are Tk. 1,000 and Tk. 900, respectively.

[11] A technical evaluation of a joint ILO/UNDP project (BGD/85/153) computed that person-minutes required per basic product in Bangladesh's RMG sector is 25.0, while it is 14.0 in the United States, 19.7 in Hong Kong, 20.7 in the Republic of Korea and 24.0 in Sri Lanka.

changes. Furthermore, complaints by some US NGOs and the Harkin Bill (which calls for sanctions on imports to the United States from countries using child labour) forced Bangladesh to take urgent measures to enforce a Memorandum of Understanding on the phase-out of child labour in the RMG industry.[12] The threat of similar sanctions and measures underscores the need to implement policies to improve the working environment for all RMG employees in Bangladesh.

The global textile and apparel markets are becoming fiercely competitive. In the coming years Bangladesh's reliance on low paid labour-based, low productivity-induced, low value-added intensive exports, such as RMG, will be severely tested. With countries such as China, India and Viet Nam with higher productivity, albeit with somewhat higher wage rates, expected to offer stiff competition in the quota-free post-Multi Fibre Arrangement (MFA) phase, Bangladesh must ensure the competitiveness of its RMG exports through critical policy interventions and firm-level adjustments.

6.4 THE PERFORMANCE OF BANGLADESH'S APPAREL SECTOR AND FEMALE EMPLOYMENT: DYNAMIC ASPECTS

Growth of the apparel sector in Bangladesh has been supported by a regulated international trade regime and a proactive domestic policy framework. But there is growing concern that in a more liberal trading environment, as envisaged by the post-Uruguay Round provisions, Bangladesh's RMG sector may not be able to sustain and enhance its export capacity. The other concern for the sector relates to the fact that the potential for Bangladesh to assert its cheap labour-based competitive advantage is circumscribed by the modest share of labour in the cost structure of RMG products and the marginal presence of backward linkages in processing activities. The present section identifies changes in the RMG sector in the face of competitive pressure; the implications for the sector of further globalisation will be discussed in the subsequent section.

---

[12] For details, see Bhattacharya (1996b).

Strategic Choices

Bangladesh's RMG sector is encountering growing competition on a number of fronts: the threat of new entrants, the bargaining power of suppliers and buyers, and rivalry among existing competitors. If the country is to retain its competitive advantage (and, by implication, female industrial employment is to grow) Bangladesh will need to restructure its RMG sector at an accelerated pace. This would entail developing appropriate backward and forward linkages; substantially improving its capital, labour and managerial efficiency; and formulating and implementing product and market diversification strategies. In truth, prospects for expanding female employment in the RMG sector lie in implementing any or all of the following corporate approaches:

- A marketing approach (i.e., more international subcontracting and transition to direct sales abroad);
- A product approach (i.e., more production for the profitable high-value international apparel market and diversification into leather- and silk-based garments);
- A production approach (i.e., increasing value added by decreasing dependence on imported raw materials, particularly fabrics).

It has been argued elsewhere (Bhattacharya, 1996b) that current structural changes in the RMG sector encompass elements of all three approaches. Analysis has revealed that the competitiveness of RMG firms in Bangladesh is being shaped more than ever before by their ability to exploit modern technologies. In other words, the ability of Bangladesh's RMG sector to improve its global market share will largely depend on the technological capability of firms to build the human skills required to set up and operate industries efficiently over time. Clearly, generating such technological capability implies endowing female workers, who constitute the overwhelming majority of the workforce, with the necessary capacity.

Production Costs

Sample surveys show that RMG units in Bangladesh have experienced robust growth during the 1990s in terms of number of employees and wage bill, stock and flow of capital, and output. It is also documented that growth in the cost of employment exceeded the rate of employment expansion, indicating an increase in the wage level. The high levels of investment and export growth suggest substantial capacity expansion and some technological upgrading (Bhattacharya, 1996b).

Such positive trends in employment, output and gross capital formation are usually underwritten by changes in the structure of production costs, such as economies of scale and increased technological endowment per unit of labour. Consistent time series data tracing the evolution of firms are lacking, but the two sector studies referred to earlier can be used to trace adjustments in the RMG sector in Bangladesh.[13] Table 6.10 presents the shares of different items in the gross value of output as revealed by the two surveys.

TABLE 6.10

Cost Structure and Profit Margin of RMG Units

Indicators	ISS study (1992)	BIDS study (1995)
Value of output	100.00	100.00
Costs:	87.00	76.00
A. Industrial costs (excluding wage)[1]	73.00	64.00
B. Non-industrial costs[2]	03.00	05.00
C. Employment cost (wage bill)	11.00	07.00
Gross value added	23.00	31.00
Profit margin	13.00	24.00

Notes: (1)Industrial Costs include expenditures on raw materials, packaging materials, fuel and electricity, spares and sub-contracting. (2) Non-industrial costs include expenditures on overheads, i.e. costs other than direct material and labour expenditures. These costs include advertisement and facilitation expenses, selling and distribution costs, interest payments and taxes.

Source: Adapted from the survey results of 72 RMG units in 1992 (ISS, 1993) and 38 RMG units in 1995 (Bhattacharya, 1996b).

Table 6.10 indicates that between 1992 and 1994, the proportion of costs in the gross value of output has decreased from 87 per cent to 76 per cent, leading to an increase in the profit margin from

[13] See ISS (1993) and Bhattacharya (1996a).

13 per cent to 24 per cent. Concurrently, the share of industrial cost (excluding salaries and wages) has fallen from 73 per cent to 64 per cent, resulting in a growth of the share of gross value added from 23 per cent to 31 per cent. During the corresponding period, within the gross value of output, the share of non-industrial cost has gone up from 3 per cent to 5 per cent.

The shift towards a higher share of non-industrial costs is characteristic of products of high market value, which is corroborated by the increase in the share of value added. The fall in the share of employment costs does not signify a decrease in the wage rate in real terms, but it does point to an intra-firm redistribution of income from workers to owners. Since owners tend to be males and workers mostly females, there would also appear to be an inter-gender redistribution of income in the RMG sector, away from females. The cost structure comparison reveals the price-restraining measures deployed by firms and a concomitant increase in both capital and labour productivities, though they remain low in comparison to regional and global standards. Once again, this price restraint appears to have been largely realised by denying the teenage female labour force wage gains commensurate with productivity growth.

Factor Productivities and Factor Intensities

Comparison of the two surveys reveals that the factor intensity, or capital-labour ratio, may have gone down marginally in the RMG units in the early 1990s, whereas capital and labour productivities have registered a significant increase although they remain low in comparison to regional and global standards. Once again, this price restraint appears to have been largely realised by denying the teenage female labour force wage gains commensurate with productivity growth (see Table 6.11). It is worth noting that the samples drawn for the 1992 survey were biased toward larger firms (in terms of employment), which explains why upward movement of the output-labour ratio was not associated with a similar change in the capital labour ratio. But a higher rate of capacity utilisation may also explain the situation. Higher factor productivities of the units sampled for the 1995 survey may also reflect performance behaviour by size class following a path shaped like an inverted U. In other words, productivity registers growth as the scale of production increases and then falls for enterprises beyond a certain size.

TABLE 6.11

Trend in Factor Intensity and Factor Productivities of RMG Units

Indicator	ISS study (1991-92)	BIDS study (1994-95)[1]
Capital-labour ratio[2] ('000' Taka/worker)	31	29
Gross value added capital ratio (dimensionless)	1.34	3.5
Gross value added labour ratio ('000' Taka/worker)	40	79

Notes: 1. In 1991-92 Constant Price.
2. Capital cost excludes value of land and building.

Source: ISS (1993) and Bhattacharya (1996b).

Analysis of the time-series data on investment, employment and output generated by the two surveys reveals that the firms producing RMGs for export have replenished and expanded their capital stock, leading to higher partial factor productivities.[14] However, in regard to changes in the two measures of partial factor productivity, the gains accruing to capital were notably higher than those accruing to labour. From a gender perspective, the relative growth in the capital- and labour-output ratios suggests that the redistribution of incremental income did not favour women workers.

Wages

Evidence of increasing wage rates in various skill categories is shown in Table 6.12. During the period 1991/92-1994/95, the average monthly employment cost in a RMG unit increased from Tk. 1,608 to Tk. 1,717 (in constant terms) — implying a real increase in unit employment cost of about 6.8 per cent. In fact, wages across various categories of employees have increased by the same extent (just over

[14] For example, according to ISS (1993), the sample RMG enterprises invested toward gross capital formation an amount equivalent to 19.13 per cent of annual output. More than 70 per cent of this amount was attributable to investment in machinery and equipment.

TABLE 6.12

Average Monthly Employment Cost per Person by Skill Level in RMG Units

Taka per month

Category	ISS study (1991-92)	BIDS study (1994-95)[1]	Growth rate (%)
Professional	5643	6025	6.74
Skilled worker	1781	1901	6.74
Semi-skilled worker	1377	1470	6.75
Unskilled worker	923	985	6.71
Clerical staff	2665	2846	6.79
Support staff	1932	2063	6.78
Workers outside factory	772	–	–
Labour-all types	1608	1717	6.78

Note: 1. In 1991-92 constant price.

Source: ISS (1993) and Bhattacharya (1996b).

6.7 per cent). This suggests that, while benefits to female labour may not have been proportional to growth in the RMG sector, the modest rise in real wages may have marginally mitigated the situation. But it is not possible to infer from the data whether these increases have been eroded by the longer working hours demanded of these workers. Nonetheless, with the large reserve of unskilled labour in Bangladesh, real income growth is certainly a "pull" factor, influencing female employment expansion in the RMG sector.

Statistical evidence thus points to some positive processes at work in Bangladesh's RMG sector, although reality is a bit more complex. For example, favourable changes in wage rates have been accompanied by restructuring of employment composition in terms of skill categories of the workers.

In their bid to retain markets in the face of competitive pressures, RMG entrepreneurs in Bangladesh have made both price and non-price adjustments to their products. Because exogenous factors (e.g., the state of infrastructure) influence non-price adjustment behaviour (e.g., timely shipment of goods), entrepreneurs seem to have opted for a more active price adjustment strategy. The latter has entailed production of the existing range of outputs at lower cost, as well as product diversification in favour of high-value products. Both strategies precipitated an apparently contradictory situation in the

RMG units. On the one hand, labour costs were kept down by hiring more unskilled workers and, on the other, demand for skilled workers increased due to the introduction of high-value products in the output range. Since the supply of unskilled labour is more elastic than that of skilled workers, the latter group benefited more, at least in terms of wages and possibly also in terms of employment, from the restructuring process (see Table 6.13). Because female employment in the RMG sector is concentrated in low-skill jobs, the bulk of female workers could not benefit from restructuring at the firm level.

TABLE 6.13

Trend in Nominal and Real Wage in Garments by Skill Category

Taka per month

Worker Category	1980	1985	1988	1990	1993	1997	(%) change (1980-1997)
Trainee/helper							
Nominal	130	300	400	500	500	500	–
Real	195	300	267	337	296	242	24.10
Semi-skilled							
Nominal	300	500	600	800	1000	1000	–
Real	423	500	420	540	591	484	14.42
Skilled							
Nominal	500	800	1000	1500	1800	2200	–
Real	760	800	762	1012	1064	1065	40.13

Note: Figures indicate the highest wage offered to different category of workers, and real wage rates are in 1984-1985 constant price.

Source: Based on memory recall of 17 chief executives and senior executives of 10 RMG units. The interviews were carried out in 1997 for the present study.

The Gender Implications of Technological Improvements

Recent changes in the composition of outputs in the country's RMG sector have led to a diffusion of technological innovations. These innovations, such as computer-aided design (CAD) systems for grading patterns and marking, have been concentrated in the pre-assembly (pre-sewing) phase of garments manufacture, where female employment is marginal. As a result, if gender segregation in the manufacturing process cannot be dismantled, women workers will simply be bypassed by the introduction of these new technologies.

The key to breaking down this gendered division of labour lies in enhancing the skills of the female workers in the RMG sector, particularly through:

- Increased formal schooling (to improve language and mathematical skills);
- Enhanced availability of RMG-oriented training facilities at an affordable price (such as a market-responsive, publicly funded training programme); and
- Greater possibilities for on-the-job training (geared to facilitate upward occupational mobility).

Thus, developing the capacity of female workers will allow them to take advantage of the opportunities offered by the introduction of new technologies in garments manufacturing. For example, the computer-controlled automated cutting systems replacing manual cutting techniques are more gender friendly but require special training. Such techniques diminish the need for physical strength and, thus, will not drive away female workers from this segment of the garments processing chain. Similar examples may be cited for the post-sewing phase.

In other words, enhanced educational qualification coupled with targeted skill development of the female workers in the RMG enterprises constitutes the real basis for sustained access to more remunerative jobs. Incidentally, success in the unfolding global economic scenario will increasingly require firms to foster such skills; those failing to do so will have to accept an erosion in their market share and depressed rates of return. The inability of entrepreneurs (and the government) to elaborate forward-looking (positive) restructuring strategies based on enhancing the skills of female labour will lead to redundancy for their workers.

Thus the response to this fast-evolving situation in the RMG sector must come from both government and entrepreneurs. It is imperative that the government increase gender equity-sensitive allocations, particularly social sector expenditure targeted toward female education and skill development. The picture emerging in countries where industrial restructuring has taken place without attention to gender concerns is a swing back from female intensity in manufacturing, where women have been effectively replaced by male workers (Joekes, 1995; Pearson, 1998). Entrepreneurs, on the other hand, will have to appreciate that they tend to lose out in the long run by not investing in the capability development of women workers. However, entrepreneurs can argue for a cost sharing arrangement with the government in order to underwrite the risks of seeing trained female workers desert to their competitors.

6.5 THE IMPLICATIONS OF GLOBALISATION FOR FEMALE EMPLOYMENT IN BANGLADESH'S APPAREL SECTOR

As indicated above, the phenomenal growth of the export-oriented RMG sector has led to a high degree of feminisation of formal manufacturing employment in Bangladesh. The sector retained its growth momentum in the face of stiff competitive pressure and, in fact, has been able to offer increased wage rates to its workforce over time. However, the female workers remain trapped in the low-skill/low-wage segment of processing activities in RMG factories. Whether current RMG growth rates will be sustainable in the future, whether women will be able to continue to access employment opportunities stimulated through such growth, and whether there will be transfer of technology and increase in productivity to the extent that will lead to wage increases in real terms are important issues of concern for Bangladesh's RMG sector. Some of them are taken up in this section.

The Post-MFA Textile and Apparel Trade

The dynamics of global trade in textiles and apparel has important ramifications and implications for Bangladesh's export-oriented RMG sector. World trade in textiles and apparel developed since 1974 under the restraining rules of the MFA. The nine developed-country signatories to this agreement were Austria, Canada, the European Community (EC), Finland, Norway, Sweden, Switzerland and the United States. During negotiations of the GATT Uruguay Round, it was decided to integrate the MFA into the GATT (WTO) over a transitional period of 10 years (in four phases) beginning on 1 January 1995. According to the Agreement on Textiles and Clothing (ATC) of the Uruguay Round, the MFA phase-out schedule is as follows:

1. At the beginning of the first phase on 1 January 1995, each country would integrate products from the specific list in the Agreement accounting for not less than 16 per cent of its total volume of imports in 1990;
2. At the beginning of the second phase on 1 January 1998, products accounting for not less than 17 per cent of the 1990 import volume would be integrated;
3. In the third phase starting on 1 January 2002, products accounting for not less than 18 per cent of the 1990 import volume would be integrated; and
4. The remaining 49 per cent of the volume of 1990 imports would be integrated at the end of the transition period on 1 January 2005.

Following full integration, trade in these products will be governed by the general rules of the WTO. In each of the four phases, products for integration are chosen from the following categories: tops and yarns, fabrics, made-up textile products and clothing. Importing countries determine the schedule of integration.

During the transition period, quotas are increased for items remaining outside the integration process according to the following schedule:

1. From 1 January 1995, the annual growth rates applicable to these quotas would be increased by 16 per cent;
2. From 1 January 1998, the annual growth rates applicable to these quotas would be increased by 25 per cent; and
3. From 1 January 2002, the annual growth rates applicable to these quotas would be increased by 27 per cent.

In 1994, the GATT Secretariat projected phenomenal growth in world trade in textiles and apparel once the restraining rein of the MFA was phased out. Annual growth rates from 1.2 per cent to 4.3 per cent for textiles, and 4.1 per cent to 8.6 per cent for apparel are projected through 2005. As Table 6.14 shows, global trade in textiles and apparel combined is expected to increase from approximately US$ 199.5 billion in 1992 (base year) to between US$ 289.2 and 469.9 billion by 2005. The table also indicates that the global trade in apparel is expected to rise from around US$ 105.6 billion (in 1992) to between US$ 178.9 and 307.9 billion by 2005, and that of textiles from US$ 93.9 billion to between US$ 110.3 and 162.0 billion over the same period.

TABLE 6.14

Expected Annual Growth Rate of World Trade in Textiles and Clothing (1992-2005)

Projections	1992 (billion $)	2005 (billion $)	Growth rate (percentage change)	Annual growth rate during 1992-2005 (%)
Version 1				
Textiles	93.9	110.3	17.5	1.2
Clothing	105.6	178.9	69.4	4.1
Total	199.5	289.2	45.0	2.9
Version 2				
Textiles	93.9	111.4	18.6	1.3
Clothing	105.6	197.6	87.1	4.9
Total	199.5	309.0	54.9	3.4
Version 3				
Textiles	93.9	162.0	72.5	4.3
Clothing	105.6	307.9	191.6	8.6
Total	199.5	469.9	135.5	6.8

Source: GATT (1994).

The Future of Apparel in Bangladesh

Will Bangladesh be able to share in the gains from the expansion of the global apparel market? This will depend, in part, on the extent to which MFA phase-out affects the performance of the country's textiles and apparel sectors. At present, a quota is imposed on Bangladesh's apparel exports in only two of the nine countries signatories to the MFA: the United States and Canada. Market access is restrained on 31 categories of RMG exports in the US market and nine categories in the Canadian market. These two markets currently account for about 60 per cent of total RMG exports from Bangladesh. Quota utilisation in these countries has been around 85 per cent and 65 per cent respectively, indicating that the quotas did not have a restrictive impact on Bangladesh's RMG exports (World Bank, 1993). As a matter of fact, the quotas have played an important role in providing Bangladesh with a guaranteed market in these two countries.

With the phasing out of the MFA and the elimination of quotas on these major categories of exports, some of the traditional RMG exporters, such as Bangladesh, are expected to face serious competition from a number of newcomers, which, under the MFA, faced restricted entry in the US and Canadian markets (Blackhurst *et.al.*, 1995). Bangladesh's RMG firms currently import a large proportion of their raw materials (grey fabrics) from countries such as India, China and Thailand under back-to-back L/Cs. In a quota-free environment, however, these countries may increase exports of finished apparel to North American markets. Whether Bangladesh's RMG sector will be able to withstand the challenge from these countries in the post-MFA period is thus an issue of critical significance for the future of the industry. The key issue here will be the competitive strength of Bangladesh's textiles sector in general, and its RMG sector in particular.

If we juxtapose the phase-out programme on the structure of apparel exports from Bangladesh, we find that most items of export interest are to be integrated into the WTO in the last year of the phase-out (2004). Bangladesh thus has about five years to prepare for the post-MFA trade regime.

Other market access problems may also threaten the future performance of Bangladesh's RMG sector. For example, Bangladesh's exports enjoy preferential access in many European markets under the EC's Generalised System of Preference (GSP) schemes. These provide Bangladesh access to the EC market at zero tariffs. It is notable that, although substantial across-the-board reductions in tariff rates were negotiated in the Uruguay Round, reductions on textiles and apparel were relatively low. For example, tariff rates on imports of textiles and apparel by EC countries have remained relatively high, at about 12.5 per cent. Preferential treatment under the GSP allows EC importers to claim a duty rebate equivalent to 12.5 per cent of import value on imports of garments from

Bangladesh. In recent years this preferential treatment has contributed to robust growth of Bangladesh's apparel sector through substantial market expansion in the EC market. The EC accounts for about 35 per cent of Bangladesh's global exports of apparel.

However, problems of market access recently faced by Bangladesh indicate that such facilities cannot be expected on a guaranteed basis. For example, access to the EC's GSP scheme is subject to compliance with "rules of origin" (ROO) requirements. Under these requirements, a two-stage transformation is required for woven RMG and, for knit RMG, a three-stage transformation (cotton to yarn, yarn to fabric, fabric to RMG) is required. Since Bangladesh's indigenous capacity in spinning is negligible (about 5 per cent of total requirement), it is not possible to comply with the three-stage criterion. At present, most of the yarn used by the knit RMG factories of Bangladesh is imported (mainly from India). Although the EC ignored this non-compliance until recently, it has had to revise its position under pressure from Bangladesh's competitors. In October 1997, the government of Bangladesh reached agreement with the EC under which Bangladeshi entrepreneurs would refund the duties (amounting to about US$ 60 million) previously waived by the EC. Although the EC has agreed to a flexible approach to this issue,[15] the incident reveals the types of problems countries like Bangladesh may encounter in the global market — despite trends toward liberalisation in the post-MFA phase.[16]

There is every indication that Bangladesh's apparel sector currently stands at an important crossroads. As we have seen, the wages of RMG workers in Bangladesh are the lowest in South Asia. But because backward linkages in the RMG sector are few, the local value addition has so far been very small — only 25-30 per cent of gross exports. Bangladesh can produce locally only 4 per cent of the 2.2 billion square metres of fabric required by its RMG factories. With quotas phasing out, and preferential treatment for exports

---

[15] The EC agreed to a two-stage conversion (the so-called derogation). However, the derogation will be time-bound. Moreover, there is a possibility that a quota will be imposed on exports exceeding a certain amount. For details, see Rahman (1997).

[16] For example, under the current rules of SAPTA, a 40 per cent local value addition is required to benefit from a preferential import tariff.

coming under threat, continued vibrant growth of Bangladesh's apparel exports hinges on the creation of backward linkage in the textile sector. It has been estimated by the Ministry of Textiles (1993) that the country needs to set up, by the year 2000, 146 yarn units to meet 40 per cent of related demand, 109 fabrics units to meet 100 per cent of domestic demand and 199 dyeing/finishing units to fully absorb locally made fabrics. This would require an investment of more than US$ 4 billion.

Relevant in this context are the composite textile mills that have recently been commissioned by the private sector in Bangladesh. A number of export-oriented textile mills are also being set up. Import data supply evidence of this trend: in 1995-96, Tk. 5,579 million worth of L/Cs were opened for textile machinery; the corresponding figure for 1996-97 was Tk. 5,776 million. Between 1994-95 and 1996-97, Tk. 12,061 million-worth of (both woven and knit) textile-related machinery was imported by the private sector (CPD, 1998). This is an indication that the private sector is indeed responding to opportunities for enhancing backward linkages in the textile sector in Bangladesh. Furthermore, negotiations under the aegis of SAPTA (the South Asian Preferential Trading Arrangements) also envisage duty-free access of Bangladeshi products (including textiles) to the SAARC countries, which may be expected to expand markets within the region.

The Ministry of Textiles projects that, if sufficient investment is made in the spinning and weaving sub-sectors, Bangladesh can build a competitive export-oriented RMG sector with strong backward linkages to the textiles sector. Bangladesh will thus need to pursue a pro-active industrial policy if such investments are to be realised by 2005. If Bangladesh is indeed able to make such investments, opportunities for absorption of additional female workers in the textiles and apparel sector can be expected to improve. In the absence of a pro-active policy favouring establishment of backward linkage industries, however, Bangladesh may be marginalised in the global apparel trade, leading to an erosion of the country's current share in the global market. And because female employment has failed to expand in other sectors, collapse of the RMG exports would have a disastrous impact on female employment in Bangladesh.

Employment Opportunities Post-MFA

From the above discussion, it is clear that withdrawal of the quota system, erosion of GSP margins, and increasing competition from both "old" (previously restrained by MFA) and "new" (such as China, Viet Nam, Cambodia) competitors are three major factors with serious implications for Bangladesh's apparel sector in the foreseeable future. Capacity to translate the static comparative advantage of cheap labour into dynamic competitive advantage is severely constrained by the textile and apparel sector's narrow production base with low technological capacity.

However, there is also a brighter side to the story. Projections confirm that adequate investments in backward linkages in the textile sector have the potential to enhance Bangladesh's apparel exports significantly. Bangladesh can remain competitive in the global market, and potentially increase its share in the global textile and apparel trade, provided appropriate policy initiatives are undertaken.

In the above context and with competition likely to increase once the textiles sector is fully integrated under the WTO, enhancing the competitive strength of Bangladesh's apparel sector is critically important. When local value addition is low, the scope for reducing the cost of the final product by using cheap labour is limited — since the inputs that constitute the major part of the cost are sourced at global price. On the other hand, when backward linkages are established (in spinning and weaving) and inputs are produced at lower prices domestically, the relatively low wage level of a country can play a more important role in enhancing competitiveness of the final product in the global market. However, this approach also requires taking adequate steps to raise the level of productivity in upstream activities.

The Ministry of Commerce (1996) recently carried out a study on prospects for the country's textile sector in the post-MFA period. The study made projections from two perspectives. In the "normal scenario", production in the sub-sectors of dyeing-finishing, weaving, handloom, silk, knit-hosiery and spinning is expected to grow at 5 per cent per year during 1995-2005, while consumption/use of fabrics in the export-oriented RMG industry is assumed to increase at the rate of 10 per cent per year during 1995-2000 and 5 per cent per year during 2000-2005. Under the "self-sufficiency scenario", 40 per cent of the domestic and export-oriented requirement of yarn will be locally produced by 2000; by 2005, the level of local sourcing will reach 100 per cent.

Estimates made by the Ministry of Commerce also show that employment in the textile and apparel sectors may rise from 3.5 to 6.2 million under the "normal" scenario, and to 9.7 million under the "self-sufficiency" scenario (see Table 6.15). A large part of this increase is expected to be constituted by women (see Annex Table 6.4).

TABLE 6.15

Projection of Employment in Textile Sector Under "Normal" and "Self-sufficiency" Conditions (1995-2005)

(million person years)

Sub-sectors	1995 (Base year)	2000		2005	
		Normal Conditions	Self-sufficiency Conditions	Normal Conditions	Self-sufficiency Conditions
RMG					
Local	0.836	1.071	1.071	1.366	1.366
Export-oriented	1.200	1.935	1.935	2.469	2.469
Dyeing-finishing	0.217	0.279	0.634	0.356	1.282
Weaving (powerloom)	0.103	0.129	0.425	0.165	0.991
Handloom	0.733	0.938	0.938	1.197	1.197
Silk	0.230	0.296	0.296	0.375	0.375
Knitting and hosiery	0.051	0.065	0.065	0.083	0.083
Spinning	0.133	0.170	0.622	0.217	1.985
Total	3.503	4.883	5.986	6.228	9.748

Source: Ministry of Commerce, 1996.

According to projections, the share of female employment (90 per cent) in the export-oriented RMG sector will be protected, and the proportion of female workers would register some increase in the non-export-oriented RMG sub-sectors (see Table 6.16). As mentioned earlier, the proportion of women in the total workforce of the textile sector is very low in Bangladesh, even when compared to other developing countries. As most of the incremental labour force is expected to be employed in the upstream textile-related activities

TABLE 6.16

Projection of Share of Female Labour in the Textile/Apparel Sector (1995-2005)

(in percentages)

Sub-sectors	1995 (Actual)	2000 (Projected)	2005 (Projected)
RMG			
Local	10.0	15.0	20.0
Export-oriented	90.0	90.0	90.0
Dyeing and finishing	2.0	5.0	10.0
Weaving (powerloom)	3.0	80.0	15.0
Handloom	44.0	47.0	50.0
Silk	52.0	55.0	60.0
Knitting and hosiery	14.0	20.0	30.0
Spinning	10.0	15.0	20.0

Source: Ministry of Commerce, 1996.

(part of which caters to local demand), women will not be able to fully exploit the potential employment opportunities if present patterns of female employment in the textile sector persist. By 2005, the share of female employment is projected to rise from 10 to only 20 per cent in non-export-oriented RMG, while in the dyeing/finishing sub-sectors the share is expected to rise from 2 to 10 per cent, in the knitting/hosiery sub-sectors from 4 to 30 per cent, and in the spinning sub-sector from 5 to 20 per cent. However, Ministry of Commerce projections do not say whether specific policies will be required to provide employment, or whether low relative wages are expected automatically to ensure enhanced female employment.

Ministry of Commerce projections also foresee female employment rising from 1.6 million (in 1995 base year) to between 3.4 million (under normal conditions) and 4.0 million (under self-sufficiency conditions) (see Table 6.16). However, for such projections to materialise, substantial resources will have to be directed toward the textiles sector through both public and private investment, and foreign direct investment. Moreover, the protection of quantitative restrictions (QRs) on imports and high levels of tariffs may also need to be continued until 2005. Projections show that if QRs on imports of textile products are withdrawn (as stipulated in the ATC), then about 180,000 women workers will be retrenched immediately.

Table 6.17 suggests that if the protection enjoyed by the textile sector is withdrawn, employment creation for women will be 250,000 less in 2000 and 360,000 less in 2005 compared to the projected figures of female employment in the textiles sector under normal conditions.

TABLE 6.17

Impact of ATC on Employment of Women in the Textiles Sector (1995-2005)

(million person years)

Sub-sectors	1995 (Base year)	2000 Normal Conditions		2005 Normal Conditions	
		With ATC	Without ATC	With ATC	Without ATC
RMG					
Local	0.084	0.161	0.161	0.273	0.273
Export-oriented	1.080	1.742	1.742	2.222	2.222
Dyeing and finishing	0.005	0.007	0.014	0.018	0.036
Weaving (powerloom)	0.003	0.005	0.010	0.013	0.025
Handloom	0.324	0.221	0.441	0.300	0.599
Silk	0.120	0.147	0.163	0.203	0.225
Knitting and hosiery	0.007	0.007	0.013	0.013	0.025
Spinning	0.013	0.026	0.026	0.043	0.043
Total	1.636	2.316	2.570	3.085	3.448

Source: Ministry of Textiles, 1996.

Bangladesh's policy makers are thus faced with a dilemma. If the phenomenal growth of the RMG sector is to be sustained, and if the scope for women's employment in the manufacturing sector is to be enhanced, resources must be found and committed to the development of the textile sector. The textile sector must also be given some protection in the interim period. As a least developed country (LDC), Bangladesh is granted some leeway as regards protectionist policies which are WTO-legal; however, such protection may become untenable in the medium and long term.

The projected investments also imply substantial transfers of technology into the country's textile-related sectors. Tomorrow's competitive factories in Bangladesh will require more skilled and semi-skilled workers, with higher literacy rates and the capacity to carry out mechanical operations and quality control in the production process (CPD, 1998). If conscious policy interventions and training programmes are not undertaken by the government to educate and train women, they cannot be expected to fully exploit the opportunities which will open up in the backward linkage industries. Women workers are currently concentrated in the low skill-intensive operations, and the projected industrial restructuring will demand an important shift from this structure of employment.

Even if tomorrow's competitive factories do become more skill-intensive, there is no guarantee that women will be trained and hired for these more demanding jobs. In developing countries such as Bangladesh, gender norms and biases regiment the definitions of skilled and unskilled labourers, the value given to work experience, the delegation of workers for on-the-job training, etc. In such a context, there is genuine apprehension that women may be marginalised as technologies transform factories and working methods. Bangladesh will thus need to combine structural, institutional and human resource development strategies to ensure that current women workers, as well as new female entrants, possess the necessary skills and training to service the changing labour requirements of the emerging textile and apparel industries.

A concerted and conscious effort by both public and private sectors will be called for. The government will need to design appropriate incentive packages to encourage the private sector to promote gender-sensitive, action-oriented activities. Translating such an approach into macroeconomic policies is a challenging task in itself, but a few policy measures in this respect do present themselves.

First, there is a need to reconsider public expenditures with a view to a gender/equity-sensitive allocation pattern. Emphasis has to be placed on social sector expenditures targeted toward female primary education, as entrepreneurs prefer to hire literate and numerate female workers. The demand for basic educational competency will increase further as new technologies spread throughout the apparel sector. Such expenditures must be protected in the face of pressures to balance budgets under stabilisation and adjustment policy requirements.

Second, a mechanism has to be devised to share the costs of on-the-job training of female workers between the government and entrepreneurs. The public contribution would underwrite the potential risk of workers leaving a firm after receiving training. It is unlikely that the task of skill enhancement of female workers would meet with success if left to any one of the two actors exclusively.

Third, the government's labour market policies will have to be guided by the goal of promoting flexibility. Under no circumstances should labour market intervention make female labour costlier to the employer (e.g., by emphasising maternity benefits and restrictions of women working at night) than male labour. However, this is not to underplay the need to enforce the current statutory provisions relating to female industrial employment.

Fourth, in order to counteract gender discrimination based on social prejudices, the government must step up the public information campaign aimed at changing people's perception of women's role in society, particularly in the workplace. Such an awareness-building exercise aims to counteract perceptions that contribute to a "compartmentalisation" of female participation in production processes and perpetuate wage biases against female workers. Involvement of trade unions and NGOs should strengthen this sensitisation exercise.

6.6 CONCLUSION

Large-scale entry of women into the labour market has been one of the most striking features of recent industrialisation in Bangladesh. A supply of cheap and readily available female labour has provided Bangladesh with a competitive edge on which the success of its flagship export-oriented industry, RMG, was built. The growth rate of the RMG sector over the last decade was almost 25 per cent; in the 1990s the sector has registered an average growth rate of about 20 per cent. Creation of employment opportunities, mainly for the women constituting about 90 per cent of the sector's workforce (i.e., about 1.2 million people) has been a striking feature of the rapid expansion of the RMG sector in Bangladesh.

However, the female labour in this sector is concentrated mainly in the low-skill/low-wage segment of the production process, limiting local value addition in, and future growth of, the sector. Globalisation of the textiles market is likely to test the limits of such low skill-intensive export-oriented manufacturing activities in developing countries such as Bangladesh. At the same time, unshackling of global markets provides Bangladesh with a unique opportunity to capitalise on expanding market access by restructuring its domestic apparel sector through introduction of new technologies. Diffusion of such technologies is expected to further increase the growth momentum of the RMG sector and, consequently, female industrial employment in the country.

The phasing out of Multi-Fibre Arrangement is expected to bring new challenges as well as new opportunities for Bangladesh in the medium to long term. Analysis shows that in order to remain competitive in the apparel market, Bangladesh must build backward linkages in the RMG industry. And evidence suggests that investments in upstream activities have indeed been picking up in recent years. However, if female workers remain concentrated in the low-skill/low-wage segment of the production cycle, even if the number and share of female workers in the labour force increases, this is unlikely to result in income growth for the female workers. A conscious public policy package aimed at encouraging skill development, facilitating technology transfer and raising of the productivity level of female workers thus needs to be put in place to translate Bangladesh's comparative advantage into competitive advantage. This will facilitate sustainable improvement of the earning opportunities of the female labour force in the country's textiles and apparel sector.

The feminised labour force in the export-oriented RMG sector of Bangladesh is perhaps at a threshold between significant reduction in market share under pressure of competition and globalisation, or enhanced market opportunities induced by a move toward higher value-added products. The actual outcome hinges on the efficacy of the policies implemented to steer the outcome in the country's medium- to long-run interest. Such interventions will have to embody women-oriented social sector allocations and must be supported by a conscious effort by the private sector to train the female labour force in order to raise their productivity and stimulate backward (e.g., spinning and weaving) and forward (e.g., fashion and design) linkages in the apparel sector. The effectiveness of these measures will depend on the ability of the government to develop policies aimed at dismantling the gender segmentation of the labour market. Our analysis has shown that, irrespective of humanitarian considerations, gender-sensitive interventions are justified because of the revealed comparative advantage of female labour in textile-related activities, which can be enhanced if appropriate policy inducements are put in place.

References

Bangladesh Garments Manufacturers' and Employers' Association (1997). Quarterly Reports of the BGMEA.

BBS (1996a). *Census of Manufacturing Industries 1991-92*, Dhaka.

—— (1996b). *Report on the Labour Force Survey in Bangladesh 1995-96*, Dhaka.

Bhattacharya, Debapriya (1994). *Women and Industrial Employment in Bangladesh: Challenging and Opportunities in the Era of New Technologies*, report prepared for United Nations University — Institute of New Technology, Maastricht.

—— (1996a). *Search for Breakthrough: Twenty Five Years of Bangladesh's Industries*, paper presented to the international conference on Bangladesh 1971-96: Past, Present and Future, held at Institute of Commonwealth Studies (London, 13-15 December 1996).

—— (1996b). *Climbing up the Value Chain: RMG Sector in Bangladesh*; paper presented in the Seminar on Export Competitiveness in Bangladesh Industry: Achievement and Policy Agenda, Dhaka, No. 10-11.

—— (1996c). "International Trade, Social Labelling and Developing Countries: The Case of Bangladesh's Garments Export and Use of Child Labour", in *Annuaire Suisse-Tiers Monde 1996*, IUED, Geneva.

—— (1998). *Export Processing Zones in Bangladesh: Economic Impact and Social Issues, Multinational Enterprises Programme*, Working Paper No. 80, ILO, Geneva.

Blackhurst, R., A. Enders and J. François (1995). *The Uruguay Round and Market Access: Opportunities and Challenges for Developing Countries*; paper presented at World Bank Conference on The Uruguay Round and the Developing Economies, Washington, D.C.

Centre for Policy Dialogue (1998). "Governance of the External Sector", in *Crisis in Governance: A Review of Bangladesh's Development 1997*, University Press Limited, Dhaka.

Export Promotion Bureau of Bangladesh (1996). *Annual Report on Export Performance.*

—— (1997). *Monthly Report on Export Performance*, May.

GATT (1994). *The Results of the Uruguay Round Multilateral Trade Negotiations: Market Access for Goods and Services — Overview of the Results*, GATT Secretariat, Geneva.

Industrial Surveys and Studies (ISS) Program (1993). *The Structure and Performance of Bangladesh Manufacturing, 1992*, World Bank and USAID, Dhaka.

Joekes, S. (1995). *Trade-Related Employment for Women in Industry and Services in Developing Countries*, UNRISD/UNDP Beijing Occasional Paper Series, No. 5, UNRISD, Geneva, August.

Ministry of Commerce, Government of Bangladesh (1996). *The Impact and Implications of the Agreement on Textiles and Clothing*, report prepared for the Uruguay Round Study Project, Dhaka.

Ministry of Textiles, Government of Bangladesh (1993). *Textile Industry of Bangladesh: Problems, Issues and Sixteen-Point Programme*, TSMU, Dhaka.

Pearson, R. (1998). "'Nimble fingers' Revisited: Reflections on Women and Third World Industrialisation in the Late Twentieth Century", in Cecile Jackson and Ruth Pearson (eds.) *Feminist Visions of Development: Gender, Analysis and Policy*, Routledge, London.

Rahman, M. (1997). *EU GSP Scheme and Market Access Problems of Bangladesh's RMG Products*, paper presented at the conference on Trading Out of Poverty, London, March, 1997.

Stichele, M.V. (1995). *A Gender Perspective on International Trade*, report of ICDA 1995 Annual Conference, Brussels, October, 1995.

World Bank (1993). *Study on Export Prospects of Garments Industry* (mimeo), Dhaka.

—— (1995). *Bangladesh Labour Market Policies for Higher Development*, Report No. BD-13799, Washington, D.C.

Yang, Y. (1993). *The Impact of MFA Phasing Out on World Clothing and Textiles Markets*, National Centre for Development Studies, Australian National University, Canberra.

Annex

ANNEX TABLE 6.1

Gender Composition of Manufacturing Sector (1991-92)

Ind Code	Industry name	All employees				Operative			
		Male		Female		Male		Female	
		No.	%	No.	%	No.	%	No.	%
311	Food mfg.	40575	4.14	3430	1.94	29239	3.61	3370	1.93
312	Food mfg.	59892	6.12	2207	1.25	40744	5.03	1905	1.09
313	Beverage ind.	1569	0.16	146	0.08	731	0.09	142	0.08
314	Cigarettes	30232	3.09	2597	1.47	27661	3.42	2579	1.47
315	Animal feeds	63	0.01		0.00	42	0.01		0.00
321	Textiles mfg.	554762	56.65	9207	5.21	491853	60.73	8897	5.09
322	Textiles mfg.	17903	1.83	1300	0.73	15106	1.87	1284	0.73
323	Wearing apparel	66062	6.75	149776	84.68	51584	6.37	149490	85.4
324	Leather & its prod.	10786	1.10	16	0.01	8791	1.09	16	0.01
325	Footwear except rubber	5155	0.53	135	0.08	4089	0.50	135	0.08
326	Ginning pressing	3986	0.41	11	0.01	3177	0.39	11	0.01
327	Embroidery of textile goods	17	0.00	512	0.29	7	0.00	503	0.29
331	Wood and cork prod.	10004	1.02	3248	1.84	8163	1.01	3194	1.83
332	Furniture mfg.	2303	0.24	1	0.00	1930	0.24		0.00
341	Paper and its prod.	16512	1.69	231	0.13	11060	1.37	78	0.04
342	Printing and publishing	15368	1.57	79	0.04	10639	1.31	7	0.00
351	Drugs and pharma.	17079	1.74	1024	0.58	6981	0.86	866	0.50

(Contd.)

(Continued)

Ind Code	Industry name	All employees				Operative			
		Male		Female		Male		Female	
		No.	%	No.	%	No.	%	No.	%
352	Industrial chemicals	9474	0.97	292	0.17	5475	0.68	134	0.08
353	Other chem.- products	14947	1.53	359	0.20	11487	1.42	307	0.18
354	Petroleum refining	875	0.09	14	0.01	620	0.08		0.00
355	Misc. petroleum prod.	204	0.02		0.00	113	0.01		0.00
356	Rubber prod.	3635	0.37	28	0.02	3029	0.37	28	0.02
357	Plastic prod.	3185	0.33	29	0.02	2363	0.29	28	0.02
361	Pottery and chinaware	3336	0.34	51	0.03	2547	0.31	51	0.03
362	Glass and its product.	1835	0.19	216	0.12	1534	0.19	212	0.12
369	Non-metallic mineral prod.	20250	2.07	317	0.18	17858	2.21	196	0.11
371	Iron and steel basic indus.	14781	1.51	14	0.01	10689	1.32		0.00
372	Non-ferrous metal ind.	459	0.05		0.00	324	0.04		0.00
381	Structural metal prod.	13086	1.34	69	0.04	10880	1.34	69	0.04
382	Fabricated metal prod.	6113	0.62	42	0.02	5300	0.65	42	0.02
383	Non-electrical machinery	6526	0.67	68	0.04	4366	0.54		0.00
384	Electrical machinery	12671	1.29	350	0.20	9426	1.16	307	0.18
385	Transport equipment	12543	1.28	45	0.03	9530	1.18		0.00
386	Scientific precision etc.	162	0.02	10	0.01	120	0.01	10	0.01
387	Photographic optical goods	117	0.01		0.00	91	0.01		0.00
389	Mfg. of sports goods	198	0.02		0.00	170	0.02		0.00
391	Decorative handicrafts	120	0.01	15	0.01	108	0.01	12	0.01
393	Other mfg. industries	2276	0.23	1036	0.59	1834	0.23	1036	0.59
394	Other mfg. industries	286	0.03		0.00	220	0.03	174909	0.00
	Total	979347	100.0	176875	100.0	809881	100.0	174909	100.0

Source: BBS, 1996a.

ANNEX TABLE 6.2

Level of Wages and Salaries by Sex in Manufacturing Sector (1991-92)

Ind Code	Industry name	Total wages and salaries paid (000 Tk.)				Per employee (Tk.)			
		All employees		Operative		All employees		Operative	
		Male	Female	Male	Female	Male	Female	Male	Female
311	Food mfg.	743914	30167	418845	29172	18334.29	8795.04	14324.87	8656.38
312	Food mfg.	1740736	37057	1052188	18995	29064.58	16790.67	25824.37	9971.13
313	Beverage ind.	54066	1005	19085	941	34458.89	6883.56	26108.07	6626.76
314	Cigarettes	347791	11163	285531	10990	11504.07	4298.42	10322.51	4261.34
315	Animal feeds	886		416		14063.49		9904.76	
321	Textiles mfg.	12506641	128039	9889202	112206	22544.16	13906.70	20106.01	12611.67
322	Textiles mfg.	338586	10021	270714	9665	18912.25	7708.46	17920.96	7527.26
323	Wearing apparel	1104935	1760883	675294	1753268	16725.73	11756.78	13091.15	11728.33
324	Leather and its prod.	244381	278	155745	278	22657.24	17375.00	17716.41	17375.00
325	Footwear except Rubber	280916	397	157244	397	54493.89	2940.74	38455.37	2940.74
326	Ginning pressing	63886	82	38494	82	16027.60	7454.55	12116.46	7454.55
327	Embroidery of textile Goods	182	3058	127	3029	10705.88	5972.66	18142.86	6021.87
331	Wood and cork prod.	188808	24780	132548	23823	18873.25	7629.31	16237.66	7458.67
332	Furniture mfg.	41784	57	30897	18143.29	57000.00	16008.81		
341	Paper and its prod.	877810	67680	515957	403	53161.94	292987.01		46650.72
342	Printing and Publishing	440940	2044	262831	262	28692.09	25873.42	24704.48	37428.57
351	Drugs and pharma.	863469	49562	276255	40099	50557.35	48400.39	39572.41	6303.70
352	Industrial chemicals	532667	40290	263471	3110	56224.09	137979.45		48122.56
353	Other chem. Products	675147	13555	356217	7287	45169.40	37757.66	31010.45	23736.16
354	Petroleum refining	149312	845	98366		170642.29		60357.14	58654.8

(Contd.)

(Continued)

Ind Code	Industry name	Total wages and salaries paid (000 Tk.)				Per employee (Tk.)			
		All employees		Operative		All employees		Operative	
		Male	Female	Male	Female	Male	Female	Male	Female
355	Misc. petroleum prod.	5019		2243		24602.94		19849.56	
356	Rubber prod.	68743	299	54167	299	18911.42	10678.57	17882.80	0678.57
357	Plastic prod.	90585	333	59468	284	28441.13	11482.76	25166.31	0142.86
361	Pottery and Chinaware	56188	940	35700	340	16842.93	18431.37	14016.49	6666.67
362	Glass and its product.	70954	1710	41687	1527	38667.03	7916.67	27175.36	7202.83
369	Non-metallic mineral prod.	255789	4957	151611	1545	12631.56	15637.22	8489.81	7882.65
371	Iron and steel basic indus.	589925	461	392604		39911.03	32928.57	36729.72	
372	Non-ferrous metal ind.	15772		10410		34361.66		32129.63	
381	Structural metal prod.	218736	546	160733	546	16715.27	7913.04	14773.25	7913.04
382	Fabricated metal prod.	120519	486	88655	468	19715.20	11571.43	16727.36	1142.86
383	Non-electrical Machinery	239340	2454	128283		36674.84	36088.24	29382.27	
884	Electrical machinery	349662	10119	207543	7193	27595.45	28911.43	22018.14	3429.97
385	Transport equipment	432524	1939	248502		34483.30	43088.89	26075.76	
386	Scientific precision etc.	3238	90	2391	90	19987.65	9000.00	19925.00	9000.00
387	Photographic optical Goods	1764		1204		15076.92		13230.77	
389	Mfg. of sports goods	3920		3238		19797.98		19047.06	
391	Decorative Handicrafts	998	281	842	246	8316.67	18733.33	7796.30	20500.00
393	Other mfg. industries	35072	6841	25393	6841	15409.49	6603.28	13845.69	6603.28
394	Other mfg. industries	4139		2806		14472.03		12754.55	
	Total	23759744	2212419	16516907	2033386	24260.80	12508.38	20394.24	11625.39

Source: BBS, 1996a.

ANNEX TABLE 6.3
Growth of RMG Exports (1977-1997)

Year	RMG exports (million US$)		Share in total exports (%)	
	All RMG[1]	Knit RMG	All RMG	Knit RMG
1976-77	0.07	–	0.02	–
1979-80	0.67	–	0.09	–
1982-83	10.8	–	1.58	–
1984-85	116.2	–	12.44	–
1986-87	298.7	–	27.81	–
1989-90	624.1	14.8	40.95	0.97
1992-93	1444.9	204.5	60.64	8.58
1994-95	2228.2	393.3	64.17	11.32
1995-96	2547.1	598.3	65.61	15.41
1996-97[2]	3001.2	763.3	67.92	17.28

Notes: 1. Exports include both woven and knit-RMG.

2. Exports of 1996-97 are estimates based on export performance between July-April, FY 1997.

Source: Export Promotion Bureau, Annual Report (various years).

ANNEX TABLE 6.4

Projected Female Employment in Textile and Apparel Sectors Under Normal and Self-sufficiency Conditions (1995-2005)

(million person-year)

Sub-sector of textiles/apparel industry	1995 (Base year)	2000		2005	
		Normal conditions	Self-sufficiency conditions	Normal conditions	Self-sufficiency conditions
RMG					
Local	0.084	0.161	0.161	0.273	0.273
Export-oriented	1.080	1.742	1.742	2.222	2.222
Dyeing and finishing	0.005	0.014	0.032	0.036	0.128
Weaving (powerloom)	0.003	0.010	0.034	0.025	0.149
Handloom	0.324	0.441	0.441	0.599	0.599
Silk	0.120	0.163	0.163	0.225	0.225
Knitting and hosiery	0.007	0.013	0.013	0.025	0.025
Spinning	0.013	0.026	0.093	0.043	0.397
Total	1.636	2.570	2.679	3.448	4.018

Source: Ministry of Commerce, 1996.

Index

105671